The Eyes Have It

Techniques of the Moving Image

Volumes in the *Techniques of the Moving Image* series explore the relationship between what we see onscreen and the technical achievements undertaken in filmmaking to make this possible. Books explore some defined aspect of cinema—work from a particular era, work in a particular genre, work by a particular filmmaker or team, work from a particular studio, or work on a particular theme—in light of some technique and/or technical achievement, such as cinematography, direction, acting, lighting, costuming, set design, legal arrangements, agenting, scripting, sound design and recording, and sound or picture editing. Historical and social backgrounds contextualize the subject of each volume.

Murray Pomerance
Series Editor

Wheeler Winston Dixon, *Death of the Moguls: The End of Classical Hollywood*
Murray Pomerance, *The Eyes Have It: Cinema and the Reality Effect*
Joshua Yumibe, *Moving Color: Early Film, Mass Culture, Modernism*

The Eyes Have It

Cinema and the Reality Effect

MURRAY POMERANCE

Rutgers University Press | New Brunswick, New Jersey, and London

Library of Congress Cataloging-in-Publication Data
Pomerance, Murray, 1946–
The eyes have it : cinema and the reality effect / Murray Pomerance.
p.   cm. — (Techniques of the moving image) (Vivid rivals — The two of us — Being there —
A fairy tale.)
Includes bibliographical references and index.
ISBN 978-0-8135-6059-5 (hardcover : alk. paper) — ISBN 978-0-8135-6058-8 (pbk. : alk.
paper) — ISBN 978-0-8135-6060-1 (e-book)
1. Realism in motion pictures.   I. Title.
PN1995.9.R3P66 2012
791.43'612—dc23   2012023499

A British Cataloging-in-Publication record for this book is available from the British Library.

Visit our website: http://rutgerspress.rutgers.edu

Manufactured in the United States of America

For
Eugene Weiner (1932–2003)
in grateful memory
and to
Doug and Catherine McFarland
in grateful reflection

It would seem, however, that if analysis seeks to be exhaustive (and what would any method be worth which did not account for the totality of its object, i.e., in this case, of the entire surface of the narrative fabric?), if it seeks to encompass the absolute detail, the indivisible unit, the fugitive transition, in order to assign them a place in the structure, it inevitably encounters notations which no function (not even the most indirect) can justify: such notations are scandalous (from the point of view of structure), or, what is even more disturbing, they seem to correspond to a kind of narrative *luxury*.

—Roland Barthes, "The Reality Effect"

When you're on the inside, even the phony things on the outside seem wonderful.

—Jules Dassin, *Brute Force*

Contents

Acknowledgments

I have been helped extensively by a very large number of kind people, to whom I owe a very sincere debt of gratitude. These include Sandra Joy Aguilar, Columbia Broadcasting System, Los Angeles; Patty Armacost, American Society of Cinematographers, Los Angeles; Jonathon Auxier, Warner Bros. Archives, Los Angeles; Hazel Bateman, Edinburgh College of Art; Lauren Buisson, Powell Library, University of California at Los Angeles; Seaver Bulbrook, Toronto; Brian Cameron, Ryerson University Library, Toronto; Ned Comstock, Cinema-Television Library of the University of Southern California, Los Angeles; David Cronenberg, Toronto; Terry Dale, Los Angeles; Joe Dante, Los Angeles; Erica Farber, Los Angeles; Raymond Fielding, Gainesville; Jean-Michel Frodon, Paris; Louis Garrel, Paris; Catherine Gillam, AFI Library, Melbourne; Alexander Gionfriddo, AFI Library, Melbourne; Samuel Goldwyn Jr., Los Angeles; Alan Goouch, Toronto; Patricia King Hanson, Louis B. Mayer Library, American Film Institute, Los Angeles; Lauren Hermann, Charleston, Illinois; Peter Higdon, Toronto; Frieder Hochheim, Los Angeles; Eben Holmes, Toronto; Carla Holt, Warner Bros. Music; Beth Howland, Los Angeles; Andrew Hunter, Toronto; Charlie Kimbrough, Los Angeles; Elizabeth Knazook, Special Collections, Ryerson University Library, Toronto; Bill Krohn, Los Angeles; Christopher Lacroix, Toronto; Matt Leggatt, Bournemouth; Zachary Liebhaber, Davidson Library, University of California at Santa Barbara; Glenn Man, Honolulu; David Martin-Jones, St. Andrews, Scotland; Paul Moore, Toronto; James Naremore, Bloomington; Jenn Nolan, Louis B. Mayer Library, American Film Institute, Los Angeles; the late Ronan O'Casey, Los Angeles; Polo Ornelas, Sony Studios, Culver City; Victor Perkins, Warwick; Eugene Polito, Irvine, California; Barry Salt, London; Keilana Smith, The Chateau Marmont, Los Angeles; Vivian Sobchack, Los Angeles; Matthew Solomon, Ann Arbor; Carol Tavris, Los Angeles; George Toles, Winnipeg; Terry Trotter, Los

Angeles; Beverly Walker, Los Angeles; Melanie Weismann, Davidson Library, University of California at Santa Barbara; Keith Zajic, Warner Bros. Music.

In addition, a group of devoted staff at the Margaret Herrick Library, Academy of Motion Picture Arts and Sciences, bore with my excessive and too often inchoate demands, with grace and great insight: Sondra Archer, Andrea Batiste, Barbara Bunting, Bob Dixon, Michael Francis, Russ Good, Sue Guldin, Barbara Hall, Mona Huntzing, Don Lee, Linda Harris Mehr, Charlie Qualls, Jenny Romero, Faye Thompson, Jonathan Wahl, and Libby Wertin. And my friend and colleague Jerry Mosher (Long Beach) has helped far beyond the call of duty.

My colleagues at Rutgers University Press make the life of a bookster grand and beautiful. These are Lisa Boyajian, Marilyn Campbell, Anne Hegeman, Andrew Katz, Liz Scarpelli, and Eric Schramm, and my indefatigable and nurturing editor, Leslie Mitchner.

My assistants, Ian Dahlman, Matthew Thompson, and Nick White, are the most eager of 100 percent bona fide Canadian beavers, able to track down remote sources in a single bound, and faster than a speeding text message. They have worked with great patience and care in the face of my hopeless need.

Finally, to Nellie Perret and Ariel Pomerance, who love film with me, and who are, indeed, the love of my life—my thanks for unbounded support and encouragement.

The Eyes Have It

We are such stuff
As dreams are made on

—*The Tempest*, IV.i.156-57

Prelude: Corn

"Reality," no less an expert than Liza Minnelli opined to *Vanity Fair* in November 2010, "is something you rise above." In saying this, and without being philosophical, she invokes "reality" as a weight, the humdrum oppression of the everyday. Liza imagines herself—and us—striving to reach some almost-imperial artistic plateau resting "above the clouds," from which perspective the vulgar, quotidian, and workaday world "down there" looks small and banal and impure. Of course this is a very Romantic view. It embodies, perhaps especially, the artist as an isolated and distinguished figure, subject to different laws of gravity, thus able to fly.

By contrast, Edmund Husserl made bold to disclaim the real existence of "reality": "We can no longer say that the world is real—a belief that is natural enough in our ordinary experience—; instead, it merely makes a claim to reality" (7). *Makes a claim.* Even wallowing in the world one might already be capable of escaping it, if only one could share this observation, and acknowledge a transcendence one was called upon to achieve. William James would come to twiddle this same thread, that it is only our convictions that make things real. "Belief, or the sense of reality, is a sort of feeling more allied to the emotions than to anything else" (283). "Reality" onscreen is thus no simple measurement of film's reproducing the world we live in outside the theater. It is yet one more of the "effects" of cinema, a cultured stylization that must change with the knowledge, desire, and expectations of those who appreciate it. And the terms in which "reality" is manifested will shift with what is technically, materially possible in the means of reproduction. When, broadly as a culture, we took painting

1

seriously, filmic settings had to be painted, or otherwise hand-made, to seem "real." Now that we spend our time looking at digital graphics, the "real" is wondrously digitized. "Reality" isn't really *there* in the depiction, it's *here* in our way of accepting, interpreting, moving through, and moving on. Walter Benjamin notes how in filmmaking, we have "a process in which it is impossible to assign to the spectator a single viewpoint which would exclude from his or her field of vision the equipment not directly involved in the action being filmed—the camera, the lighting units, the technical crew, and so forth (unless the alignment of the spectator's pupil coincided with that of the camera)" ("Work of Art" 115). The viewer is inextricably embedded in the action. What seems "real" to the viewer is bound up in its "reality" with a viewing position that excludes contradictions.

"Reality" has been a perduring theme for cinema scholarship and has obsessed filmmakers from early cinema onward. Georges Méliès, for example, wanted to both embrace and elude it with magical tricks, as did Buster Keaton with choreographic movement and Charlie Chaplin with his plastic body. David Bordwell reflects upon Gregg Toland's assertion that in order to make *Citizen Kane* (1941) seem real, many of the sets "were designed with ceilings, which required him to light from the floor" (347–48); these places seen on the screen would look like comparable places seen in the actual world. The screenwriter Frances Marion is pointed to by Bordwell as well. She "claims that the strongest illusion of reality comes from tight causal motivation" and points to the audience "demanding" an illusion of reality (19). Bordwell and Janet Staiger show that the Society of Motion Picture Engineers worked from the early 1930s at "the presentation of a real or imagined happening to the audience in such approach to perfection that a satisfactory illusion of actual presence at the corresponding event is created" (Goldsmith 350, qtd. in Bordwell, Staiger, and Thompson 257). Further, the Bazinian fondness for depth of field came to be associated with the representation of "real" space and the "real" event onscreen.

Yet at the same time film artists have worked against a kind of journalistic "realism." For one salient case, we might consider Alfred Hitchcock's ripostes to François Truffaut about the presence of an ornery old ornithologist in the middle of *The Birds* (1963).

> She happens to be there by pure chance! . . . To insist that a storyteller stick
> to the facts is just as ridiculous as to demand of a representative painter that
> he show objects accurately. . . . I don't want to film a 'slice of life' because

people can get that at home, in the street, or even in front of the movie theater. They don't have to pay money to see a slice of life. . . . The only thing
that matters is whether the installation of the camera at a given angle is
going to give the scene its maximum impact. (Truffaut 102–03).

Hitchcock is thus utterly unconcerned with, even unaffected by, the
plausibility that some early screenwriters and filmmakers insisted upon
capturing for their audience ostensibly hungry for reality. What Hitchcock was giving onscreen was "reality," not reality; a simulation artfully
constructed and evident as such, reflective of what we understand to be
real and yet at no time presuming to claim for itself the same status. "In
the fiction film," Hitchcock said, "the director . . . must create life."

In raising once again this issue of "reality" and our experience of it, must
I inevitably seem to be reconstituting the "rather lame Romantic revival"
that Peter Gay positions around the time of World War I, and into which
he incorporates Madame Blavatsky's "theosophical dogmas" (just as he
might also have woven Arthur Conan Doyle's spiritual divagations and
commitment to a fairy world) (133; 131)? Must we think of the triumph
of feeling and desire as an opposition—and only an opposition—to the
"naturalist" display of factualities? In *Abstraction and Empathy*, Wilhelm
Worringer discussed the centrality of "naturalism" in the Renaissance, as
art worked to fulfill an "ultimate goal" through the mysterious "power of
organic form" (29; 28). In later centuries, Worringer complains, "art still
employed reality as an artistic means in the loftiest sense" and for us now,
with a relatively "slackened artistic instinct," the real "inevitably appeared
. . . as the criterion of art; truth to nature and art gradually came to be
looked upon as inseparable concepts. Once this fallacious inference had
been drawn it was a short step from regarding the real as the aim of art,
to *looking upon imitation of the real as art*" (29, my emphasis). At its most
urgent, however, and its most pure, the "real" in art is something gripping
and powerful in its own right, something stunningly relieving and pleasur-
able, a response to "an immense spiritual dread of space" (15). The effect
of seeing the "real" in a bounded work is that our vitality is triggered, our
sense of being in the world—and at the same instant outside of it—made
palpable and present. Essential to this approach is the understanding that
what one calls "real"—points to with delight as "actual" and possible even
"authentic," although of course even falseness can be actual—is something
that turns us on in a particular way; and further, that being turned on *is* at
that breath, if for only a flash, the sense of "reality."

Filmic representation is one form of pictorialization, a very old human process and obsession. Jacques Aumont very helpfully points out how in the forty years before 1820, "a veritable revolution occurred in the status of the nature sketch: the *ébauche*, an attempt to register a reality predetermined by the project of a future painting, gave way to the *étude*, an attempt to register reality 'just as it is' and for no other reason" (232). (We may imagine the twin pleasures these forms would have brought, that of anticipating a resolution presently suspended and that of seizing and holding what passed quickly before the eye.) In the *ébauche*, form predetermined vision, and it was form that was ultimately real. With the *étude*, reality was—precisely as Balzac noted—the grasp (see Benjamin 41). "The essential trait of the *étude*," continues Aumont, "is not exactitude . . . [but] its rapid execution. Never to be retouched, the *étude* remains a work destined to capture a first impression that it fixes in a record of artistic directness" (232). He could be writing of the fleeting images inside digitally animated action sequences today, in the way that they are also designed to capture a viewer's first impression. At issue with the *étude*, Aumont summarizes Peter Galassi, "is a conception of the world as an interrupted field of potential tableaux, scanned by the gaze of the artist who, exploring as he travels through the world, will suddenly stop in order to cut it up and 'frame' it . . . the photographic apparatus as incarnation of this mobility finally discovered" (232). The "reality" of the *étude* lay in the sense of immediacy, of a blossoming of the world that was ready to be seen in passing, one could even say a world of the quotidian made available to the passer-by.[1]

And Rudolf Arnheim quotes Leonardo espousing the value of movement as a symptom of the real and vital. "If a painted figure lacks it, it is . . . 'doubly dead, since it is dead because it is a figment and dead again when it shows neither movement of the mind nor of the body'" (*Art* 335). With the Puginist movement of the mid-nineteenth century, Arnheim shows us, the use of nature as a basis of decorative art was entirely dismissed as bogus, and what was "real" was a figuration that could be found only in the design that contained it. Fact should be clearly distinguished, always, from fiction; Turkish rugs should be admired, for instance, "because 'they have no shadow in their pattern but merely an intricate combination of coloured intersections'" (*Sense* 34) and one had to keep one's distance from pretenses of the imagination. As Dickens put it, "You mustn't fancy" (in *Hard Times*, qtd. in Arnheim, *Sense* 35). Our idea of "realism" now is a return to Vitruvian values, in which the elemental forms of the natural world reduced to a framed pictorialization are regarded as essential keys to the truth, in which the addition of "fictitious . . . features" was to be encouraged, not abhorred (*Sense* 34).

Since "reality" in perception is in combat with the perception of illusion, also to be acknowledged is the role played by theater design in fostering a keen focus of attention upon the created figure. In a brilliant analysis of the modern theater, Lary May shows how if talking films "rooted characters and audiences in the vernacular art of a diverse people" (102), it was also true that theater spaces could work to alienate viewers from such attachments. "Official institutions of the middle class," he writes, had "excluded the images and desires of workers" as the nineteenth century disappeared (107). But under the leadership of William Fox, among others, new theaters were built where, decorative and divisive balconies and loges having been superseded by sweeping curvatures and functional seating, "the rich rub elbows with the poor and that is the way it should be. The motion picture is a distinctly American institution" (*Fox Exhibitors Bulletin*, June 1914, qtd. in May 107). In the new picture house, built of "steel, Formica, chrome, and glass" and where "throughout the structure, colored lights remained hidden behind walls, exuding tints that blended white with gray, brown, and beige into a dynamic, flowing whole" (117), an end was put, too, to that fragmenting concoction, the decorative proscenium: "Like a painting frame, the proscenium separated the viewers from the art, making them spectators who accepted the moral lessons unfolding in a world of 'illusion' " (118). (We can see how already from the mid-1880s, with *Un dimanche après-midi à L'Îsle de la Grande Jatte*, Seurat had begun expressly to signal the importance of critically examining, and thus disincorporating, the framing "proscenium" of a vision.) With the new theaters, a new dramatic "reality" had to unfold, something less mythic, less archaic, less ostensibly performed (or orated), more down to life even in its special optical glory. *Taxi!* (1932), *Lady for a Day* (1933), *The Grapes of Wrath* (1940), *They Live by Night* (1949)—these films had to play without "art" or pretense, had to affect audiences as straightforward visions of the world they lived in. "Real" stories recounted what happened to ordinary people carried away by extraordinary events, yet in a way that borrowed fluidity from music and illumination from Impressionist painting.

The "reality" of the screen image is, perhaps more than anything else, influential. Expostulating on the semantic marvels effected through vocal coach Tim Monich's work with screen actors—this is the man who made Brad Pitt's speech fit the character of Aldo Raine in *Inglourious Basterds* (2009); he made Matt Damon into François Pienaar for *Invictus* (2009);

he made Shia LaBeouf sound as though he grew up on Long Island for *Wall Street: Money Never Sleeps* (2010)—Alec Wilkinson admonishes us to remember that "to be *persuasive*, characters in a film should sound as if they lived in the same place or at least inhabited the same period" (36; my emphasis). Characters would be persuasive, then; and in its "reality" cinema would attempt to persuade. Let us zoom in and focus on that word *persuasive*, without further specific regard to voices, sound, or coaching, since it is evident—from this usage and its many reflections in critical and popular discourse—that beneath film work and film performances as we find them, a structure of *persuasiveness* sits, like a gravitational system, a structure by and through which one can be drawn toward the world of a film and encouraged to be convinced by, and satisfied with, the "reality" a filmmaker offers. Evidently it is by *persuasion* that when viewers watch movies they are brought into narrative and taken for a pleasant ride. What is it to seek "persuasiveness" in a performance or a scene? How is persuasiveness fostered and managed? And as to the peculiar pleasure of being persuaded, because surely being persuaded brings relief from the agony of doubt, what is it like—if not always and in every instance, then in some particularly fascinating filmic moments? These are the questions that deeply underpin my explorations in this book.

We can probably take the *New Yorker*'s Wilkinson as a person who certainly does not mean to suggest that what the actor says alone convinces the audience of its importance, its truthfulness, its logic, or its moral value. What persuaded audiences are persuaded *of* by the kind of shaped speech that Monich helps produce is the very reality of the character who emits it, his palpable belongingness to a carefully depicted social world. It is not that the world of the screen story is necessarily a wondrous world, or even an interesting one, nor certainly that it is actual; but its parts fit together in a credible way. For an extreme and weird example: watching civilians trapped inside a diner in Irvin Yeaworth's *The Blob* (1958), I can believe that they really are there: there in a diner, in a diner that is "real" (if not indeed actual), and there as the sorts of people who might "really" (if not actually) inhabit such a world as this, who would flee hysterically from a giant purple entity from outer space (all this in the face of my undoubting knowledge that there are no giant purple entities traveling here from outer space). In the same way, when I watch Matt Damon as François Pienaar on a rugby pitch in South Africa, I must believe he really is there, there not only in the rectangle of cinematic space but in that nation, playing with boys who are really there, too, and who are as South African as he (Pienaar, not Damon) is.

It is not only Coach Monich but all of cinema that strives toward persuasiveness, this, as Worringer warned, in the face of our increasingly
scientific way of apprehending the world and addressing our unceasingly
"heaving breast" (132, 134). If occasionally when we see a film the fiction
fails, and we are spectacularly not persuaded, this lapse hardly detracts
from the centrality of persuasiveness in cinema generally, from viewers' desire to see and become involved in worlds that, even for only the length of
a breath, inspire belief.

Stalking: Construction and Variation

In *The Wizard of Oz* (1939), after our heroine Dorothy has found herself stranded in the strange and marvelous land of the Munchkins, either
in a concussion-induced delirium or in a phantasm caused by a magical
tornado, she comes to be marching down a yellow-brick road and soon
enough discovers . . . a cornfield. On the other side of a wooden fence that
borders the road, the cornstalks commence, and they stretch off away and
away, up and up, as far as the eye can see until the distant horizon. Nearby
upon a post is, of course, a Scarecrow—"partly inspired by the brainless
populists of the Farmers' Alliance who wouldn't vote for women's rights in
the South Dakota campaign of 1890" (Schwartz, *Finding Oz* 276)—who
will soon sing and dance as nobody but Ray Bolger can, making Dorothy
feel it is far more fun to be her, and to be heading off to Oz, than to be
poor Frances Gumm sequestered at MGM and laboring on all this frou-
frou every day with not enough to eat and insufficient sleep. That cornfield: it strikes one as having a certain peculiar reality.

The corn looks, perhaps, like what we saw growing by the side of the
road in rolling tufts, as, on summer Sunday afternoons in the days before urbanization overtook the pastoral, we went with our families for a
little country spin in the new car. Or like what was pictured on the box of
Kellogg's Corn Flakes that eager children chomped for breakfast. Golden
speartips and broad green leaves mounting upward like ladders; and underneath all this the solid dark loamy delicious earth, mother of us all.

Dorothy's stalks are rather neat—in fact, rather orderly—planted by a
sensible farmer. They are colored rich brown and green and they roam off
in legions in undulating greenish waves against the blue, blue, blue of the
magical unchanging sky. Any viewer knows well enough that cornfields as
vast as this, fading off into such touching infinitudes, do not exist in the

everyday world right next to gleaming yellow-brick roads, nor are the perfectly starched quality of Dorothy's blue-and-white gingham dress and the spangly red of her newly inherited shoes the sort of effects to be seen in everyday life either (at the National Museum of American History, the ruby slippers are available to be gawked at, but without Dorothy in them they don't look right). All this, for its verisimilitude, is a bit contrived, a bit sequestered. It has the look of studio make-believe—which, of course, it is—except that at the same time it purports to be nothing else than Munchkinland and the viewer has neither reason nor will to offer disbelief of that. Who, after all, would really *not* like to visit Munchkinland, where the Lollipop League might offer welcome? In watching Dorothy at her cornfield, then, one is having a hypothetical experience of a hypothetical world. Further, if the corn in this cornfield is something less than edible, it is at least the stuff of which—when it has dried—Scarecrows can be made, and the stuff that—while it is green—they can guard, and therefore the cornfield is as real as one needs it to be for one's own purposes, which are, needless to say, the purposes of the happy imagination.

What I wish to point to is not that Dorothy's cornfield is contrived but that even having recognized aspects of its contrivance, and having acknowledged that it is like no cornfield in the real world as we know it, we remain comfortable taking it as real. Our belief has a limited duration, but it is thoroughgoing. And it's belief we have; not suspension of disbelief, that cynical by-product. When we look by comparison at *The Corn Harvest (August)* of 1565 by Pieter Bruegel the Elder, we see a picture, a rendition, of corn (perhaps a rendition that for some of us has texture and smell); but here in *The Wizard of Oz* we see what seems to be corn itself, the substance of a rendition, or at least "movie corn," which, being photographic and not painterly, or at least not detectably painterly, suggests itself as borrowing from the same reality as the little girl who stands next to it. And the suggestion is sufficient. The corn as one sees it need not index a true agricultural product. Mary Ann Doane invokes the problem of "extricating the real from the business of realism" ("Indexicality" 4) and Tom Gunning asserts that "the index may not be the best way, and certainly should not be the only way, to approach the issue of cinematic realism" ("Moving" 31). When we stand next to the Bruegel canvas (at the Metropolitan Museum), regardless of its stunning color and light the depiction does not seem to borrow from the same reality as we do; the viewer or reader needs to cross a kind of "bridge" to enter the reality of that painted corn and its earnest gatherers, yet willingly does cross it. With Dorothy's cornfield, however, no bridge seems necessary, albeit much of the stuff we are looking at is part of an enormous painted muslin backing worked by George Gibson and his scenic art department team in early fall 1938 on Stage 26 at MGM (Scarfone and Stillman 126); the remainder is a 75 × 50-foot "plantation" of "resilient Celluloid cornstalks" (116)—celluloid on celluloid!

In an important essay, "An Aesthetic of Astonishment," Gunning describes how throughout early cinema, but also in more contemporary film, there are moments when the audience is confronted with a visual experience that contradicts the viewer's understanding of the world, leading to a double resolution: "I know—but I see!" Here with the cornfield, then, although the viewer realizes she is watching a filmic entertainment; although she is aware that it is through an industrialized process that workers and materials have been brought together by investments of high capital to produce the startling effects that yield the sight; although she knows that she is engaged in a fiction—neither Dorothy nor the Scarecrow being, in everyday truth, real; still, there it is, that cornfield, stretching off to ever, and there is that poor Scarecrow about to be freed from it. (To find a brain!) We know, but we see!

Flimsy as he seems, that Scarecrow is one of the principal hooks for credulity, since if he does not seem real to the story happenings, Dorothy in treating him as real will diminish in reality as well. If she and he diminish in reality, there is little hope that the audience will accept as anything but crass, arbitrary constructions a Tin Man who can squeak symbolically and a Lion who talks with a Brooklyn accent and is afraid of his own tail. However, the reality of the Scarecrow, his fear, his clumsiness, his good will, his combination of spastic posture and exceptional grace, the palpable presence of this first principal clown (and artful projection), depends hugely on the reality of that cornfield, since no believable stuffed man inhabits an unbelievable plantation. That plantation must catch belief first, and then one is ready to grasp anybody stranded within it. Having believed in him, the viewer will dance with him, as he leads Dorothy along to meet her Wizard (and then, of course, to fly home and awaken from this extended—and ultimately horrifying—dream).

Like Dorothy and the Scarecrow, skip off for a moment (possibly singing). It is October 6, 1958, and Alfred Hitchcock, by now one of the most celebrated filmmakers on earth, is at work with his crew and actors, in front of a few hundred locals who have come to patiently gawk, on a highway near Lost Hills in the San Joaquin Valley, near Bakersfield, California (Shanks Communication), to simulate what his script for *North by*

Northwest (by Ernest Lehman) refers to as "Prairie Stop 41," in the wilds of Indiana a few hours out of Chicago. The film's protagonist, Roger O. Thornhill, an advertising man from New York, has been plagued in being mistaken for an operative of the U.S. government named George Kaplan. The real Kaplan (a voice on a telephone) has now asked him for a rendezvous at this unlikely place. Thornhill, more than eager to see his elusive doppelgänger once and for all, shows up, as people used to say, "with bells on." But for Cary Grant, the other cast members, and the technical crew, this location was hardly a *gemutlich* place to work. "I personally *hated* it more than any other sequence I've ever worked on," said Peggy Robertson, Hitchcock's assistant:

> We were getting ready to go on location, we were in wardrobe getting outfitted for it and one of the men who'd been on the location said to me, "Don't forget your boots." I said, "What boots? We're shooting in the fields, why do I want boots?" He said, "Just take boots with you," and walked away. Well, I thought it was a joke and didn't pay any attention and I got out there in the truck and got out, and as I was getting out I looked down on the ground and saw the place was swarming with tarantulas and cobras, it was alive with these terrifying things. So I said, "I'm not moving from this spot unless I get some boots at once!" (Hall 187)

In the sequence, finally, Kaplan does not appear, but a pesky cropduster, "dusting crops where there ain't no crops," does — appear, indeed, and blast our hero with machine-gun fire as he dashes for safety across the road and throws himself into the dirt (in his elegant slate gray Italian silk suit). Then, as the plane circles for another run and zooms in with a kind of anthropomorphic malevolence, Roger spies . . . a cornfield!

To it he races, and among its protective, if rather dry, stalks he makes to secrete himself. This move buys a little time, but the pilot is no slouch and he circles yet once more, this time releasing pesticide, a dense and asphyxiating white cloud that drifts down among the cornstalks. Roger must make a run for it, into fresh air and onto the highway, where he narrowly avoids being squashed by a tractor trailer hauling gasoline just as the plane swoops in and crashes into the truck (a collision and fireball shot with miniatures). This is one of the great set pieces of Hitchcockian, and all contemporary, cinema (see Pomerance, *Eye* 41–43), poor lovable Roger trying to hide from nefarious assassins in the least amenable sort of place on earth, this vast empty space with nothing beyond the little stand of corn as far as the eye can see. He is a man, as Robert Boyle put it, "in jeopardy with no cover" (Turner 174). But what about that cornfield?

It is the dry season, well past harvest, and the fields around the Tulare lakebed ("which is about the flattest, barest place on the face of the planet" [Boyle 174]) are generally bleached and burning. They had the idea of "doing the Van Gogh, otherwise you'd have a swarm of green, grassless hills, not nearly as interesting, but making it orange, Van Gogh orange, helped a lot" (Hall 188). When the wind shuffles through them, the dry cornstalks rattle with a hollow, creepy sound. And standing neatly at the edge of the road, the stand of corn looks utterly part of the place, its coloration absolutely in tune with the yawning orange-brown fields, the shocking nullity of the stalks' posture a bold refusal of statement in the face of the dry white sky.

For achieving this cornfield, considerable work had to be done, because even though, as Robertson recalled it, "Hitch drove past this [place] on the way to his ranch, his country home, every weekend he was going up there, and he was very familiar with that country. And *he* said, 'We might shoot that sequence there, it's got a large expanse of corn fields and we can grow some more there'" (Hall 262), there was nevertheless no corn in the particular spot that was eventually chosen. Corn itself had been decided early on, as the result of researching the agriculture of Indiana: "What crops grow within 2 hours automobile drive of Chicago that a man could run into and be hidden from a diving airplane? Wheat? Corn? Others? Are any of these crops normally crop-dusted in the fall, or at any time of the year?" (undated memo). And by August 1958, a budget had been arrived at for three days' work cutting corn and delivering it to the location site, preparing the ground for the corn crop, and then paying and transporting greensmen, propertymen, and assorted laborers so that they might "'plant' corn on location" (Horton Communication). The photorealism of the cornfield, in other words, was artfully contrived and accomplished, so that as we look at the scene, rather than seeing a studio construction we see authentic outdoors reality caught on film precisely as such. This sequence makes an entirely different appeal to the viewer than the cornfield sequence in *The Wizard of Oz*, albeit at a later time in the history of studio film production; and the audience has no trouble responding with an almost automatic credulity. Nor—because of the rhythm of the editor's cutting and the artfulness of the design work—do viewers hesitate as they smoothly bypass the kind of critical perception that might reveal the artifice.

The cornfield in *North by Northwest*, fake as it is, bears all the telltale traits of untransformed reality and is accepted as such. Twin readings match in perfect overlap: Roger has found himself out in the middle of nowhere, thankfully with a little cornfield to give him protection from the marauding plane; and Hitchcock, in order to film all this, serendipitously found the perfect country crossroads, where the eye could look in every direction forever, and where lingers a charming little stand of corn at exactly the right place to support the action. A similar logic would lead anyone watching this film to believe that Eva Marie Saint and Cary Grant were really in love; that James Mason had an evil streak; that the diegetic train trip from New York to Chicago on the Twentieth Century Limited really was filmed on a train (it was, but not in the way we might think), and so on. The corn "really happens" to be there for us, even though much labor effected that "happening."

Now jump forward again, thirty-five years. Midway through Emir Kusturiça's *Arizona Dream* (1993), a wannabe actor/failed used car salesman named Paul Légère (Vincent Gallo) is onstage at the Manhattan Club of Tucson in front of a panel of aging, overweight judges and an audience of raucous innocents, competing in a talent contest. His "act" is a mimed replication of the cornfield scene from *North by Northwest*, this deriving from his utterly passionate devotion to films but playing out to a viewership that doesn't recognize, and surely doesn't value, the source he is working with. With four stalks of corn, well past ripe, fixed to wooden stands in a tidy line behind him, now in perfect silence Paul does a flawless imitation of Cary Grant standing befuddled beside the road, waiting, waiting, then finally seeing a cropduster aiming toward him. Paul throws himself down on the stage, at which point, having no faith in his viewers' willingness or ability to appreciate the delicacy of Gallo's work, Kusturiça cuts to insert shots from *North by Northwest* that perfectly fill in between Paul's gestures. The performer's rendition is so precisely calibrated for angle of head, facial expression, and posture that there are brief flashes when we feel Paul is more Grant-like than Grant is. As he makes to dive into the corn, he suddenly realizes—"Oh, fuck!"—that the little girl in the fancy dress who set the stage for him didn't have a clue what she was doing and put the cornstalks in the wrong place, so he improvises and moves them into a "stand," in which, again perfectly imitating Grant, he hurls himself. "Tch-tch-tch-tch," he whispers, exactly getting the sound of the machine gun fire, "Tch-tch." As the "aircraft" is swooping in for the fatal crash with the invisible "truck"—Paul, on the stage floor, is making appropriate growling noises—and while the ignorant audience howls at his "ineptness," the hostess, standing behind him uncomprehendingly in a black sequined ball gown (of all possible garb), takes his leg and tries to pull him away from the corn, signaling that his performance is done. But he is still wrapped in the characterization. Needless to say, the applause for Paul is tepid, and the numbers hoisted by the judges into the air are low indeed.

While as a talent routine Paul's performance is, to put it mildly, strange; while his calibration of the knowledge and pleasure of this Tucson bar audience is entirely off; while he is certainly carried away in a narcissistic bubble by the pleasure of his own imagination and desire (his desire to get out of here and exist in the Hollywood of the screen if not Hollywood itself); still, all this taken as given, what he does on this stage is nothing short of marvelous: if Paul is not, as he claims, "born to act," Vincent Gallo surely is. And anyone with a treasured appreciation of *North by Northwest* will find his moves as hilariously precise as they are fantastically bizarre and twisted.

My point, however, resides in those cornstalks. Paul's antics constitute a scene within Kusturiça's scene, his cornfield a kind of stage-within-a-stage. The stalks he has had "planted" behind him are nothing but the artifice sufficient to support his frail pantomime. Slim as they are as a reminder of what we can find in the Hitchcock scene; outrageous as is their misplacement on the stage and his need to readjust them in mid-performance, when we ask whether they function adequately to suggest a cornfield for current purposes "here" and "now," we must find that they do. No other setting, in fact, would work quite as well for Paul. One stalk alone would be too self-consciously symbolic; two would be too aesthetically balanced; three would seem conventional, as though both sides and the center of the stage needed to "say" something. But four is perfect, as is the fact that the stalks are both "real" and "unreal" at the same time, just like Paul.

These stalks, once they are repositioned, constitute the perfect and ideal "cornfield" into which this "Roger" should "run," in the same way that the corn stand planted near Bakersfield by the Hitchcock team constituted the perfect and ideal cornfield for Grant's Roger and the construction on Stage 26 at MGM constituted an ideal for Dorothy's eager eyes.

One cornfield more. On Monday, Tuesday, Wednesday, and Thursday the 27th, 28th, 29th, and 30th of June 1988, at the Lansing Farm, 28995 Lansing Road, Dyersville, Iowa, Kevin Costner made a field of dreams by plowing part of a cornfield under ("Field of Dreams" file). This had been a real enough stand of corn to start with, and was worked through under the shadow of a Louma crane in a two-camera setup. The transformation of the corn was shot in temporal sequence, with Costner's Ray Kinsella seeing a vision and trying to figure it out on the Monday; hearing a voice while he worked on the Tuesday; plowing corn under and seeing the size of the field on the Wednesday; then plowing under more corn, seeing butterflies, putting up the light poles, and seeding his field on the Thursday. So "realistic" did this field seem onscreen (it had been lit by a team from Musco Mobile Lighting and shot by John Lindley) that viewers assumed a kind of transference of realism, coming to believe in full force that there was a place in the actual universe that could look just like this. The film was released April 21, 1989, and within six months, "5,000 pilgrims . . . made the trip to the real-life field of dreams" (Donovan and Nelson).

Can we say, however, that the voyage any spectator might have made from the theater to Iowa, from the screen "reality" to the farm itself, was more direct, more perduring, or more affecting than the voyage viewers of *The Wizard of Oz* and *North by Northwest* made into the depths of their own imagination? Was Paul in *Arizona Dream* having a shallower, less potent relationship with that cornfield in his mind—he symbolized any viewer of *North by Northwest* who was swept away by the film—or had he become, in ways too complex to set forth yet mirroring our own attachments, corny because of movies?

The "Reality Effect"

All four of the cornfields I have described above are "unreal" in the specific sense that while we are watching them they exist—rather than in the *n*-dimensional world where we live our lives and munch on cornbread—within a reduced and bounded pictorial flow that we call cinema. We cannot be nourished, literally, on the "corn" that grows in them, we do not shuck it, it does not stick in our teeth; and there is no highway on which we could journey to find any one of these spots. The corn in these fields is thoroughly and genetically fictional corn, the lush bounty of fictional cornfields. We "eat" it with our eyes and imaginations, we "digest" it with our interpretive powers, we "taste" it through our diegetic engagement.

Beyond this, however, it is fascinating to consider the salient fact that each of these very different constructed realities seems full and apt and believable in its context as we attend to it. Each of these "cornfields" successfully subtends a story. There is no prevailing rule or measure as to what constitutes the "real" in the cinematic frame, what a "cornfield" ought to be. When I listen to people casually discussing films they have seen—students, colleagues, strangers—I note a recurring tendency to disparage certain works, or scenes within works, as being "bogus," "ridiculous," "stagey," "unreal," "artificial," "unbelievable" ("cheesy," a fashionable word now), and this without recourse to any discussion of what the film generally intends, what make-believe world it asks us to accept. It is as though, quite independently of the intention of any filmmaker, the perceivable physical "reality" of filmic material can sensibly be measured indexically, against the perceivable physical "reality" of the everyday world that film ostensibly depicts.

But each of these cornfields partakes of, or exhibits, its distinct "reality effect." Each works in relation to the action taking place, to the light, to the angle of vision, and to other factors, in such a way as to mobilize belief momentarily—that is, within the filmic moment: not, as one might ideally like, in perpetuity but for the span of time in which one is invited—and offers oneself—to be engaged. They are all "real" in the watching. Or: the audience experiences them as real, regardless of what they are.

Consider, in this light, a short sequence that was aired on the "BBC Late News" for Saturday, October 3, 2009. A French dramatic troupe was marching through Berlin, marshaling a puppet of a sad little girl "who had lost her family." In a culminating moment at the end of the day, at the Brandenburg Gate—symbol of unity—she miraculously found them. Crowds had gathered and were following the girl's trek up the broad Unter-den-Linden, and the commentator interviewed one young woman who looked into the camera with a face on the verge of tears and said, "I love this. She's so real looking, and it's so touching!" This touching, real-looking puppet was made of wood, like Pinocchio, and stood some forty or fifty feet in height. The contrivance had been rigged to a large mobile platform within a semi-circular vertical wooden frame that projected noticeably outward into the air near the head, for structural support. From various spots on the arms, shoulders, neck, legs, and head, thick ropes projected upward to pulleys on the moving vehicle, then dropped down into the hands of a team of some half dozen or so operators who walked along beside the "girl," dressed in everyday clothing. (It was impossible to avoid seeing these ropes, and also the mechanical structure.) She wore a pretty green pinafore and had her golden curls in twin pigtails, and her face was designed so that the lips and eyelids, moving with tugs on the ropes, would make various "expressions." Papa, as it turned out, was equally huge, dressed in an astronaut's suit (don't ask). To grasp what the cheerful young observer—clearly by no means unintelligent—could possibly have meant by saying the girl looked "real" or that she was "touching," we may have to discount the fact that the puppet was superhuman in size, and indeed the fact that the puppet was a puppet. "She looks so real" doesn't mean "She looks so very much as I look, standing in front of you here and talking"; but does it mean, "She looks just like a beautiful puppet mimicking a living girl, which, I know, is what she is"? In some sense we say something is "real" when it elegantly or powerfully suits our tastes, when it strikes us as amazing or fascinating, or when we are galvanized in our gaze at it. "Real" doesn't actually indicate a closeness of match with any comparative entity in a world we take for granted, yet it may indicate a similarity. The "girl" that was being marched through Berlin looked more like a normal girl than like a normal boy or a normal elephant. Beyond that, she was made of wood, period, and actually (it could therefore be said) looked more like a tree. Unlike Pinocchio, she didn't whine that she wanted to be "realer" than she already was.

It may be that we would commit a fundamental error in making the assumption that in 1939 and the years immediately following, as viewing audiences raved about Dorothy, her Scarecrow, and their cornfield, they were somehow actually thinking the cornfield looked exactly like cornfields did at the time, sweeping the side of the road in the countryside where farmers had planted them: that viewers were especially gullible in accepting this obviously bogus construction as authentic. Perhaps no artist intended that the cornfield should look like anything but a bogus construction, a "baseless fabric" that, when the show was done, would melt and "leave not a rack behind." If the artificially created cornfield at MGM certainly looked more like an everyday cornfield than like an automobile assembly plant, a wooden puppet forty feet tall, or an elephant, still, beyond that relatively superficial assessment, what it really resembled—rather magnificently— was the sort of construction that a group of devoted artisans might believably have put together on a soundstage in Hollywood out of soil, paint, canvas, wood, and the lens's ability to trick the eye. Again, "I know—but I see!" Audiences then—and later—were perhaps not gullible at all; they were willing.

In *North by Northwest*, the cornfield matches beautifully with all the other authentic locations by seeming "found," or "artfully used," in the face of its entirely natural preexistence. Just as Hitchcock, not only a master of suspense but also a master tour guide, went to the trouble to bring his audience into the real Grand Central Station; or—as it seemed—the real United Nations; or a real secluded estate in Long Island; or the real

Plaza Hotel; here he was bringing viewers to a real pastoral setting where Americans could see America stretching out in all directions as far as the eye could measure. The cornfield sequence, indeed, was one that could have taken place only in America, that land of boundless aspiration and unlimited freedom—where there are no nooks in which to hide (nor—faced everyday with liberty and the self-made man, as Americans were, by contradistinction against their European cousins—much need to). If that cornfield didn't, for viewers in 1959, seem as real as the cornfields of their countrysides, yet it did seem as "real" as could be effected in a Hitchcock movie, a genre that held rather high standards for screen "reality." Roger's cornfield was "real" enough to please. Indeed, it was "real" enough to hide Roger, who was also not real.

And in *Arizona Dream*, Paul's silly little "cornfield" obviously isn't a cornfield at all; although what pleasure can anyone have confessing this? It manifestly *is* the sort of cheap little construction that a desperate young man who wishes he were an actor would have nailed together in order to cheat the sensibilities of his critical, hyperjudgmental audience (the un-educated yahoos to whom, in his day job, he must sell Cadillacs) in the least expensive, most convincing way. It is perfectly "real" as the circum-stances demand, as "real" as that puppet in Berlin.

What is most centrally important about all these screen cornfields, however, is something else again: that distinct as they are from one another in modality and design, these fields all produce a striking and contextually appropriate "reality effect" as they are watched. The reality that stands be-neath representation is multiple, not unitary; nor is there one ideal way of making a representation. One can thus discuss these "reality effects" best by not attempting to collapse them into a single category of cinematic manifestation, by not eliding their telling (and tickling) difference.

Measured indexically against the everyday world, every dramatic con-struction inevitably falls short, and its "lack" of reality can seem to be rather spectacular. The same hyperrealism that is achieved by the light-ing in *Field of Dreams* is used to construct a cornfield that hides invading aliens in M. Night Shyamalan's *Signs* (2002), and seems even more believ-able there because the patina of romanticism that lay upon Costner's base-ball field, derived from its life-changing effect on our baseball-loving hero, seems, retrospectively, less journalistic, less to be merely "happening." By the time of the 9/11 era, journalism and its ability to report "ongoing pres-ent actuality" was a dominant public myth (no matter what it reported), and so for all its culminating nonsense, *Signs* has, at least in its décor, a presence for contemporary audiences that is overbearingly strong and thus preemptively "real": not because of anything achieved in the film, but because of the rhetoric through which addiction to journalism has cultivated the way audiences see. It can very easily seem that as the history of motion pictures develops, filmmakers find newer and more effective ways to make up "reality" onscreen, with the inevitable result that earlier depictions begin to seem hollow, false, contrived, precious, and unbelievable. In order to understand that a judgment like this is only a rationalization, we must grasp the formative link between the "realism" of present-day screen—or dramatic—configurations and the prevailing myths that organize our social action, social thought, and aspiration. When Hitchcock made *North by Northwest*, when Fleming made *The Wizard of Oz*, and even when Kusturiça made *Arizona Dream* and Phil Alden Robinson *Field of Dreams*, nobody was looking for emerging facts, hidden truths, and "developing news" at every conscious moment, and certainly not as an organizing principle while watching motion picture fantasies. Indeed, in the response of the girl in Berlin to the puppet that so entranced her one can see a fervent and nostalgic desire to return to a condition of make-believe, in which a character's resemblance to a spirit of the imagination is more authentic than its connection to the facts of daily life.

The "reality" of the screen experience goes beyond topography, space, and what D. H. Lawrence called the spirit of place. If setting can culture cinematic action, action can also culture setting. Our point of bedrock, our telltale clue, the tiny *punctum* (as Roland Barthes would have put it) that seems to leap out of a cinematic moment and give coherence and depth to the whole construction as *real* can be: a gesture (in *The Queen* [2006], Helen Mirren taking a half-beat to look at her desktop telephone before answering it); a tone of voice (Marlon Brando, very softly, in *On the Waterfront* [1954]: "It was you, Charlie"); a look in the eye (Richard Burton, having tea with Claire Bloom in *The Spy Who Came in from the Cold* [1965], seeing at a glance the entirety of her social setup). The telltale point might even be an acted moment that is palpably simple, pure corn (in *Saturday Night Fever* [1977], the way John Travolta preens with his hair before coming down to dinner). The point isn't depth of feeling, it's feeling at all. When Gunning considered the response, "I know—but I see!" he was not only working to contradict a received wisdom about technological application in film—that, in effect, the viewer's rationality always trumped his experience: "I see—but I know!"—but also focusing his thought on cinematic aspects of all proportions, since what it is that we may see, the vision that can eclipse training and preparation, may be of a mountain, of a village, of an object, of a human hand, of a face blankly staring. His formulation, which directs us to the compound glories of cinematic experience, is absolutely essential and foundational to a serious study of cinema's history, its form, and its effect.

Orson Welles once gave Peter Bogdanovich a kind of riddle that will intrigue anyone concerned about the profession of acting. "There are very few actors," Welles said, "who can make you believe they think—not that they're thinking about what they're saying, but that they think outside of the scene" (302). For an example of the way "realities" of the screen stem not only from designs of the narrative surface but also from invisible, perhaps unknowable depths, I offer the case of Mervyn LeRoy's *Random Harvest* (1942):

Playing the role of a man apparently named John Smith—"a highly unimaginative incognito"—Ronald Colman spends most of his time in the film wandering around in an amnesiac fog. Shell-shocked, he has been sequestered in an asylum in the little town of Melbridge as the film begins, and when in 1918 the town breaks out in pandemonium at the ending of the First World War, he escapes through the gate, finds a tiny tobacco shop on a back street, and is there rescued and befriended by a singer, Paula Ridgeway (Greer Garson), who takes him under her wing and nominates him "Smithy." The two eventually take up life together in Devonshire, first at a charming little inn and then, nearby, in an even more charming cottage where, when he is not dozing by the pond with a lazy fishing line, "Smithy" begins to write for a newspaper up in Liverpool. This oasis is powerful and compelling, even facing the fact that the pond would have looked ersatz: "One idyllic set," gushes Greer's biographer, "complete with shady trees, a running brook, and trained fish," as he ruminates that the encounter there between "Smithy" and Paula "remains one of the most memorably romantic scenes in cinema history" (Troyan 140). Asked now to come to Liverpool for a possible permanent position, "Smithy" travels alone, and in that urban setting, as he walks toward the newspaper offices, he is struck in the street by a passing automobile. When he recovers consciousness shortly thereafter, he has lost all his memory of the past several years, and identifies himself as Charles Rainier, the heir to a major local fortune. Agonized at his disappearance, the loyal and loving Paula trails him and takes up a position as Rainier's secretary, taking the name of Margaret Hanson and helping him to win a local election and take a seat in Parliament. Aside from the fact that he has an unidentified latchkey in his pocket, and that now and then he has a snatch of memory related to some unknown past, he has no recollection that he knew Margaret before, or that he led another life. The two loyal companions marry, and at every available furtive moment she snatches a glance at him to see whether he is remembering the past, whether he knows that they have been together before. But nothing. Agonized, and hopeless, she plans an extended visit to South America, but arranges first to stop in Devon, to visit a charming little inn she stayed at once before. Charles is called to the little town of Melbridge to negotiate a labor disturbance and there he leads his assistant to an obscure tobacco shop on a back street, the assistant being stunned because Charles insists he has never been to Melbridge before. "But," says the assistant, "You said, 'There's a little tobacconist just around the corner.' That shop is away from the main street, you couldn't have seen it from the station." Charles responds in shock: "I *did* know. I don't know how, but I did." That his past is slowly reemerging is signaled by a snippet of music from the sound track of his first visit to the town, after escaping the asylum, now mixed underneath the passing traffic sounds of the "present." The assistant, playing detective, leads him to the asylum, still shrouded in mist and shadows, and memory starts to flood back. "There was a girl!" We cut to Margaret, looking wistfully out of the window of the Devonshire inn and announcing that she will walk to the station, it's such a lovely walk. She brings up the name of the former proprietor of the place, who is dead now, and is told that a gentleman was asking the same thing, just a short time before: he's renting a cottage, near the mill. We cut to the cottage. He is there, standing on the tiny bridge over the chuckling stream. He walks along the picket fence, opens the gate, moves under a blossoming cherry to the door, reaches into his pocket, and withdraws the mysterious key. It fits the lock. As the door swings open, she has come up to the little fence behind him.

This last sequence was filmed May 8, 1942, a day both actors apparently found emotional:

> "We were meeting at our once beloved little cottage, in the country," Greer recalled. "All the lost years of our love, and all the hopes for the future are crowded into that one scene. It hit the deepest emotional point I've ever experienced in a picture—and it remains a thrilling memory." [Director Mervyn] LeRoy recalled, "We all got on so well, it was a wonderful picture to make. When we did the last scene at the cottage gate, which was also the last scene we filmed, Ronnie said to me, 'This is one picture I hate to finish!'" (Troyan 145)

The moment as captured on film, "real" for the characters, was thus also real for the actors, if we can believe what they said in interviews. It is true that watching *Random Harvest* one is stunned by the hauntingly simple and profound sense of relationship between Garson and Colman, "the screen idol of her youth" (Troyan 138); but it is also interesting that the construction of filmic "reality" might depend to some degree on real personal feeling and sensibility, transcending performance technique.

The social theorist Georg Simmel (1858–1918) saw "sociability" as a certain freeing of concrete interactions "from any reality," by which he meant gravity, social structure, contingency. But for Simmel, sociability emerged from a "deep spring which feeds this realm," one that lies "exclusively in the vitality of concrete individuals, with all their feelings and attractions, convictions and impulses." As sociability symbolizes life, it "does not change the image of life beyond the point required by its own distance to it." And thus, "if it is not to strike one as hollow and false, even the freest and most fantastic art, however far it is from any copying of reality, nevertheless feeds on a deep and loyal relation to this reality" (55). We may think of the "reality effect" in cinema, as I am calling it, as a form of sociability, an enticement to and engagement with a certain interactional play. Art, writes Simmel, "seems to reveal the mystery of life, the fact, that is, that we cannot be relieved of life by merely looking away from it, but only by shaping and experiencing the sense and the forces of its deepest reality in the unreal and seemingly quite autonomous play of its forms" (57). In this shaping and experiencing, in this grasping some force of "deepest reality" even in the perfunctory and wildly simulatory fakeries of cinema, our knowledge of "reality" onscreen becomes, at the time, a foothold on reality itself.

A scarecrow really might dance. A man might secrete himself in a cornfield momentarily to escape death from the air. A would-be actor might pretend in front of a live audience to be a figure from the silver screen. And the long-gone baseball heroes of yesterday, corny figurines, might emerge from a cornfield and tell again the windy yarns of their heroic youth. But by contrast, Simmel warns, something far less engaging and much more dispiriting might also occur: The sociability of our relationship with cinema might go off-key, and we might find ourselves sensing that "it ceases to be a play and becomes a desultory playing-around with empty forms, a lifeless schematism which is even proud of its lifelessness" (56). It is on a voyage between these two remarkable and inexorably distant poles, lifeless schematism and the vivid sense of "reality," that my thought now sets out.

The image of happiness we cherish is thoroughly
colored by the time to which the course of
our own existence has assigned us.

—Walter Benjamin, "On the Concept of History"

1

Vivid Rivals

Seeing Time: Technical Effects and Historical Emplacement Onscreen

When things look real at the movies, one can be so enthralled as to lose a sense of reality in the "reality" of the experience. I sat in an audience far below Times Square to watch *Star Wars* in the summer of 1977, and at the moment—that glorious and epoch-marking moment—when Han Solo and Chewbacca threw the *Millennium Falcon* into hyperdrive, the twelve hundred or so captivated souls all leaned back and shouted "Wohhhh!!!" in one single, gargantuan breath. It was an embodied experience of "reality," not reality, we were having together down in that darkness, as no such acceleration existed in the real world any of us knew or had imagined looking like this. Surely at the same moment that we fell for it, we were aware that this was a trick. But the "truc," or "trick," was an agency of the marvelous, a harbinger of delight and wonder, not a mechanism for manipulative and immoral deception. To be deceived here was to see the light.

While studies of screen technology by such scholars as John Belton, Joel Black, Leo Enticknap, Raymond Fielding, Barry Salt, and most recently Stephen Prince have in various ways addressed how, why, and to what general effect widescreen and digital technologies emphasize the cinematic experience—especially, perhaps, during the 1950s and after 1995 or so—what remains to be understood and appreciated is the way it is possible for a viewer to respond to realisms of the screen. Such an understanding need not limit itself to any particular theoretical approach,

23

for example to swimming in the depths of psychoanalysis, since it is with strangers, whose biographical and historical relation to the screen differs from one's own, that one experiences cinema. Nor do prevailing social and cultural circumstances neatly enough explain what it is that happens to anyone who is provoked by the screen, what viewers are doing in their watching. What that "Wohhh!!!" constituted—and how, as selves facing otherness, as modern folk, as neurotics, as willing believers, viewers make meaning as they scream it—is the pressing question here.

Screen "reality" can be utterly confounding. A case in point, that will require a small but patient analysis:

Early in 2009, David Denby reviewed Edward Zwick's World War II adventure *Defiance* in the *New Yorker*. The film is an exposition of the brave exploits of three Jewish brothers resisting Nazi tyranny in the Lithuanian forests. Denby was openly amazed by some aspects of the depiction of early 1940s Belarus. He goes so far as to rhapsodize, recapitulating the long-lived wonder experienced by viewers at cinema's screen magic and also the now increasingly popular lingo of digital effects technology that abounds in the press, on Facebook, and in conversations around the world. "The beautiful light—a little dryer than life," he writes, "has *obviously* been digitally altered" ("Survivors" 72; my emphasis). Like many a filmgoer, however—and paid to be more articulate than most—well-intentioned Denby has been artfully misled about this digital "alteration." Everything one sees in film, "alterations" and straight images, is light. One could even say "beautiful light," without troubling to invoke prevailing aesthetic sancta or the waffling of personal opinion. What Denby can only mean by pointing to the "obvious alteration" of the "beautiful light" is that the quality of Zwick's images has led him to suspect or intuit that they are manipulations *as images*, that they have been tinkered with "backstage." He is telling us, in short, that he is viewing a special effect.

To commit the act of pointing to a cinematic frame being "digitally altered" is certainly to show a contemporary piety, now early in the twenty-first century. Yet it is hardly necessary to use digital effects to achieve the crisp color we see in this film and that Denby (sensibly) adores: an appropriate choice of film stock, the right fabrics for costumes, an evocative location, and a balance between artificial light and natural (available) light in the forests of Lithuania (where almost every minute of this film was shot) would have done handsomely. But if one possibly can, apparently, one should give the nod to electrons. "Digital alteration." The same kind of stunning sense of "real" and yet slightly "unreal" light was achieved by

Robby Müller in his black-and-white photography at Arizona's Coconino National Forest for Jim Jarmusch's *Dead Man* (1995), and by William N. Williams, Wallace Kelley, and Irmin Roberts at the Big Basin Redwoods State Park for Alfred Hitchcock's *Vertigo* (1958): no "alteration" there. What Denby reveals by raving as he does about the light in *Defiance* is his penchant, vastly distributed among the critical and lay population in the age of computer-generated imagery, for invoking the computer as cause: to some degree this is due to the fact that computers are at the root of much that occurs in global society today, but one could also argue that viewers—who do not use them for making films and thus do not fully understand how, where, and why computers are used by people who do— attribute a certain magical potency to the "computer-generated effect" and having invented this potency tend to discover it wherever they look. A notable exception is Stephen Prince, who in his brilliant *Digital Visual Effects in Cinema* explicitly sets the challenge of examining computer-generated effects. This task he accomplishes with inspiring scholarship and clarity, noting (for just one of many examples) how "the luminous, sumptuous imagery in *Che* [2008] and *Zodiac* [2007] show what can be accomplished with the new generation of data cameras, making these among the most beautifully rendered digital films yet produced" (84).

Most aficionados of computer effects, however, merely assume the need for them, and whine at more primitive accomplishments. We always worship our own technologies. In the 1990s, "green screen technology" was invoked with similar rapture by the untutored multitudes, while in the 1980s and before the "screen" was blue. In the 1930s and 1940s people invoked "visual tricks," a somewhat nondescript yet ticklish term that had at least the facility of covering a multitude of blessings and sins.

As he goes on about *Defiance*, Denby becomes still quainter and more revealing:

> At the beginning of the movie, some *standard, blurry black-and-white documentary footage* of German troops killing unarmed people glides smoothly into the staged action, filmed in sharp-focus full color, which is Zwick's way, I think, of telling us that the dramatization and the fictional invention are about to begin, but that they will remain close to the facts. (72, my emphasis)

Calling the black-and-white footage of German troops "standard" is at best an ambiguous way of speaking about what is onscreen here. The "standard" in "standard, blurry black-and-white documentary footage" can mean—and I do believe Denby intends this choice—"the sort that we have become utterly habituated to seeing": conventional, even hackneyed, routine depictions, playing to predictable audience expectations for post facto visualizations of World War II: somewhat grainy—thus presumably authentic—newsreel footage of soldiers in curvaceous hats, their shoulders slung with rifles, their gazes slavishly vacant and dull-witted. "Standard" can also mean "regulation," as in depictions that have been placed in the historical record. Official photographers work according to certain "standards" of depiction and verisimilitude. A short form: "original German propaganda footage." Is Denby suggesting viewers should tell themselves that what they are looking at is indeed authentic war footage, cut into the film? Or that it is, yet once again, the predictable fabrication now accepted as the best way to simulate—to hand over—the real?

A clue: to catalog these shots Denby uses the word "documentary," thus suggesting that, having been created a long time ago by (often nameless) others, they have now been culled methodically from repositories that specialize in hoarding such stuff. The shots are "real" in the sense that they were filmed at the time in which the story is set, roughly 1941, and in the place or places the story indicates. Thus, they represent the story space differently than fictional material would. The filmmakers would undoubtedly have been German officers of the Ministry of Information or their subordinates, and the original purpose of making the shots was to give the German army a visual record of what it was doing. Because as we watch them we take these shots as constituting "reality" in that way, and because REALITY, whatever exactly it is from case to case, has a certain preeminent value for us—as Baudrillard and others have pointed out (see, for example, *Demon*; Debord; Black; Jameson), one is swamped these days by so much empty simulation—it is worth offering the warning that even as documentaries, the pictures could be false. Many times during the Second World War "documentary" footage was manufactured through express acts of fakery and reconstruction—all necessary in order that choreography, lighting, staging, and performance should be ideal for the camera (see Frodon for numerous examples of this, and for commentaries on the German Reich's tendency to film itself). But Denby's intent in invoking "documentary" is not to suggest fakery or artifice. He wishes to lead us to the conviction that at the beginning of *Defiance* one is not watching *references to* the Nazi atrocities of World War II; one is watching *the atrocities themselves*, and has been transported through historical time in order to do so.

More: the word "blurry" creeps in to describe these opening shots that "slide" into a dramatically contrasting "sharp full focus." The word "blur" has technical meaning in matters photographic, and actually none of the shots in this film, save one, are "blurry": that one shows a long trench in the middle of the forest, in which the Germans have deposited, pink and naked, hundreds of executed bodies; the focus is swiftly pulled once the camera settles on this horror, so that a little boy who is seeing it and the theater full of viewers who are sharing his innocence (by way of the syntax of cinema, their gaze is his) should not be painfully contaminated.[1] The film's opening shots, by contrast, are not blurry—that is, missing focus through a lens effect or camera movement (such as in a whip pan)—they are *grainy*. A shot may be grainy because original footage was photographed on grainy stock (cheap material, or stock intended for very fast exposure); or because footage shot first in 8 mm or 16 mm (at any time) was blown up to 35 mm, thus magnifying its intrinsic grain. The effect of the graininess, which is here amplified to the point where it seems to be a visual trick, is to suggest a poor quality picture, that is, a poor image—as vanity might see it—manufactured before contemporary excellent materials and methods of image production existed. The graininess adds to the ability to believe that one is looking at "real" film shot in awkward lighting conditions and with unsophisticated film stock, way back in 1941. To say the shots are blurry is to suggest that history is a blur.

The Denby review now proceeds to amalgamate a number of discrete shots as "documentary footage of some German troops killing." Zwick has worked his assembly so that viewers will make exactly this reading, a reading that describes (and leads to) what I would call a "reality effect," a particular concoction that is savored for its particular taste as a quintessentially artful depiction of the world as we understand it, the real. We are traveling back in time and now stand to witness some German troops, in the year 1941, killing people in front of our eyes, all this thanks to our (magically) having access to footage shot by someone who *did* witness in this way, and who recorded everything with a camera. (One shot and only one shot in the film need have been taken from documentary footage—could not, that is, have been reenacted much later in the proper style—and that is the very first one in the film, a close-up of Adolf Hitler making a speech.[2] The image of Hitler, by now a universal icon, immediately cues the viewer to the epoch and the situation, and prepares her to unconditionally accept any footage attached to it—following Denby's lead—as bearing the same hallmarks of historical "truth.") The succeeding shots, showing officers killing Jews, pushing them around, walking around the frame, and speaking *in clearly recorded sound* (a sound effect incommensurate in its sharpness with the graininess of "old" film)—shots that finally "slide" into color—were staged as part of the current film production, with extras wearing German military uniforms or dressed as Jewish civilians. Through selection of film stock and by "pushing" the negative in development (shooting with less light than needed, then compensating in the laboratory), a grainy effect is produced that can easily be magnified by using 8 mm or 16 mm for the original photography and blowing it up. Some of these shots, including the one that the editor will finally choose as the transitional shot of the sequence, are shot originally in color; but in processing, the color information is filtered out of a duplicate copy, so that it seems to have been made in black-and-white. (Computing can be used here, as when color is added or subtracted in Adobe PhotoShop; or the shot can be duped onto black and white internegative.) The two strips of film, one in color and one in black-and-white, are now run through an optical process that, frame by frame fading out the black-and-white and fading up the color, "dissolves" or "slides" one into the other. I discuss the optical process further in chapter 2.

In such optical transition, it's worth noting, the viewer's thrill may inhere in the ability to discriminate black and white from color as a visual experience, and from some sense of color enriching or enlivening the formal but aesthetically distant rendition possible in black and white. The sliding into color seems to awaken—or reawaken!—life.

What one ends up with, then, as *Defiance* begins, is footage that suggests poor conditions for photography, old (thus inversatile) film, and verisimilitude of performance: the "actuality" of the Holocaust. And when—Denby is quite correct in suggesting this—these shots "slide" into a full color that signals a "fiction . . . that will remain close to the facts," one has been prepared to buy into the "reality" of the film story. The fiction seems not to be fiction. Denby's open celebration of his own attachment to this filmic material as "real" is a cue and guide, as well as a delightfully articulate report of how the film actually worked for a real viewer. That as a story *Defiance* openly borrows from such unabashedly constructed Holocaust invocations as *Fiddler on the Roof* (1971) and *Schindler's List* (1993) is guised under the unimpeachable authenticity of this opening sequence, which makes Denby, even the Denby who knows that "'Defiance' is a Hollywood product, with decades of storytelling know-how behind it," finally conclude that the film offers "the most moving account we've ever had of how an ordinary, rather disagreeable man . . . grows into a great leader." *Account*, note; not *tale*. And this at a time in history when Wall Street executives were being called on the carpet for telling tales but calling them "accounts," for producing purportedly bona fide accounts that turned out to be mere fictions. Very broadly in our culture, even in our astute critical literature, "reality" and "fiction" were (and remain) up for grabs. While in his book *The Reality Effect* Joel Black observes how reality and fiction besmudge, dilute, or confuse one another—"Unable to establish documentary evidence for Sergei's [the Wolf Man's] primal scene, Freud found it necessary to insist on its virtual reality. And so, despite his avowed distaste for the cinema, he resorted to many of the same techniques and effects that filmmakers at the time were experimenting with (persistence of memory, composite images, double exposure) in an effort to produce a vivid and compelling semblance of reality" (80)—there is more to the similarity of fiction and nonfiction than the audience's consternation. I think the challenge of the similarity is posed as a call for increasingly subtle discrimination on the viewer's part; corresponding tactics of subterfuge on the part of some expressive artists; and in general a newly sophisticated way of appreciating what seems to be "real" in cinema.

Since the perception of Zwick's ostensibly "documentary" footage as "real" involves a particular receptive pleasure—not that reality is essentially pleasing, or that every observation of it brings delight, but that in the catalogue of delights a very particular formulation applies to the perception of "reality"—it may be well to note that each shot is composed in such a way that everything a viewer might deem important is focally clarified and centralized in a "holy" crux around which the organization is displaced, an aesthetic center, while whatever can be deemed marginal is banished to the shady extremities. As a documentary—a recording of happenings—this filmic material is all strangely composed, controlled, shaped, even artfully framed. More: the shaping and framing serve a specific formation that gives us a sense of completion and fulfillment, that brings the satisfaction of plenitude. Thus, the "documentary cameraman," wherever he is in time and space, thinks the way his viewers do, or—since we are to believe some of these shots were made more than sixty-five years ago—"did presciently think" in the 1940s as future viewers would after the millennium. Perhaps all reasonable people think this way, desire this way, gain pleasure this way, and always did. At any rate, these produced images are not only attractive and affecting but also sufficient and satisfying. The truth, of course—the reality—is that the cinematographer, Eduardo

Serra (b. 1943), wasn't distanced from his audience by time at all. A man of our time, he was shooting for people educated and cultured by the same films as had affected him. These images only pretend to eventuate from a real scene through the agency of a camera looking forward in time. History is an appearance.

At Home in "Reality": The Many Realities of Cinema

The use of technical effects to achieve a look of historical emplacement or situational actuality is an innovation neither recent nor exclusively cinematic. Vanessa Schwartz discusses the artifice used in the Musée Grévin's 1868 reconstruction of the mine disaster depicted in Zola's *Germinal*, for example. In a discussion of television news film about a hundred years later, Gaye Tuchman notes that cameramen *learn* techniques for producing the look of objectivity (including maintaining a constant film speed and head-on alignment of the lens with the subject's face, "similar to a person of average height confronting another person eye to eye" [7]). Occasional jiggling of the camera can also aid in suggesting a situation which is so overwhelming as to disengage the cameraman from secure footing, a "real world," not fiction; the cameraman is understood as encircled and enmeshed by unpredictable ongoing happenings. This technique is borrowed in, for instance, *Cloverfield* (2008), where filmmaker Matt Reeves has his cinematographer Michael Bonvillain simulate jerky camera movements to replicate the vision of a New York college student caught up in a horrifying and destructive cataclysm, where the ground shakes, thousands of civilians run helter-skelter in panic all around, and skyscrapers tumble (and, ironically, where he is trying through the perturbation to shoot a personal film with a hand-held camera that sometimes protrudes unprofessionally into the frame). In *Cloverfield*, "reality" is being played with onscreen in a way directly opposite to what can be seen at the beginning of *Defiance*. *Cloverfield* would have viewers believe there is no professional cinematographer recording most of the film; instead, an untrained youngster has picked up a camera and out of loyalty to his friends is trying to capture everything as best he can. The beginning of *Defiance* offers poor, but professional, images as evidence of authenticity and the passage of time. Both professional filming and unprofessional filming are "realities" that have a "look." Each of these looks can provoke, if not, perhaps, cinephilia, at least a pleasure of recognition.

There are legion other cases in which the look of an image is meant to be convincing of unmediated presence, emphasizing the link between the audience's participation and sense of involvement on one hand—two more or less constant features of film spectatorship—and a conviction in "reality" on the other. In *Picture Snatcher* (1933), a man walks through a doorway bearing tearsheets "hot off the press" and behind him we see the spinning machinery of a big newspaper producing today's edition: the man and the doorframe are built on set, but the machinery beyond the door is a rear projection (thrown onto a relatively small screen). In Preston Sturges's *The Sin of Harold Diddlebock* (1947), Harold Lloyd and Jimmy Conlon throw themselves around on a high window ledge in pursuit of Jackie the Lion, who is leading them on a merry chase. Jackie is hardly worried about falling from a height, being an actual cat, but we worry on his behalf, becoming especially terrified as the camera presents a view downward into a street bustling with pedestrians "far below."[3] In Frank Tashlin's *The Disorderly Orderly* (1964), Jerry Lewis is so anxiously self-absorbed on his date with Karen Sharpe at an Italian restaurant that he twirls his spaghetti all the way up his forearm like a cast: spaghetti for real, or so it seems, so that when Jerry screws up his face and whispers "Heat! Heat!" one believes him. At the ending of *Thelma & Louise* (1991), Geena Davis and Susan Sarandon, having decided to transcend male-dominated society by taking responsibility for their own lives, drive their automobile off the edge of the Grand Canyon: really off the edge; really into thin air. And in *The Talented Mr. Ripley* (1999), Matt Damon, wounded and humiliated in forbidden love, smashes Jude Law's head in with an oar, on a boat afloat under Mediterranean blue skies: a real oar, it seems, and real bludgeoning, so that the body, really bloodied to death, seems to weigh the boat down as it sinks pathetically into the sea.

Certainly in all these moments, and countless others, something deemed to be valuable is at stake for filmmakers, a certain purportedly unquestionable authenticity of place and action: that Jackie the Lion is actually high up on a ledge; that Jerry is twirling real steaming spaghetti; that Davis and Sarandon have really gone over a cliff; that Law's body is really being turned to pulp. Film workers collaborate in using technical devices or carrying out operations toward realizing shots that will "work" successfully to engage viewers.[4] Yet in proposing that it is "reality" that is generally at stake I mean to point to only one of many realities that obtain for any engaged viewer. First, and beyond much of my consideration here, is the real fact that, very much at work themselves, viewers actively inhabit a bounded environment furnished with some kind of screen. This particular reality, a complex one to be sure, is expressly not what most filmmakers would like their audiences noticing,[5] since it includes the fact of the theatrical design—say, the translucent, high-transmission material out of which the screen is made (see Fielding, *Technique* 272)—as well as the capitalistic substructure of theatrical operation: that one is here to watch only because one has paid to have a seat; that the seat is rented and not owned, so that one's occupation of an ideal viewing position is limited in time as well as in space; that there are only some legal claims a patron can make as to the sort of experience that must be provided in exchange for the entry fee; and therefore that the money one has paid is refundable only under certain conditions of complaint, and not merely because one ends up disappointed with the product. Theatergoers (as Erving Goffman names them [see *Frame Analysis* 129–30]) are not to be aware that while the fourth wall purports to open up a "real world," in truth a mere series of photographs is being thrown onto the screen by means of a projector lamp the power for which is paid for by the establishment. Nor should viewers recognize, swept away by pictures of the world, that these pictures are all contractually controlled for exhibition rights, whether they originate in documentary footage now marshaled and rented by the foot or in live-action footage for which paid and contracted performers appeared at a site pre-announced on a date set months beforehand, then did what they had agreed to do in front of a device manned by experts who understood how to illuminate them in such a way that they would handsomely show. No one has more faithfully described the existential pains of this process than Pirandello, whose operator Gubbio confesses to the reader what he accomplishes by turning the crank of his camera:

> Here they feel as though they were in exile. In exile not only from the stage but also, in a sense, from themselves. Because their action, the *live* action of their *live* bodies, there, on the screen of the cinematograph, no longer exists; it is *their image* alone, caught in a moment, in a gesture, an expression, that flickers and disappears. They are confusedly aware, with a maddening, indefinable sense of emptiness, that their bodies are so to speak subtracted, suppressed, deprived of their reality, of breath, of voice, of the sound that they make in moving about, to become only a dumb image which quivers for a moment on the screen and disappears, in silence, in an instant, like an unsubstantial phantom, the play of illusion upon a dingy sheet of cloth. (68)

All of this is part of what *can* be thought "real" for someone who is watching a film; but not part of the "reality" apprehended in a "reality effect."

Beyond this material reality—yet also not my focus here—is the fact that the movie has been advertised at some real expense to the producer and distributor and is being attended only because viewers were somehow lured: by the exoticism of the title and theme (as conveyed by graphic representations) or by the fame and exclusiveness of particular performers (the star system) or by the reputation of the filmmaker or screenwriter or genre in which the film story is cast. Equally seductive is the social reality of filmgoing: the class relations that obtain between characters and viewers; the problems of navigating city space to and from a theater; the friends with whom one goes to see the film and to whom one will later make a recommendation (imitating the review process on lay turf); the restaurant at which one sits afterward over an expensive latte to commit a postmortem; the reviewer (David Denby, for example) who offers a professional comment that one can read as gospel; not to mention the warehouses full of ancillary merchandise one can acquire as a souvenir of the filmgoing experience, such as, in the case of the late Heath Ledger who appeared in *The Dark Knight* (2008), a fourteen-inch-tall ceramic figure in "full costume and makeup." There are billboard advertisements, television spots, casual references to films in popular discourse, and, once the original passion has cooled, DVDs one can acquire and warehouse, directors' cuts, twenty-five-year anniversary celebrations, and so on. All these are as "real" as I am, sitting here writing about them, but in pointing to a "reality effect" I don't look their way, either.

To the degree that he gives attention to any of these technical, economical, or sociological "facts," the viewer is turned away from the diegesis onscreen, convinced that everything he sees depicted there has only a kind of sham or perfunctory existence as a hook. Present in any viewer's "real" perspective, but not more than a distraction from the cinematic experience, is the world itself—its state of perturbation, its long past, its ecology. Cinema is historical, and occurs in the context of surrounding, if not prevailing, biological, cultural, climactological, political-economic, and global circumstances. There is war, poverty, killing, struggle in this or that bounded geographic territory and involving this or that ethnic or religious or racial group: drought and famine in Africa, flooding in China or Latin America, financial crisis, fraud, murder, active or portended conflict. It is not difficult to link the motifs of a film with these pervasive overriding themes, since obviously those who made the picture live in the same world viewers do. A film can seem to be "about" a global conflict or economic situation or technical development or even about a news story, regardless of whether "From a True Story" appears on the credits or not. A film can be about the making of a film like itself.[6] But this immanent, surrounding, inescapable "real world," the space of biography, is also not what I mean to point to when I say film conjures a "reality effect." In light of any "external" reality conceived globally or culturally, large or small, the characters in whom one fully believed a moment ago are transmogrified into mere workers caught in a mere mobilization. In addressing the "reality effect," it is not this disabling, quotidian existence that I have in mind, this very material existence subject to gravity, death, and taxes and structured by political, social, economic, and psychological forces, and that, displacing the cinematic effect, generally substantiates little more than a picture of one's own gross manipulation through the "apparatus" of cinema. With this grounding paramount, cinema can be only an opiate that has been foisted upon the viewer in order that he may be distracted; distracted in order that he may be held off from power.

Opiates not only captivate, however; they also nourish. To the extent that the viewer recognizes himself as only a dupe, only a patsy, he is deposited in a world that may be real but is not, in truth, fully cinematic.

Nor, as part of what viewers consciously appreciate as a "reality effect" when they watch films, am I pointing to another distinct set of conditions, those that obtain for film workers in the phases of their work while they are working—conditions that surely merit serious discussion (such as can be found in Clark; James and Berg; and Horne). A director, for instance, must deal with a recalcitrant actor who won't make a move in front of the camera without consulting a coach he has brought to the set (Alfred Hitchcock working with Montgomery Clift on *I Confess* [1953]), a coach, further (here Mira Rostova), for whom the director has no particular respect; or must haggle with an actor who at a crucial moment just says "No" (George C. Scott, working for Arthur Hiller in *The Hospital* [1971], as Hiller recounted to me). A studio boss must put up with a box office winner who spends his time off-camera pilfering props and costumes from soundstages, as did Louis B. Mayer with Wallace Beery (Eyman, *Lion* 222–23). A cinematographer must achieve a shot in limited available light before the sun sets, which is to say, inside the next three or four minutes, or must, as Nestor Almendros did working with Eric Rohmer for *Claire's Knee* (1970), invent a way to shoot outdoors over a period of several weeks with extremely variant weather conditions, yet obtaining a uniform and matchable quality of evenly diffused and unreflective light (he tied a huge white cotton sheet to four poles and had it held up over the shooting area for the whole film, thus producing "filtered" light no matter what the sun was actually doing [see Almendros]). Actors must appear to be strangers or antagonists while in fact being married and/or living together (Richard Burton and Elizabeth Taylor in *The V.I.P.s* [1963]); or must appear to be intimate lovers when they have only recently met (Michael Pitt and Eva Green in Bertolucci's *The Dreamers* [2003]). If a "reality" obtains for those who labor to make a film, something that is for them not the fake construction they are mounting but an actual, quotidian working life, audiences watching films do not usually trouble to grasp it; and our pleasure in filmic "reality" does not depend on having access to the facts of a production, fascinating or alarming as these facts might be (and controversial as this thought might seem to those who program entertainment television). While he performed as cheerily as a parrot in *The Band Wagon* (1953), for example, British song-and-dance man Jack Buchanan was suffering from excruciating dental pain, but we don't care, and knowing about it doesn't sharpen our engagement as he sings "I Guess I'll Have to Change My Plan" or "That's Entertainment."

In *The Reality Effect*, Black uses the phrase in a way quite different from what I am attempting to do with it here. For him, the viewer of cinema is committed in a general way to the reality of what is purveyed by way of cultural norms, values, orientations, attitudes, and desires, so that cinema becomes, as I would put it, a form of news broadcasting about the deep structure of our social experience. What, then, can we apprehend about our world if we take media seriously? An important question to ask. But by putting the words "reality effect" into quotation marks, I am meaning to suggest, first, that not everything one sees onscreen strikes the same chord of response—that there are moments of palpable falseness, designed to be read as such; and moments in which what one might take to be "reality" is not up for grabs at all (animation is full of these); and also moments that work only because somewhere in the screen construction is a node that is interpreted as strictly real. I see the "reality effect" as precisely an effect, not a general contingency or result of the cinematic process. Any sort of screen moment, "real" or not, can lead to a condition of cinephilic devotion, or can fail to; and so this analysis does not at all mean to probe the viewer's more diffuse commitment to the screen and what is purveyed there. The intent here is to examine some particular reality "effects" in some depth, to turn them in the light, as it were, and perhaps reveal elements of structure, nuance, and ornamentation.

As audiences watch movies, the "reality effects" that tickle and captivate lead them to take circumstances as being situated, if not exactly in the everyday world then at least in a world that can be reached from it—perhaps based upon it, extending off reasonably and logically, even to the immeasurable distance of a galaxy far far away, yet approachable by some wishful route. If in fictions of the literary page the sense of happening and place is ultimately a verbal matter; if in fictions of the stage that sense depends upon the proportions and delicacies of performance, in film one is presented with an opportunity for *residence*, since viewers are in stasis or motion inside the space of the filmic event. Thelma and Louise are having a culminating moment, perhaps suicidal, perhaps transcendental, but whatever it is, the audience is there not merely symbolically but also spatially, gravitationally, sensually. The audience hovers near Tom and Dickie's boat not just as witnesses but as accomplices to the violence; or rides on the ledge with Jackie the Lion, desperately thankful that lions know how to handle heights. As the viewer is at home in the scene he has a license to watch invisibly. In this way, sensing and appreciating moments of dramaturgical reality onscreen invokes the deepest roots of homeliness, *heimlichkeit* but also *unheimlichkeit*, since every soothing comfort is, at its depths, a terror. "Nothing," writes Hélène Cixous, "turns out less reassuring for the reader than this niggling, cautious, yet wily and interminable pursuit (of "something"—be it a domain, an emotional movement, a concept, impossible to determine yet variable in its form, intensity, quality, and content). Nor does anything prove to be more fleeting than this search whose movement constitutes the labyrinth which instigates it; the sense of strangeness imposes its secret necessity everywhere" (525). Home, as Freud's thought suggested, is canny and uncanny together and at once, and that is the feeling of placement inside the filmic tale: canny, because one recognizes and understands as though having been here forever; and uncanny because somehow it is all much too clear.

Looks of Truth: Establishments and Transformations of Consciousness

Absent obstructions—failures of fit that do not account for themselves—one enters into the filmic world for its duration. And now arrives a fascinating challenge to the sense of embodiment and placement: spatial jumping, technically speaking, the edit. What is it to experience the jump of an edit? Any edit. It is easy enough to recognize that the leap between the final frame of one shot and the initial frame of another is taken in something less than a twenty-fourth of a second, thus so rapidly that it transcends the limits of perceptual acuity. But still, through the mechanism of the edit the viewer moves from one place to another, or one view to another, and the jump is inherently shocking. When viewers enter Thelma and Louise's convertible and roll along with them toward the edge of that precipice at the Grand Canyon, accelerating, so convicted is the sense of presence in bond with the women's condition that when the editor cuts to a long shot of the car lifting off, flying away from the red rock into the vast stretches of the air, gravity has kept the audience pinned to a seat behind the two women even though viewing consciousness is now floating as one observes from outside. The viewer has a safe position hovering away from the vehicle, yet gravity draws her backward in time, into the vehicular space itself, by way of a trace synaesthesia, a body memory from the immediate past. This "immediate body memory" is like an afterimage, but expands beyond vision into one's other senses, especially one's proprioceptive reaction to spatial presence (the reaction that makes us feel an awareness that we are feeling an awareness). Since the viewer is both in the car and not in the car at the same moment, she experiences ecstasy. The rolling car and the flying car: somehow they are the same car. The flat earth under the wheels, the termination of the precipice—the same. A coherent feeling that the two vantage points are linked, however smooth the transition, is effected through a deliberate and careful leap of consciousness between two senses of embodiment (while, technically, two pieces of film have been spliced together that were carefully shot to achieve a balance in lighting intensity, color, and direction of movement, thus making possible an exact match in the configuration of diegetic space). This particular edit was a special challenge since the "airborne" shot is hardly a straight record of physical reality; it is a matte composite involving both location and studio work. The camera's precise angle of vision in the two shots is a critical matter, since the shift from one perspective to another must not strain orientation, and must seem rational to that very deeply concealed, calculating self that endures and regales in the rigors of narrative.

Regarding this potential "strain on orientation": a general predisposition toward narrative progress—that action should move on and move forward—does not always obtain for viewers, who sometimes cherish the ability to pause at a moment and examine action from multiple points of view (we may think of that pioneering insertion of the close-up of the ankle in D. W. Griffith's *The Gay Shoe Clerk* [1903]), but when it does, the forward movement of thought, the leap from point of view to point of view must seem—in some logical sense—fluid if it is to seem logical. (The consciousness that regulates and permits accession to such leaps resides itself in fluid depths.) To such fluidity of narrative movement—I am talking about conceptual movement, the movement of awareness—people became increasingly habituated after the development of railway travel (Truffaut once commented that cinema was like a train in the night) but only in the sense that frames shift smoothly in projection no matter what their contents. In considering shot transitions one must think through the many ways in which the change in the angle of view represents an alteration in stance, all this related to the way logical transitions really do "move" people to shift frames of reference sequentially. The will plays an important role in charging us for such transitions: film viewers participate with a kind of determinate collaboration, wanting to take up new perspectives on action and space even as they are offered.

Every edit requires some transformation of consciousness.

When perspectival shifts surpass the limits of a viewer's imaginative strengths, when they are too great to fit the "map" she etches as she works through a narrative, they may invoke a "dream" or "insanity" coding. Consider as an example the extreme perspectival shifts in the various shots edited together by George Tomasini to fashion Scottie's dream sequence in *Vertigo* (1958), shots including animations by John Ferren and live footage by Robert Burks.[7] This assemblage of shots, jumping from unfolding animated floral patterns to monochrome tinted shots of Carlotta Valdes gazing into the camera and matte composites of Scottie falling away, could only, it would seem, be a dream. A contrast can be found at the conclusion of *Invasion of the Body Snatchers* (1956), where Miles (Kevin McCarthy) has seen the alien pods taking over Santa Mira *and so have we*. Although he appears "insane" to drivers on the highway as he races between their cars, screaming, "You're next!" Robert Eisen's editing never loses perspectival match, and thus never hints to us that our identification with him as sane is groundless.

Character eye lines can be of central importance in building a sense of socially "real" space. In that spaghetti scene in *The Disorderly Orderly*, we enter a little restaurant with Julie and Jerome, watch them become comfortable at their table, watch Jerome stride over to the jukebox and call up

Doris Day singing "Que Sera, Sera," see their platter of spaghetti being delivered (by the incomparable Benny Rubin), and engage with hapless Jerome as he pitches in and winds those saucy strands up his arm. As the film cuts away to Julie's astonished and entertained face, then back to the now trapped young man, one knows how to read the line of her gaze inside the "box" of one's narrative home: with a certainty, it was Jerome and only Jerome she was looking at just now, Jerome who, even out of shot, was still here (eating while Julie is not). Read in terms of compositional grammar, this is a perfectly standard pair of matching one-shots—Julie looking/Jerome eating—but to make any "standard" shot is not the simplistic matter it might seem. From where, after all, is the audience looking at this looker looking? Given the camera's position, what can be the space that she is taking in with her gaze? Jerry Lewis himself is a master on the subject of shot construction:

> The first film I did with Norman [Taurog], I watched him say to a cinematographer, "I want a two shot." I later learned the reason I was upset about that was because there are thirty thousand two shots. Which two shot? What kind of two shot? Straight two shot, fifty-fifty? Over-on, over-on? Single pull? Single to a deuce? Start the deuce, stay with the deuce? How many two shots does the cinematographer have to choose from? I said "No, that'll never do." When I started to direct, I sat on that camera. I made the two shot and built the marks and the moves for that two shot. And anyone that didn't do that, couldn't be taught to do that on the spot, so I would very diplomatically say, "Norman, this is a three-camera shoot. You need the whole thing, 'cause there's a hundred girls. You need the deuce of Dean and Jerry, but you better have a single on the fuckin' money. Get a single on the kid. And we got it all. The two of them, beautiful. Oh, and the single on the kid is a transport. Get him for thirty feet, get Dean for thirty feet. Transport. We'll have all we want of the singles." I told Norman about it; [he said,] "That's very good." He never argued with me about the technical. (Fujiwara 103–04)

In this *Orderly* scene, there is a clear affinity between the camera's angle on Jerome eating, a second angle of Julie's gaze into offscreen space as we focus on her, and the third, pick-up angle of Jerome that follows (to show us what she is seeing). Is the pick-up on Jerome from precisely the point in space occupied by Julie's eyes? (If it were, the audience would suddenly be on the date, a position too compromising.) And do we see her seeing a Jerome who is intelligible to her, or a Jerome who is intelligible to us? (That is, who must legitimize and authenticate the Jerome being seen, Julie or the viewer of the film?) While on one hand it is true that all gazes off- can be thought of as being directed to an anywhere/everywhere, an absence of place, the understanding of offscreen space as constructed through shots like these actually denies the nullity produced by the screen boundary; actually invokes memory traces and constructions that fill in this area one cannot actually see. Also: when Julie looks at Jerome, is she seeing all of him or only his arm, or only his face? She must "see" only what the viewing audience can also see, since the cutaway will give her vision of Jerome over to that audience; and what that audience sees must be enough for filling in the dramatic contingencies of the moment.

To be "at home" in a narrative, one need not be chained to a particular vantage point but may inhabit a "body" that stretches and jumps, that extends itself willfully as needed. But a further issue concerns the extent to which, residing in that motile "body," one is morally implicated in the action watched. In order to see the murderer Tom Ripley put an end to Dickie Greenleaf the viewer has been situated in their rowboat, bobbing on the dark blue Mediterranean in the heat of the full sun. This being a cramped space, in which Ripley and Greenleaf must find room to move, the audience must occasionally vacate its position and hover above the waves just beyond the gunwales or wait above, looking down: when this happens, the action becomes more objective, thus more and less realistic at once: more because it plays to us as a given; less because our ideal viewing position is better than we would find in real life. Experiencing the scene depends on tacitly agreeing not to wonder how at certain instants one can be hovering around the craft like a hungry shark, or circling above it like a vulture. Being another passenger in that boat and floating above it to peer down have to be interpretable as synonymous experiences, one always able to stand in for the other. The boat is our home only when the body is being ravaged there—this even though our identification is with the murderer Tom; once Dickie is dead, there is no further reason to be near him, and the film cuts twice: first to a high angle from which we gaze down upon Tom embracing the corpse, perhaps sleeping with it; and then to a position on the rocky shore where Tom is seen pulling on Dickie's jacket as in the background that boat slowly sinks away. While they could literally cut any piece of film to any other, in practice filmmakers are sensitive to an expressive grammar that limits and shapes their cutting (see, for some examples, Bordwell and Thompson).

Establishing shots have signal power to focus the imagination, since among their other features (of aesthetic and dramatic quality) they stand as transitions between the viewer's alert everyday consciousness and the relaxed state of mind that must be adopted in yielding to the embedded seductions of the narrative. As we learn from Kristin Thompson, the abstracting definition of space itself is a relatively late development in establishing shots, which in early films contained most of the action (Bordwell, Staiger, and Thompson 196) but in later films contain very little, if any, action at all. Establishment turns at once in two directions, toward the outside practical world that the viewer inhabits and can recognize and toward the interior make-believe world of the narrative. Yet any shot might function to establish the grounds of the "reality" to be invoked in shots to come, thus to be a grounding "reality effect." In *The Mummy* (1932), once filmmaker Karl Freund has used a plaster model of the Temple of Dendur, then followed it immediately by an exterior stock shot or two, he can proceed with studio sets or California locations dressed to simulate Egyptian ones, importing extras who speak proper Egyptian Arabic for some daylit shots of diggers unearthing a burial mound; and, later in the film, he can insert a single point-of-view stock shot of the pyramids, made during the day but filtered in the lab to appear as though lit by moonlight. At more or less the same time, W. S. Van Dyke was filming *Tarzan the Ape Man* (1932), using inserted stock shots of animals rushing toward a camera to simulate the hero's position as he is attacked in the jungle. Later, trained animals and a professional wrangler in costume could be used on a soundstage to simulate the actual fighting without jeopardizing the star's health and future contractual opportunities.

In John Ford's *Mogambo* (1953), color process plates (rear projection images) of gorillas (made by Jack Whitehead, Freddy Cooper, Doug Wolf, Jackson Drury, and Johnny Pallatt under the direction of Yakima Canutt) are intercut and sometimes combined with color portraits of Clark Gable, Grace Kelly, and Donald Sinden (made by Robert Surtees on location and Freddie Young in the studio [see Eyman 422–23]): as the novice white hunter Donald Nordley, Sinden is, in fact, "filming" the gorillas! Tag Gallagher astutely observes how "reality" was an immediate issue for viewers watching this material; the apes, he writes, "prompt us to question ourselves (man/beast) and to wonder what is real"; then he takes pains to note how they "were photographed . . . with 16 mm equipment using the same methods Donald does": "What is curious, however, is that these

16 mm shots (recognizable by their paler color) are *almost* (the operative word in discussing *Mogambo*) always crosscut with Donald's Bolex 16 mm movie camera, so that the cinematic result *suggests* we are seeing the film he is taking" (309–10). The lack of color match may have arisen from the fact that the film proper was shot in Technicolor three-strip (with black-and-white separation negatives and a full set of color matrices produced in the lab) while the gorilla plates were made on Eastmancolor negative, on which the dye couplers had a tendency to fade. Perhaps the audience's desire for a coherent continuation of the story blends the two "halves" of the scene into a unified whole: people see Sinden attacked by a gorilla and Gable swiftly reacting to protect him (while Kelly falls to the ground screaming) in the same frame context as they see the documentary shots of the menacing gorillas. The experience of reality is a product of the desire to see.

Locational Transforms

With regard to the setting of dramatic action, it is not against cultural or geographic facts that realism is measured but against the viewer's (often limited) knowledge and (often exaggerated) expectations. For Freund to take filmgoers to "Egypt" in 1932, for example, was to reinvent the "Egypt" of their present-day imaginations. And what was Egypt for American audiences in 1932? When *The Mummy* was released by Universal, only a decade had elapsed since the discovery of King Tut's tomb by the Londoner Howard Carter, and the general public in America and Europe, titillated by the mystery of mummification and golden ideas of immortality and untold funerary wealth, "wonderful things" as Carter saw them (Reeves and Taylor 141), was hardly equipped to claim familiarity with the subtle and manifold details of Egyptian culture. Viewers were in no position to complain (correctly) that the Egyptian Museum—as depicted in the film—bore no resemblance to any museum actually operating in Egypt. Nor were they familiar with the Egyptian personality, such as it was, or with the arcane details of ancient Egyptian funerary rituals (which are openly suggested in the film). What was called for to seduce belief in the proceedings narrated, then, was a set of scripted happenings commensurate with what might have been conceived by someone for whom "Egypt" meant nothing more than "the untold past," "the desert," or "mystical obsession," all of this gilded with a certain romantic patina that linked together female weakness, male chivalry, and the yearning voice of Time.[8] With the sixteenth-century European mystical idea of the Golem here transposed onto the mummy (Boris Karloff), a non-European figure (Egypt had been part of the Ottoman Empire until only eight years before the discovery of Tutankhamen's tomb), it could seem possible and reasonable for this undead priest of ancient Thebes to achieve a semblance of life some 3,700 years later, to prowl through the shadows of nocturnal Cairo with a stultified, entranced gait, and to mutter sparse phrases half incoherently and in a drone. Nor is it difficult in such a visual and tonal context to imagine a primitive sacrificial killing with a jeweled dagger, just as we see attempted by the mummy's agent upon a hypnotized princess (and once again in 1984, following the same formula, in Steven Spielberg's *Indiana Jones and the Temple of Doom*). It can seem credible and "real," too, that a character deeply involved with esoteric practices might possess a tool for seeing across space and time, such as a magical pool in which, like a movie vision, an execution and burial from almost four thousand years in the past is made available in the "here" and "now" of the film's present. The recursion of Imhotep's vision of his own long-past death, appearing just like the film in which we watch him watching it, is part of a structure that lulls viewers into belief, since if what the priest sees in his pool is only nonsense, what can be claimed of the picture of him watching the nonsense but that it is nonsense, too, this degrading the viewing experience to a mere con? Far less self-negating is to accept the tale, which means accepting the tale-within-the-tale that Imhotep is being offered.

The "reality effect" of Imhotep's magical pool is thus garnered through a negotiation (swift and sweet) between credulity and sobriety. It has a basis in structural arrangement. Further, the film generally presents a "realism" that moves in two directions. In purveying only a minimal simulation of what can be taken as a world, it forbears to overtax the viewer's credulity or presume upon rarefied knowledge, tendering only bare facts (in a way that is largely false, technically speaking, no matter how authentic it might have seemed at the time to viewers who had never been to Egypt).[9] The "realism" of guised locations offers but simultaneously declines to offer. The actual geography that underpinned Freund's "Egypt" was local, not foreign: the excavation scenes were shot at Red Rock Canyon State Park at Cantil, California, itself an ancient geological formation but not the one watchers surmise in their engagement. This technique of locational masquerade is often to be found in cinema of the classical period and beyond, when there were strong preferences for shooting as much as possible on studio soundstages with their meticulously controlled lighting and the easy support of professional expertise in every creative area, and a general reticence to risk insurance costs and other possible obstructions by traveling far from home or to locations controlled by people unfriendly to American production. In the early summer of 1955, filming "unmasked" scenes of *The Man Who Knew Too Much* in Marrakech, Hitchcock and his team were continually subject to the whim and permission of the Glaoui, for example, and indeed there erupted a revolution against him just at the moment the production packed up to leave; yet shots were actually made in the *souk*, in the Place Djemaa el Fna, and outside the Mamounia Hotel. For *Dr. Zhivago* (1965), masking was used. David Lean filmed his Russian steppes in Alberta, not very far from the foothills where Ang Lee would shoot the Wyoming of *Brokeback Mountain* (2005). The Gotham City of *The Dark Knight* is Chicago's Loop, with key scenes shot on Lower Wacker Drive and East Wacker Place. For *The Paper Chase* (1973), the ivied precincts of Harvard were shot not in Cambridge, Massachusetts, but in downtown Toronto—one of the great urban character players, often guised as other cities onscreen (and profitably so, since widely distributed commercial cinema has not yet educated international viewers about what Toronto looks like "as itself"). In the late winter and spring of 2007, Adam Shankman used some of the same streets as Baltimore for his remake of John Waters's *Hairspray* (and still, every morning as I ride to work, I can see a ghost image of John Travolta in drag only blocks from where I live).

What counts in the end is not how real a place is, but how real it looks, *even if it is what it claims to be*. Appearance, after all, does not spring spontaneously and naturally out of existential being, as the looks of any recognizable movie star should testify (but if they do not, peek at the makeover sequence in *A Star Is Born* [1954]). If the "Sicily" of Michael Cimino's *The Sicilian* (1987) is indeed Sicily itself (the village of Sutera, southeast of Palermo), still—and notably—it looks remarkably like Sicily; like the Sicily of our imagination. Given that most viewers were not in a position to recognize the location one way or the other, "authenticity" in using it could have been a personal comfort for Cimino or a value he sought after for other reasons, but it was hardly a requirement of filming, since what reads onscreen here is only what predominantly ignorant audiences imagine the look of Sicily to be. In simulating settings the principal issues are optical, not geographical, as we can see easily enough from the opening pan shots depicting a charming Alpine village in Hitchcock's *The Lady Vanishes*

(1938), made in complete geographical abstraction on a studio table with a miniature set carefully lit and photographed with a lens that could give a "proper" bird's-eye view. The same technique was used, with a much larger and more elaborate model, in the Coen brothers' *The Hudsucker Proxy* (1994) to simulate a snowfall in midtown Manhattan. Here, as with Ishirô Honda's Tokyo in *Gojira* (1954), the buildings were about four feet tall. Richard Rush's *The Stunt Man* (1980) plays effusively with this theme of geographical transformation, putting an open assertion about movie manipulation into the mouth of a zany film director (Peter O'Toole), who in shooting an antiwar war film is using as his own location the same one Rush employs in filming him, the Hotel del Coronado just outside San Diego (which in 1959 was magically in Florida, as a principal setting for Billy Wilder's *Some Like It Hot*). And in *Close Encounters of the Third Kind* (1977), Steven Spielberg mocks up the idea of locational masquerade by having Roy Neary (Richard Dreyfuss), who has dug up his garden and those of his neighbors to fabricate in his middle-class playroom a huge rendition of the Devils Tower, actually pose next to his sculpture in a shot that, because of the lighting, camera position, and lens, makes the "mountain" go utterly real. We think for a brief instant that there has been an edit, and we have been transported to Wyoming. One "is" looking at Devils Tower; at least until the phone rings and, called away from his work, Roy cannot see the television news broadcast glaring behind him with photojournalistic images of the "real thing" (see Pomerance "Man-Boys").

In general with locational transforms, when well-known monuments or recognizable buildings are excluded from a shot the very simplest of adjustments can effect a wholesale construction of the "real": a little paint on the front of a building, a change of signs, a smooth movement of the camera during the shot so that no particular structure gets enough attention to make close scrutiny possible. For *The Incredible Hulk* (2008), the street outside my office was turned into 125th Street, Harlem, merely by a change of street signs and the addition of smoke bombs, exploded vehicles, and actors running amok as the camera swooped around. In watching films, viewers make cursory inspections for detail early on, looking for internal consistency more than factual truth, and when they are satisfied they take what they are given as logical, substantial, and authentic: thus the relative importance of the establishing shot. Even when a location is used to stand in for itself, these operating rules apply: Hitchcock wanted a sequence for *Stage Fright* (1950) staged at the Royal Academy of Dramatic Arts on Gower Street in Bloomsbury (staged, indeed, on a little stage there!), and he shot on the real location. Most viewers, never having been to RADA, do not recognize this: the place looked "right enough," it conformed to expectations about a drama school, and that was all that counted.

Realities of the Screen Body

Perhaps nothing is as real for any viewer as her body, nothing as artificial as the body of the other. Another way to say this: when we touch ourselves we reach an ultimate depth, but the inside of the other is (only) a spectacle for the eye, something we can urgently want to see in action. This makes the body of the self socially alien, an inward-facing being, and also contemplative. The other can be penetrated, and in that penetration, implied and invoked by it—is action. Marc Augé:

> The distinction between places and non-places derives from the opposition between place and space. An essential preliminary here is the analysis of the notions of place and space suggested by Michel de Certeau. He himself does not oppose "place" and "space" in the way that "place" is opposed to "non-place." Space, for him, is a "frequented place," "an intersection of moving bodies": it is the pedestrians who transform a street (geometrically defined as a place by town planners) into a space. (64)

Those pedestrians: they from whom we learn. As space is an "animation" of place through the action of "moving bodies," that action and those bodies provoke us through a narrative that is only "real" while we sit in stolid observation, from a position we consider ultimate. To look at the body is not the same as to feel oneself looking. To look is to begin to open, and to feel oneself looking is to be neither open nor closed.

Action, zombie, and horror films depend for their bite on some manifest evidence of the other's punctured embodiment, an irruption or a sudden glimpse past the decorous surface of the skin and into the seething bowels of the "pure."[10] Such films utilize the "reality" of the leaking body as a staple ingredient. When one sees actors onscreen, then, they are typically manifested through a veil of distance, which is the simple fact of their appearance inside a diegesis in a performing role, a fact made plain in every sighting. At the moment it is broken open by a bullet, a hatchet, or a bomb, however, that body becomes "really" itself, a vulnerable being more than a "believable" surface, if only for a flash. The constant technical improvement of latex appliances is aimed at the project of sustaining the moment of viewer belief over longer and longer shot durations and through progressively closer points of vantage. The "reality effect" of the wounded body is thus constantly in development as a site of increased concentration and analysis, as though the film viewer, in watching the story, is performing a kind of on-the-spot autopsy (seeing with his own eyes).

We can all agree that in the past fifteen or twenty years, the screen depiction of maimed, opened, suppurating, dismembered, and hideous bodies in the name of situational "realism" has increased exponentially—obviously mirroring progress in special effects technologies. In this area, one cannot show with the camera what cannot be demonstrated by backstage artists. The idea of a link between disease, debility, disintegration, and vision is an old one. Barbara Tuchman notes that in the plague-ridden fourteenth century it was believed, not least by noted medical experts, that "people fell ill . . . not only by remaining with the sick but 'even by looking at them.' Three hundred years later, Joshua Barnes, the seventeenth-century biographer of Edward III, could write that the power of infection had entered into beams of light and 'darted death from the eyes'" (102). The body's contagion—that is, the contagion of the body of the other—was produced through the spectatorial gaze; but an ultimate reality could have been achieved when the sensorium took in mechanisms or produce of the body that, due to their liminal qualities, could not be denied. The stench of feces in the street, the presence of privies, cesspools, and drainage pipes, then the synaesthetic linkage between what might be observed and what had to be smelled, all still combine to produce, even as we read Tuchman's twentieth-century observations, the piquancy of the real. If the body, wounded and infected, suppurating and bleeding, was especially "real" to those who needed not share its fate, because they stood apart and observed, a specially embodied realism would be engendered in cinema, with its augmenting lenses and rich capacity to display the flesh on hand and provide for viewers an unobserved sanctum from which to gaze upon disease.

Take the onscreen medical procedure, formal or informal: one of the recurring rituals of cinema. The eviscerated, probed, autopsied, slashed, amputated, essentially defenestrated body, the body open to inspection, the body dumping its containment is the body in ultimate action, and when such bodies intersect—certainly inside a single film but also, more profoundly, in the marketplace of global distribution—we have the creation of one powerfully credible space of the "real." In *Commando* (1985), Arnold Schwarzenegger hacks off a man's arm with a machete and we are permitted to stare at the spraying arteries and bleeding muscle. This sight is repeated in Spielberg's *Saving Private Ryan* (1998). Fellini spares his viewers some of the gore as he shows such "surgery" used for simultaneous corrective punishment and entertainment in *Satyricon* (1969). While patricians mumble in the audience, a thief is walked onstage, his hand placed upon a block. As the man looks to his viewers with a shivering smile, the limb is unceremoniously hacked off. Still smiling, he is carried off the stage, all this seen in medium-long shot. In *The Cell* (2000), Jennifer Lopez confronts the instantaneous filleting of a horse. The boat murder scene in *The Talented Mr. Ripley* involves Ripley using an oar to smash Dickie's head in, on camera. While the intensification of bodily contact during cinema's golden age was handled relatively modestly, with blood-free stabbings and shootings, scarless stranglings, and tidy poisonings, the corner was more or less turned in 1970 with Mike Nichols's *Catch-22*. Captain Nately (Art Garfunkel) has crashed his plane, and the camera moves into the cockpit to see him trapped in his seat, surrounded by dead comrades. Slowly, moving down his torso, we realize something Nately does not know yet, that his ventrum has been opened in an enormous wound, and his stomach and intestines are slowly spilling out.

If the slain or wounded body, in combat or civil disorder, is a key "reality" for the screen, formal surgery in its systematized regularity points to the groundedness of embodiment. Filmmakers know that non-medical personnel are not privy to what surgery looks like to those who routinely practice it. Throughout the history of cinema, there has been a gradually intensifying visualization of surgeries—depictions have become bloodier and bloodier—but not because viewers know more and more about surgical procedure and thus demand greater "realism" in the portrayal of operations. What they have come to know more about is the way filmmakers have portrayed surgeries onscreen, always willing to move a step beyond the graphic limitations of their predecessors. The fundamental law of visual effects has been that sights are good in themselves, and so whatever can be made visible has been made visible regardless of medical or dramatic relevance. Here we see yet another reprise of the intensification of vision that Antonie van Leeuwenhoek (1632–1723) produced as, with his microscope, he made possible the observation of muscle fibers, blood cells circulating in capillaries, and spermatozoa, in short, a more detailed vision of life. In a kind of reaction, action cinema has worked persistently to multiply the quantity of visual events onscreen, and this applies to body unpackings. Like screened exorcisms (*The Exorcist* [1973]), screened initiation or torture rituals (*A Man Called Horse* [1970]), screened sacrifices, sacred or profane (*A Nightmare on Elm Street* [1988]), and screened mutilations (*Saw* [2004–2009]), screened medical conditions and procedures have developed according to unfolding conventions of portrayal. Self-surgery in *The Terminator* (1984) or *127 Hours* (2010); reparative surgery in *Ronin* (1998); eye surgery in *Minority Report* (2002); heart surgery in *Terminator Salvation* (2009): blossoming cinematic "realities" have been engendered by earlier and far less decorative cinematic "realities," like the modest and tranquil offscreen death of Kay Francis's Joan in *One Way Passage* (1932).

Medical procedure, in its historical growth, has been about progressively opening the body to the control of understanding, not just about vision for its own sake:

> The observing gaze refrains from intervening: it is silent and gestureless. Observation leaves things as they are; there is nothing hidden to it in what is given. . . . The gaze will be fulfilled in its own truth and will have access to the truth of things if it rests on them in silence, if everything keeps silent around what it sees. The clinical gaze has the paradoxical ability to *hear a language* as soon as it *perceives a spectacle*. . . . One can . . . define this clinical gaze as a perceptual act sustained by a logic of operations. (Foucault, *Birth* 107–09)

The medical gaze-*in* is produced by work, since except with rare injuries the body does not open itself automatically to view.[11] But in cinema, the work of the gaze is typically effaced, so that the body as a site seems always to have been ready, always blossoming, for inspection. Bluntly: at the moment the body is opened to view, the camera is magically there to view it and the viewing act is naturalized.

Beyond surgery, the body as a locus of wounds has been intensified as well: such spectacles as birthing a child (*Rosemary's Baby* [1968]), reaching into a cowboy to dig out a bullet (*Dead Man* [1995]) or into a skull to tweeze out a portion of brain (*Hannibal* [2001]), fishing a young man's testicle out of the dust after he has stepped on a land mine (*The Big Red One* [1980]), or nursing a man whose skin has been severely burned (*The English Patient* [1996]) have come to be described in cinema with sounds and visions that would never have been attempted in the studio age—*High Sierra* (1941), *Magnificent Obsession* (1954), or *Not as a Stranger* (1955)—but that now seem merely appropriate. We can see this development if start-ing with the treatment of Drake McHugh's (Ronald Reagan) implied amputation in *Kings Row* (1942)—"Where's the rest of me?"—we work forward through the same procedure used, with progressively more blood (or at least more elaborate demonstration of agony), on William Bendix in *Lifeboat* or Van Johnson in *Thirty Seconds Over Tokyo* (both 1944), Kenneth More in *Reach for the Sky* (1956), Omar Sharif in *The Horsemen* (1971), Bruce Campbell in *The Evil Dead* (1981), and James Franco in *127 Hours*. What prepares the audience's endurance is a mix of hunger to pen-etrate the glossy surface of the actor (to find the motive-body beneath the act) and ignorance of medical techniques as such, thus willingness to take what is given to the eye as what must be given, because it is there in so-cially organized actuality.

Because it is manifested as a total lack of performance, death is notori-ously easy to simulate with authenticity, especially onscreen where it can be shown in limited duration while an actor holds his breath and reduces his discernable movement.[12] Death performed in front of a camera has a tendency to seem real, since playing dead is such an accurate game and the limited duration of the shot and the cheat of the camera angle conspire to assist. It can be difficult if not impossible for audiences to assess vi-sions of death's reality. And just as mock-ups of death can be hard to dis-tinguish from death itself, so death itself can be hard to distinguish from mock-ups. The case of the filmmaker Nicholas Ray is instructive in this regard. Progressing on a long and terminal road with incurable lung can-cer, he agreed with his protégé Wim Wenders to participate in the film-ing of a motion picture that would feature him and his daily routine. In a climactic scene of the film, which was released as *Lightning Over Water* (1980), and playing the character "Nicholas Ray," Ray dies onscreen, but it was only viewers familiar with his life and his medical case who realized they were witnessing the performer's actual death, which he had arranged with Wenders, his close friend and professional associate, to display for the camera. Ironically, Ray's death does not distinguish itself visually from thousands of other, quite fake, screen deaths, from the lead thief's in a pile of money in *The Great Train Robbery* (1903) to Raymond Massey's in a great oaken bed in *East of Eden* (1955) to Jack Nicholson's in the scoop of a bulldozer in *The Departed* (2006). In Gore Verbinski's *Mousehunt* (1997), a brilliant performance of a man dying of emphysema is given by the actor William Hickey. Most viewers were unaware in their watching that the "authenticity" of Hickey's work derived in large part from the fact that he was, indeed, dying of emphysema as he shot his scenes; he perished soon after filming. It wasn't significant that the man was actually on the verge of death since he fully appeared to be.

In these cases, two quite distinct kinds of "reality" are in play together. There is the actual, historical reality, or everyday reality, in which death is taking place to terminate life. One might be tempted to call this an "un-cinematic" reality, except that with both Ray and Hickey it is anything but. Historical reality transcends cinema, but with sufficient devotion and concentration on the part of film workers it can be shaped for cinematic use. There is also the fictional "reality," in which characters "die" as for decades they have "died" onscreen before. These "deaths" do not look appreciably different from those that are put up with the greatest fakery by charlatans and clowns, and that is what is signally vital about them as agencies of cinema: they look as we believe they ought to look, even given that we cannot tell whether it is "death" we are gazing at, or death.

The "reality" of the cinematic body reflects what William James wrote about reality in general, namely, that rather than a property of events or circumstances, of spaces and actions, it is attributed to things by people who regard them. Reality is a mode of appreciation and understanding, a kind of "key signature" in which we hum out our perception of the world. James's question was not what reality *is*, but what the circumstances are under which we would call something "real." His suggestion that "any object which remains uncontradicted is ipso facto believed and posited as absolute reality" (289) is borne out by the cinematic image and its powerful internal coherence. Filmmakers must be successful in soliciting a reading of bodily "reality" from their audiences, who are typically building judgments upon earlier experiences of watching film. To seem "real" in itself, any single contribution to film must be in balance with what is in the dramatic surround. Every performative gesture must work with the set, the other actors, and the light, and also in the context of the history of such gestures. The set builder's nail is hammered, his paint is brushed, with a consciousness of the kind of performance that will take place here. For example, to make the conversation of Paul Newman and Julie Andrews seem appropriately adult and somber there, as he recounted to me, production designer Henry Bumstead added gray to all the colors he used in the East Berlin hotel scene of *Torn Curtain* (1966).

When the visible surround changes radically from one shot to the next, an actor's consistently strong embodied performance can be vulnerable to collapse, this even in a film that makes no particular pretense to realism.

A case in point: George C. Scott as the gum-chewing, jaw-dropping, frat jock five-star General Buck Turgidson in Stanley Kubrick's comic farce, *Dr. Strangelove, Or How I Learned to Stop Worrying and Love the Bomb* (1964). Here is a performance that wavers between hyperbolical animation and bureaucratic mundanity. When Scott is caught in long solo speeches in a single shot, without much visible background, he seems to leap outside the proper boundaries of performance, exaggerating, hamming, and railing at the heavens. But when this same demeanor is caught against other exaggerating performers or exaggerated sets he suddenly seems a natural, even unremarkable part of a world gone mad. In evaluating the "reality" of Turgidson one cannot but consider his body, the amplitude of his gestures, the modulation of his vocal tone, the range of his vocabulary, and his use of facial expression for emphasis—this latter sometimes augmented by Kubrick's use of a wide-angle lens. For wide-angle shots, performers often consciously withdraw expression to some degree, since the lens always already acts to expand and magnify it. By consciously failing to do this, an actor can physically augment the lens's work, as we see with Scott, or with Jack Nicholson and Shelley Duvall's somewhat over-the-top expressivism in *The Shining* (1980). In these performances, even enclosed the body explodes.

Invisible Witness: "Reality" and the Unseen Audience

For a moment to recall *Defiance:*

In the opening sequence of that film, as discussed above, one has a palpable sense that the action is distinctly, alarmingly present—Hitler on his podium not so far away, his murderous soldiers in the street with their guns. Viewers are positioned in proximity to events without bearing any of the weight that might, in a social world, be loaded upon such proximity. After all, to be sufficiently close to soldiers to see their actions in detail is also to be close enough for them to see their watchers, yet here they do not (see us seeing, or see the "documentary photographer" shooting them shooting; he is perhaps disattended in order that the "real" deaths the soldiers are producing can be successfully dramatized—the Nazi witnesses to such extermination footage did not want to be seen seeing, either). The present camera, at any rate, provides for a denotative invisibility on the viewer's part, an invisibility of which he can be conscious and in which he can feel relief. He "survives" by avoiding—escaping from—the gaze and focus of wanton killers: that is, actually surviving because he is in another domain, he feels unattached from threat as an engaged viewing participant because inside the closeted viewing space, which includes both him as watcher and the diegetic characters he is watching, they look past him. (The image as fetish is unconscious of its possessor.) In order for us to experience the thrill of this flight, the killers' gaze must be something merely immanent; possible yet not manifest. In an arrangement like this we have moved a great distance from the strategic relationship of performers to camera in very early cinema, where, as Tom Gunning points out, one tended to find "the recurring look at the camera by actors," a look that "is later perceived as spoiling the realistic illusion of the cinema" ("Cinema" 57).

Characters behave as though audiences are not there watching them in most narrative cinema: the prevailing fiction is that watching (from without the action) is not occurring, and viewers are not accomplishing it; the action being watched is the world. In the concluding moment of William Wyler's *The Heiress* (1949), when Morris Townsend (Montgomery Clift) is banging on Catherine Sloper's (Olivia de Havilland) door and she does not let him in, the audience sees clearly enough that, inside the great house, she hears and turns away, turns away and goes upstairs, cuts him brutally (but justly) out of her life. But she does not see him: cannot, because she does not open the door. We are outside the door watching his culminating frustration, looking straight at him, yet he does not know (while Clift, of course, knew he was having a close-up). When Gunning points to a "realistic illusion" that is spoiled by the performer's looking at the lens, he draws attention to cinema's regular artful posing of its content as unposed and unartful, as a mere eventuation in the flow of happenings. The camera by means of which we are seeing what is onscreen "is not there"—Stanley Cavell suggests that "there is always a camera left out of the picture: the one working now" (126)—nor is the screen itself, on which what the camera saw is being projected.

By calling conventional narrative cinema a "realistic illusion," Gunning also makes clear two facts: that the contents of the screen *are* an illusion, and that the illusion is manufactured in such a way as to hide its manufacture, made to seem less than an illusion. For Gunning in a way, in the exhibitionism of early cinema, in the actor's explicit turning toward the camera and confronting the lens (and its line of gaze) directly with the penetrating ray that is emitted from his own eye, inheres a shattering of the possibilities of illusion, a directness that brings to one's attention, in watching, the simple historical fact of an actor's presence; thus, the fact of technique and production, and, by implication, the corresponding fact that "diegetic facts" are on a plane different from that of everyday life. If, gazing at the screen more generally, one senses a heightening distance, an artful delirium, in seeing "reality effects" one suddenly becomes like those who, in the words of Hans Ulrich Gumbrecht, "long to perceive the world and its phenomena 'such as they are'—that is, without any perspectival distortions. They do not want such insight and understanding to be subject to revision and historical change. They still hope that the possession of truth will improve the conditions of human existence" (336).

A very delicious rendition of this "invisibility of the witness" is produced twice in John Carpenter's thrilling (and technically groundbreaking) film *Memoirs of an Invisible Man* (1992). First, having discovered that he has somehow (after exposure to mysterious radioactivity) become invisible, Nick Halloway (Chevy Chase) is running through the streets at night. It is raining. Raindrops strike him, some dripping off and some clinging, as raindrops will do, and one begins to see a beady silver sheen taking the shape of a body in motion along the sidewalk. The configuration is essentially an organization of refracted light. Here, it is as though the body of Halloway is being bombarded by particles that do not penetrate but adhere to his outer surface, and since each of these particles is a water drop that to some degree reflects available light and there are street lamps casting illumination into the area where he runs, it is possible to see by way of the reflections what appears to be a silver surface: the body made visible as a shape by being coated by reflective beads, that is, by myriad tiny mirrors. Bodies are not invisible, we know, and raindrops do not cling to their surface without being absorbed first in layers of clothing; in an earlier moment, Nick is shown to have stripped off that clothing, a hilarious play upon the convention of the strip-tease since the more he takes off the less there is to see of him. At this point on the street, given that the body itself no longer reflects light, the only thing that can make Nick "visible" is the reflection from the water drops. Because the ideology of this construction seems logical enough, and because it is represented onscreen with sufficiently detailed art, audiences can believe they are seeing an actual "invisible man" and get some inkling of what it might be like to be in his position, generally undetectable by others while "floating" in the environment and catching views of anything and everyone he wishes to see. He is the invisible viewer we so wish to be, with the movie camera's power to spy on whomever he likes; indeed it is principally in and through

cinema and its camera that such purely invisible watching is possible in
the world we know as real.[13]

A second key "invisible" moment in the Carpenter film has Nick sitting at his desk in an elaborate research facility, smoking his pipe. Or at least, this is what viewers are to interpret him as doing. What they actually see is the pipe moving jerkily through the air roughly at head height, then a packet of matches rising as though in someone's hands, a match being struck and then brought to the bowl of the pipe, and a trail of bluish smoke filling some ("oral") cavity and then descending downward (through a "windpipe"). The "invisible Nick," who is smoking while he watches, must be fashioned by audiences reading him into the picture. (He is invisible, but the smoke is not.)

Two *magics* are performed simultaneously in each of these cases. First, a character delights in occupying a position from which, unless infected by additives that give him away, he may innocently watch the world. Secondly, although we are watching pictures of absolutely no one, we coherently imagine an "invisible" character who "cannot be recorded." It goes without saying that in virtually every narrative circumstance onscreen, one might imagine such an "invisible" bystander, watching the world without being watched and also undetectable to us—who are so devoted to watching (without being watched), ourselves. This trick is performed differently in David Lean's *Blithe Spirit* (1945), with the ghostly Constance Cummings made up in gray-green and dressed in matching chiffon, all this contrasting the vivid colors of the scene in which she moves; the audience "takes her" to be invisible, while plainly she is not, and when bumbling Rex Harrison protests that he sees her he solicits the audience's sympathy of identification, yet not quite their admiration, since in this event seeing the visible ghost is no great accomplishment.

If, as in Gunning's description, some object of perception suddenly turns to look at the perceiver, or at the camera (the perceiver's factotum), the "invisibility" of sighting comes into question. He who gazes and he who is gazed at suddenly become mutually perceivable one to the other, at least logically—the performer does not exactly see the viewer seeing him, yet when he looks at the lens he knows someone like the viewer is out there, and thus for each viewer a radical experiential change occurs. As I see the eyes of the performer looking toward mine, it is *as though I am suddenly visible and to be seen*. There is an acoustic parallel. I can listen to the proceedings of everyday life without those who are making the sounds I hear recognizing that I am doing this. But under certain circumstances it

Voice

can become unavoidably apparent to a listener-in that he is being detected in his listening, indeed, that perhaps sounds are being made explicitly so that he may hear them (the stage technique of the *aside*). In such an event, what sound makers do not want heard is explicitly not what the listener takes himself to be uncovering but something else, still hidden behind or underneath. This happens regularly when one person leans forward and whispers in another's ear, whispers a "secret" that is actually a giveaway. With films, where one has the leisure of being able to think oneself an undetected hearer or eavesdropper, the illusion of one's non-presence can suddenly be violated if a character leans forward to whisper *in another character's* ear, this whispering magnified in such a way as to produce the effect for viewers of being close to the ear being addressed and thus of apprehending the whisper as being central to the moment at hand. This technique of the "stage whisper" flushes us from cover as listeners, all of us at once, who were so silent in our listening that until now nobody knew we were there. To look at this in terms of sound production, the recording of sound is normally accomplished so that all relevant sounds (which is to say, all recorded sounds) are discernable *to some presumed listening audience*, and yet at the same time under most conditions the listening of that audience is not explicitly invoked: but with "stage whispers" it is. The tone of "making sure you can hear even this" says directly, "We now admit that we know you've been hearing everything else."

Here as more generally, when conventions are violated we begin to see the structures they build. One hilarious example of a situation where listening *is* explicitly indicated as listening (and by analogy, watching explicitly indicated as watching) can be found during the key crisis moment in that film overloaded with crises, *Dr. Strangelove*. The president of the United States, Merkin Muffley (Peter Sellers), is in his War Room, a vast and shadowy underground bunker flickering with the light of huge projection screens. He is on the "hot line" to Dimitri Kissoff, the premier of the U.S.S.R., after bombers loaded with thermonuclear devices have accidentally been sent on a kill mission to Russia:

Phone

Muffley: Hello . . . uh, hello, Dimitri. Listen, I can't hear too well, do you suppose you could turn the music down just a little? . . . Uh-huh, that's better. . . . Yes. . . . Fine, I can hear you now, Dimitri, clear and plain and coming through fine. I'm coming through fine, too, eh? Good. Then, . . . Well, then, as you say, we're both coming through fine. Good. Well, it's good that you're fine and I'm fine. . . . I agree with you, it's great to be fine (laughs nervously).

Now, then, Dimitri: You know how we've always talked about the possibility of something going wrong with the Bomb. The Bomb, Dimitri. The *Hydrogen* bomb. Well now, what happened is, one of our base commanders, he had a sort of . . . well, he went a little funny in the head. You know, just a little . . . funny. And, uh, he went and did a silly thing. . . . Well, I'll tell you what he did, he ordered his planes to attack your country. . . . Well, let me finish, Dimitri. *Let me finish*, Dimitri. . . . Well, how do you think *I* feel about it!

Although we can hear only one of these speakers (Muffley), we are given grounds in his responses for believing the Russian partner is speaking, too, and thus his patiently holding the telephone becomes a signal to us that he is openly listening to a speaker. We can especially attend to the side talk about the quality of the telephone line, with each man (presumably) distinctively announcing his ability to hear the other, a demonstration on both ends of open attention to the production of sound: "I can hear you now, Dimitri, clear and plain and coming through fine. I'm coming through fine, too, eh?" In Muffley's pauses and in the Russian's—alluded to by Muffley—we can actually confront and see the demonstration of hearing, just in the same way that, in another movie and another confrontation between Russia and the West—the meeting in Istanbul of the British spy James Bond and his counterpart Tatiana Romanova in *From Russia with Love* (1963)—we can confront seeing. Half-naked in bed these two regard one another, she complimenting his good looks and he returning that she is the most beautiful woman he has ever seen—in short, each admitting to a gaze upon the other and in this affirming the act of watching (an act that we, in silent invisibility, are watching, too).

Invisible attention is itself diegetic material. At the same time that films offer their viewers the opportunity to see and listen to a diegetic world undetected, they represent dramatic situations in which, modeling what viewers do, characters see and/or listen to others without being seen or listened to themselves. Further, typically this very active seeing and listening that is involved in film viewing and modeled inside the narrative is not referred to, pointed to, indicated, labeled, or teased out as such. Films offer a specially illuminated diegetic space, in which actors narratively seen do not see; or in which sound makers narratively heard do not hear; all this in the way that film viewers sit with others to watch without being watched watching and to hear without being heard hearing. The "reality" of the diegetic world is enhanced, even stabilized, by this structured invisibility that causes it to resemble the extradiegetic world in which we live. William James suggests that what we call "real" has a sensible vividness or pungency: "No object which neither possesses this vividness in its own right nor is able to borrow it from anything else has a chance of making headway against vivid rivals" (301). The "vividness or pungency" is produced and articulated exactly by virtue of our not being detected in appreciation. Further, everything we detect and take onscreen as "real" is a vivid rival, a rival for any other attention—such as the attention that could be paid to us attending to it—and vivid as only film technique can make for. The vividness is diminished with each reference to the assessing audience outside the world of the fiction.

It is not happenstantial that in both theater and cinema there is an apparent boundary to perception, such that audiences are not distinguished in their distinguishing. A long history of the development of illumination resulted in nineteenth-century stages that were increasingly bright by comparison with auditoria, as we learn from Wolfgang Schivelbusch's extensive treatise on the industrialization of light. In 1818, the writer Ernst August Friedrich Klingemann became director of the Braunschweiger Theatre (which in 1928 was the site of the first performance of Goethe's *Faust*), and a year later published, with G.C.E. Meyer, his *Kunst und natur: Blätter aus meinem Reisetagebuche* in which he made the important observation that in theaters, the auditorium light was sponsored by the court while the stage lighting was paid for by the house management. The performance onstage, notes Schivelbusch of early eighteenth-century theater, "was matched by one put on by the audience" (204); whereas later on, audiences began to desire more separation between stage and audience and there was a clear trend toward "a brighter stage and a darker auditorium" (205–06). By the nineteenth century, a new theatrical ideal had found its place, "to achieve direct communication between the spectator and what was being presented, to the exclusion of all distracting, external factors. The idea of darkening the auditorium was to enhance this feeling of community between the viewer and the drama" (206). Once the audience could withdraw into darkness, and the drama onstage gain more luminosity, the fiction could achieve a new "reality," glowing more brightly, attracting the full sum of viewers' attention, and thus appearing more substantially rounded and three-dimensional. "Whatever things have intimate and continuous connection with my life," wrote James, "are things of whose reality I cannot doubt"; roundedness and three-dimensionality have a bluntly intimate, physical connection with the lives of viewers. Part of the effect of the brilliant stage coupled with the dark audience was a bounding off

of dramatic space, its territorial amputation. Writing of the panoramas of
the early nineteenth century, lit as they were by daylight but framed off by
a bridging black canvas, Schivelbusch quotes a contemporary report that
"the viewer experiences the most perfect illusion. It is not a picture that
he sees, but nature itself unfolding before his eyes" (215). By 1930, Béla
Balász could write of his "involvement," his being wholly absorbed, with
the action of film. Film had at least equaled theater, possibly supplanted it.
If, as Schivelbusch notes, theater was "the place with the greatest appetite
for light in the nineteenth century" (50), surely in the twentieth century
that place was cinema, especially after 1935 with three-strip Technicolor
cinema, which depended for its production on such massive quantities of
light that the procedures of soundstage filming were onerous for all involved. For Schivelbusch, in light-based media, light "does not simply illuminate existing scenes; it creates them. . . . The spectator sitting in the
dark and looking at an illuminated image gives it his whole attention—
one could almost say, his life" (220–21). One looks, that is to say, so avidly
that the very looking disappears.[14]

To say that a spectator sitting in the dark gives the intense illumination of the stage or the screen "his whole attention" is, in a way, to invoke
a profound relation between increased illumination, the concentration of
the visual faculties, cinema, and modernity. Jonathan Crary writes about
a particular form of attention that is purely modern, in which, following
the transition through the nineteenth century from folk to urban business
society (what Ferdinand Tönnies called, respectively, *Gemeinschaft* and
Gesellschaft), one "focuses . . . one's telescope on [a desired] object" (Tönnies, qtd. in Crary 52). This technique becomes shopping; and finally, by
the 1980s in cinema, it is a foundation of what some critics called *le cinéma publicitaire* (see Assayas; Bergala). There is a pervasive and ongoingly
motile surveillance, the rapt concentration upon discernable, isolable, recordable social facts or symbolic objects in the world of the surround—a
world that is always attractively addressed, pointed to, and encapsulated
by the rectangle of the frame. Rather than contemplation in tranquility of
the relations of figments and concepts in the thinker's mind and memory,
modern attentiveness urges a sharpened alertness, even a defensive annotation of facts and positions, as though everyday life were a military
endeavor. Gunning has noted, as well, the birth in modern times of the
figure of the detective, exemplified so fully, for example, in Fritz Lang's *M*
(1931): a being who shifts through the circulation of modern life with a
snatching eye that relates one to another the so-called important facts of

developing life. "Conan Doyle patterned Holmes on his professor of medicine, Dr. Joseph Bell of the Royal Infirmary of Edinburgh, who astonished students and patients with his ability not only to diagnose diseases from symptoms but also to read a person's occupation and background from details of body, gait, and clothing" (Gunning, "Tracing" 23; see also Pomerance "Significant").

Because it is linked to artistry—Walter Benjamin quotes Balzac's observation that "artistry as such is tied to a quick grasp" (41)—modern attention seems creative, and those who look can come to believe they have fashioned the object of their own gaze. The ability to see quickly, to discern without meditating, can be lifesaving. Marshall Berman describes Baudelaire's primal scene as one in which a pedestrian, crossing the busy street, is "thrown into the maelstrom of modern city traffic, a man alone contending against an agglomeration of mass and energy that is heavy, fast and lethal" (159). When viewers successfully track the thread of cinematic action through a blitzkrieg of fast-paced shots, as in much action film of the late 2000s, they demonstrate a kind of optical heroism, since the charged and rapid flow of otherwise disconnected images is a kind of traffic in itself. As in these pulsing sequences viewers fixate upon the screen, caught up in the brilliant flickering of the light that changes from quick shot to quick shot, they can feel they have seized upon action itself—that elusive beast—and can follow its movements, track it home. Very early cinema must have struck more deeply original and resonant meditative chords, as we may surmise from Maxim Gorky's famous reaction to the Lumières' films, which would begin with a still frame, "the shadow of a bad engraving," but then "suddenly a strange flicker passes across the screen and the picture comes to life. Carriages come from the back of the picture towards you, straight towards you, into the darkness where you are sitting. . . . Silently the ash-grey foliage of the trees sways in the wind and the grey silhouettes of the people glide silently along the grey ground as if condemned to eternal silence and cruelly punished by being deprived of all life's colours" (25).

For Gorky, this is no "real" *endroit* but instead a domain of "curses and ghosts, evil spirits that have cast whole cities into eternal sleep." The modern eye has leapt forward. Relentlessly it awakens to its unending task of discernment that replaces with its sharpness and alacrity the feelingful gateway of memory. Floating before the viewer is an incessant challenge to inspection, a labyrinth of masks and poses, a jungle of possibilities. The task is to see straight, to determine the event, to annotate it and be its living witness. And to do all this as though one does not exist.

"Reality Effects" and Pleasure

What makes the "reality effect" *unheimlich* is clearly not that it represents tedious quotidian reality—bookshelves, sunlight streaming through a French door—but that in it can be seen something outlandish and abnormal, something viewers would expect never to encounter in daily life, yet configured with the same detail, the same sharpness, the same roundness, the same distinctive presence as all that is disattended normally as real. The moment of perceiving the "reality effect" constitutes a transcendence of the already known artificiality of cinema, its techniques and processes, a convincing glimpse of what should not be (treated as) visible. Let us say that Kong looked like a magnified doll (and thus did not constitute a "reality effect" himself), but that the apes Kubrick worked into his introduction of *2001: A Space Odyssey* (1968) looked only like apes—except how could they have been? While I would not cite it as a genesis or locus of cinephilia more broadly, there is a distinct pleasure in perceiving "reality" onscreen, a sense of combined recognition and doubt, a flowing forward with the narrative coupled with a canny and self-mocking hesitation. This pleasure of recognition can be felt in examining hyperrealist painting, or in squinting to look at pointillism, where the world as it presents itself to the eye (the eye that sees or the eye of the imagination) seems replicated with all its nuances of illumination by a representation artfully constructed. To argue that screen "reality" is constructed by art directors, cinematographers, and performers largely in order to gracefully and seamlessly subtend certain "key" dramatic moments is to give the narrative a place of importance more central, perhaps, than it deserves; and to subtract from the viewer's direct experience of the screen images, which often tickle or soothe in their special coherence and situation of artfully effected detail. An interesting and uncontemporary example is given by the navigation screens in the cockpit of the globular shuttle in *2001*, each lively screen flashing with "relevant" and "current" navigational information in code before the eyes of a pilot ostensibly concerned with setting a spacecraft into place on an orbiting station. The viewer makes no sense of the mini-screen information, but its sheer presence and delicacy, its motility, its apparent responsiveness to "exterior" conditions all broach the subject of a direct and inherently faithful indication of "real" momentary conditions.

In Alex Proyas's *Knowing* (2009), a professor of astrophysics at M.I.T. named John Kessler (Nicolas Cage) comes into possession of a fifty-year-old document that lists in chronological order every major disaster that has occurred in the five decades leading to 2009, with a precise date, latitude, longitude, and number of dead registered for each. Trying to come to terms with the very existence of such a thing—evidence, apparently, of a deterministic universe in which until now he has steadfastly refused to believe—Kessler finds himself en route to the very next predicted event, an airplane crash at a major Massachusetts highway not far from Logan Airport.

So that the impact on Kessler's consciousness and worldview of this catastrophe should be transmitted to the audience powerfully enough to seal the dramatic authenticity of the document he has been studying, the crash must be portrayed fully, even opulently, onscreen; the audience must witness exactly what he is witnessing and with exactly the awe that he is experiencing. From a production point of view, the crash must be staged in its entirety. So: the plane comes down out of an overcast sky, far more quickly than at daydream speed, ripping through high tension lines in a twist so that one wing points into the air while the other scrapes across the asphalt between vehicles that are stranded in a traffic jam. The aircraft is at once a looming object and a dream figura. Watching, one feels paralyzed—desiring in the same breath to stop the action and to see it proceed. The craft tears across an adjacent field, breaking up there in the vast reaches of black mud, exploding, ejecting screaming passengers who run off-camera enveloped in flames. Then it explodes again, with smoke everywhere and blackness and fire and screams.[15] To speak technically: as it approaches and crashes, the aircraft seems quite as real as Kessler himself does, its grain structure wholly integrated and small enough so that we do not see compositional effects. The thing looks like a flying three-dimensional object, not a pixilated artist's rendering. The sound is deafening, as we imagine it would be in a real circumstance, and Cage's stunned, wide-eyed reaction (like that of a supporting actor playing a highway patrolman) is perfectly calibrated to demonstrate first disbelief and shock, then adrenalin-boosted energy as he runs into the wreck to try to help. When in 2005 for *War of the Worlds* Steven Spielberg required a plane crash in a suburban housing tract, he produced it through an elaborate sound effect followed a few minutes later by Tom Cruise discovering the

broken pieces of a fuselage arrayed (neatly, we might think in retrospect)
in the road outside his house.[16] Spielberg's fragmented aircraft was a constructed set. With *Knowing*, while the final shots of the torn plane on the
ground involved set construction, vapor from dry ice to simulate smoke,
controlled flames, and stunt work, the shots of the plane dropping to the
ground and scraping the highway could not have been made in this way.
The *unheimlichkeit* of the moment springs from two experiences taken together, the sense that one is standing just next to a real-looking airplane as
it crashes—a massive object plummeting from the sky, and, with horrific
improbability, heading for *this* spot—and the knowledge that one is at the
same time safely secreted in darkness, held away from all this by the net
of artifice.

To leap backward, sixty-five years:

Midway through Sam Wood's *Kings Row*, a film about life in a small
American town at the turn of the twentieth century, a young girl named
Randy Monaghan (Ann Sheridan), daughter of a railroad section boss,
is being driven in a carriage by her beau, "rich and high-toned" Drake
McHugh (Ronald Reagan), as they come to a railroad crossing where
they must halt for a passing freight train. The barrier has been lowered,
and Drake pulls the horses up just as they reach it. The train is moving
slowly across the screen from right to left, and as though to demonstrate
the thoroughly integrated and familiar quality of small-town life, in which
everybody knows everybody, one of the trainmen hanging from a ladder
at the rear of the caboose calls out a friendly "Hiii, Randy!!" and waves
his hand. "Hello, Ed!" calls she, waving back. (Something of an homage to
this shot is included repetitively in David Lynch's *Blue Velvet* [1986], this
time with a fire truck and a boy standing on a lawn as it drives by in slow
motion.) When the train has passed, Drake urges his horses onward and
they take a step or two, but Randy says, "Oh, let me out here, Drake," and
the editor cuts to a profile shot of the two of them, losing the perspective
on the railway tracks.

In *Kings Row*, the artful composition of the train shot conveys to viewers—viewers of the time and viewers today—a sense of effortless presence
in reality: carriage, train tracks, sky. But it was no more possible then than
it would be today to record both a passing train with its heavy locomotive
sound and the sound of an engineer's voice calling above it. Nor, without
committing substantial expenses—a rental contract with the railroad, ex-
port of enormous arc lights to an exterior location and powering them—
could filmmakers have obtained a crisp and readable "star" shot of the girl

in the carriage at the same time that they kept a moving train in focus in the background. Far more efficient, for a number of reasons, was photographing Sheridan on a soundstage, where lighting could be rigorously controlled and where the silence for proper sound recording was available.

What was needed, then, was a rear projection shot of the passing train, with Sheridan in a prop car in front of the screen on which this was being shown. The engineer and his wave were designed as part of the rear projection and the sound of his voice was recorded separately and mixed in. The fragments were pieced together in a skillfully realized composite shot, perfectly lit and recorded, while the film background operated to give a sense of place. I will say more later in this book about rear projection and its technical difficulties. This shot from *Kings Row*, involving the work of designer William Cameron Menzies and special effects photographer Robert Burks, is a masterpiece of rear projection technique, with the background bright enough to read crisply and without apparent differentiation from the foreground.

Structurally speaking these two effects sequences—from *Knowing* and *Kings Row*—are very distinct. In the structure of the "reality effect," two conditions are convoked. First, an actional proposition: viewers are in a position to believe that in the real world outside the cinema events do sometimes occur in the way that they are depicted occurring onscreen. (In Jean Renoir's classic *The Golden Coach* [1952], set in the early eighteenth century in South America, there are frequently scenes where we hear a baby crying, crying just as in real life a baby sometimes cries.) Secondly, an observational proposition: viewers count on the likelihood that what happens in their reality can be seen to happen, is visible, and that anyone might find himself placed—indeed, can count on being placed—so that he can watch. "Actional reality" and "observational reality" are thus two distinct facets of the "reality effect." An event can be thought "actionally real" when it strikes the audience that things like this do happen: a train will pass by a railway crossing. An event will seem "observationally real" when one believes that were it to happen it would look like this, and one would—or could—be positioned in roughly this way to watch it: Kong climbing the Empire State; Jackie the Lion or Roger Thornhill out on a ledge. Actionally, what one is watching seems plausible. Observationally, and irrespective of the plausibility of an event, one seems plausible to oneself in seeing it this way; in representation it conforms to the parameters of our expectation.

With *Knowing*, the viewer can tell herself that aircraft do unfortunately crash; but it is only in the imagination that one is placed ideally to watch every aspect of a crash play out with full optical clarity. The scene is action-ally real but observationally hypothetical. An even more extreme example is given by a view looking upward at a plummeting jet being saved by the superhero as it heads for the pitcher's mound in a major league park full of spectators, in *Superman Returns* (2006). Spielberg's "air crash" has more observational reality, since although the audience does not watch the plane coming down the idea of finding oneself wandering around the wreckage after a crash is not implausible. If air crashes are real in themselves, the air crash *as we see it* in *Knowing* is not. In the "reality" of a depiction it-self are imbricated not only the way physical events might transpire, given the laws of gravity and motion, but also the social organization by and through which one might be in a position to observe. Cinema of course provides a new form of social organization, in which observation is much more expansively possible. The scene in *Knowing* looks like a movie scene.

Both actional and observational reality may be considered to be present or absent in a film scene: events either do or do not take place as they are being seen; and people either do or do not typically find themselves in a position to watch. A fourfold table of "reality effects" can be constructed, offering a quartet of possibilities (see Figure 1).

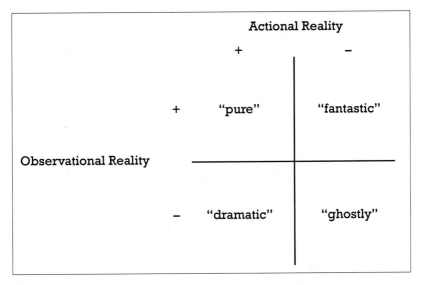

Figure 1

What we see in *Kings Row* is an example of "pure reality," since watching it operates in the context of real-world knowledge that (a) trains that look like this one pass at crossings that look like this one, and (b) people can indeed watch when they do. By calling this effect "pure" I am not meaning to suggest that onscreen it necessarily sparkles in any material or phenomenological way: a bad rear projection, a kind of contaminated vision, would still constitute a "pure" case, though perhaps a less fully rendered one. The scene in *Knowing*, by contrast, provides an example of "dramatic reality" since, although planes that look pretty much like this do sometimes crash, observers are not typically placed ideally to see. The term "dramatic reality" is meant to suggest that the realism of observation inheres in its dramatic frame, and that the dramatic frame intrudes upon the effect as it is experienced.

One could call up a case of "fantastic reality," where viewers watch onscreen an event that people (any people; some specially designated people) could be placed to watch if ever it did occur, yet it doesn't occur: the birth of the alien from the belly of John Hurt in Ridley Scott's *Alien* (1979); the landing of a "mother ship" on the far side of Devils Tower, Wyoming, in *Close Encounters of the Third Kind* (1977). Members of a surgical team do tend to surround bodies that are being operated on, as in *Alien*, and do look down from an ideal vantage point so as to see what is inside once an incision has been made—and sometimes visitors of the right rank can stand and join the observation. But alien creatures with three mouths embedded inside each other do not spring out of living human bodies,[17] screeching hideously and racing across the floor to hide in the heating ducts. (One may fear that they do; *Alien* is ultimately about feeling, not perception.)

And as a fourth type one can imagine a "ghostly reality," in which events such as are being depicted do not happen in the world where we live yet if ever they were to happen people could never be ideally placed to see them (yet onscreen, here and now, such events are happening, and we are happy to be placed ideally to watch): the dead Sam Wheat (Patrick Swayze) talking intimately to his beloved Molly Jensen (Demi Moore) through a door in *Ghost* (1990); the little hobbit Frodo (Elijah Wood) throwing the monster Gollum into the lava pit of Mount Doom in *The Lord of the Rings: The Return of the King* (2003) after a private struggle; a spaceship's cook (Earl Holliman) secretly asking his friendly robot assistant Robby to make him some bourbon on a distant orb with a green sky and two moons in *Forbidden Planet* (1956). Here, it is the "reality" itself that is ghostly, not the characters wedged into the screen representation. Lean's *Blithe Spirit* is mostly ghostly for viewers today, not only because the interactions in the plot are frequently between non-living persons but also because they take place in an English country house to the likes of which today's typical viewer has little or no expectation of being invited.

The sense of purity (or directness), the sense of drama (or contrivance), the sense of the fantastic (or extension), and the sense of ghostliness (or unworldliness) can all be evoked onscreen, then, and all constitute types of "reality effect." My point here is not to preface a careful discussion of these four types, since in themselves they are only conceptual and at any rate screen experiences often merge and blend them, but simply to illustrate how we are faced with the possibility of more than one sense of "reality" onscreen, more than one kind of experience. Nor would I claim that this typification is exhaustive. Our pleasures in thinking we are actually encountering something through the magic of filmmaking are complex and varied. The pleasure of watching Randy waving to her friend the engineer in *Kings Row* is, however dilute or minuscule, of a different kind altogether from the pleasure of watching Kessler watching that plane crash in *Knowing*, and not only because it is less morbid. It involves recognition and categorization: I know a moment like this, I know where it fits. Whereas in *Knowing* we experience astonishment: This is happening! It is happening in front of my face! I choose *Kings Row* quite intentionally as a film from Hollywood's golden age, one with which many young viewers today would be unfamiliar (or that they might watch only through a cynical lens, as a principal vehicle of its time for the competent actor-turned-politician Ronald Reagan); and I choose *Knowing* as a very contemporary—thus presumably "more advanced"—special-effects extravaganza. Given that the effects scene in *Kings Row* was not attempting in 1942 to meet the same challenge as would the effects scene in *Knowing* in 2009, the two are not comparable as being more or less accomplished or effective. Each is effective and accomplished in its way, and each gives a distinct thrill of recognition. As a realistic moment, the air crash in *Knowing* is not better than the passing train in *Kings Row*, it is a different kind of thing.

In *Kings Row*, one has to admit there is hardly a sense of *thrill* at all, simply a direct acknowledgment. This is because cinematic depictions that fit along the top of the fourfold chart above, in which observational reality is present, are not in and of themselves thrilling *as depictions*. To thrill *as a depiction*, a screen organization must show us what we cannot otherwise see at all, what only cinema can show.

Glitch and Repair: The Problem of Collapsing Artifice

One further turn of the screw. Anything made to seem flawless can have a flaw. The glitch has come under scrutiny as telltale evidence of construction, or as a pathetic failure in the simulation of reality (see Holmes). But seeing a glitch has its own committing consequences.

Given that makers of motion pictures manage the costs of materials, labor, technologies, and skills so that acceptable—acceptable but not necessarily ideal—products can be produced in a systematic, predictable, and profitable way, it develops that repetition of themes and developmental formulae, not to mention working with known personnel, is the recipe for profit. Mostly for this reason, viewers "hungry" for cinematic entertainment are offered a menu with comparatively limited choice. Confronted with scanty options, they learn to appreciate the standard fare, indeed to praise and keenly value their cinematic experiences given the practical restrictions that are in play. For most who watch films, convenience is a hallmark. Once it has become convenient to watch a particular film, inventing a way to enjoy it seems a simple act of sanity. Thus it is that we may come to appreciate the films we see not because something about them is worth appreciating but because they are the birds in hand; we would prefer to think of our lives as satisfying, our preferences as valued, our thoughts as esteemed, our experiences as validated, our tastes as nourished. George Orwell's sanguine observation that if we get what we are looking for, we get it wrapped up in the illusions our employers think suitable for us, we blithely disregard (see "Boys' Weeklies" 98).

Not only do viewers want what they get (rather than getting what they want), but they take it to have been made by estimable people who are expert at their work—part of the viewer's ritual of self-aggrandizement is a refusal to be catered to by obviously inferior workmanship. On the other hand, respect for filmmakers as the new supreme artists of our culture makes the public hunger for their product seem logical, even sophisticated. When viewers adulate relatively contemporary effects of screen "realism"—Gary Ross's *The Hunger Games* (2012), Neill Blomkamp's *District 9* (2009), James Cameron's *Avatar* (2009)—and hold them above older ones in esteem—Robert Wise's *The Day the Earth Stood Still* (1951) or, again, *The Golden Coach*, in which a woman has as many lovers as she pleases, and a baby cries—they merely boast of their own learning curve, only admire themselves for having the taste to prefer what current technical possibilities (and historical knowledge) make possible for film workers.

Given the costs of producing film and the global box office that is necessary for repaying them, much contemporary mass-marketed film is built so that it can appeal to an audience with little cinematic history under the belt. Ideal for many viewers in the new era of globalized downloading is the tactic of acquiring film for only the most tangential viewing, as with a YouTube clip that is multiply interrupted by the watcher's taking incoming cell calls, glancing at stock market quotations or sports scores, or making side trips to other platformed materials licit and illicit, not to mention texting, sexting, and recontexting. Plasticity and transformability constitute one of the powers of digital cinema, now being energetically touted as replacing celluloid: abandoning at once the large screen and the image fleshed out of chemical grain, with its haunting light not yet dominated by high-contrast hyperobjectivity, the digital image resides cozily in the fragmented, highly capitalized, multifocal commercial moment.[18] Once the digital revolution has converted the filmic image to information, it is equal, it is tantamount, to other non-cinematic information with which it can be combined or from which it can be subtracted.

With the pervasive sense of entitlement that viewers display now, their expectation for fabulous simulations always raising the ante on the simulations of yesteryear, "insufficiencies" onscreen are not only widely disparaged but condemned to spiteful vitriol. The "reality effects" that cinema purveyed once before, when current techniques were unavailable, are dismissed if they are even recognized. *Harry Potter and the Deathly Hallows, Part I* opened with $350 million in six days and some very complex effects, including a sextuple split screen by comparison with which earlier split-screen techniques (which I will discuss shortly) seem impotent and inadequate; *Part II* (2011) went further, or so it seemed as we watched. Linda Nead summarizes the particular thrill experienced by one distinctive observer to a "reality effect" we would hardly, in comparison, consider thrilling now: "When Henry Mayhew turned from his investigation of the streets of London and went up in a hot air balloon, he described the experience as exhilarating and sublime. The balloonist's gaze was no longer diverted by troubling, individual details but was able to absorb the extent of the metropolis in a single glance. The bird's-eye-view enabled a momentary, mental *control of the city*, which surpassed any possibilities for visual authority offered at ground level" (*Babylon* 84; emphasis mine). Mayhew's delight is reduced to the commonplace by the so-called superior thrills of digital action—Iron Man jetting above Santa Monica pier in a flight suit that gives a whole new control of perspective.

Although for some time cinema has celebrated the exhilaration at control made possible by the new point of view—in *The Wizard of Oz* (1939), in *Around the World in Eighty Days* (1956), and in *The Thomas Crown Affair* (1968, with delirious musical accompaniment by Michel Legrand)—pre-digital displays are seen by fanatics of the new digital empire as etiolated and pathetic. More impressive is what is current, apparently: the tidal wave sequence of *Hereafter* (2010), as well as sequences where superheroes leap up and fly at great heights (*Hook* [1991], *Superman Returns*, *The Green Lantern* [2011]) or ones in which aliens approach the planet earth from a supreme altitude. A particularly stunning "realization" is the concluding cosmic zoom-out in *Men in Black* (1997), where the "bird's-eye view," as Nead has it, is magnified exponentially until the earth and its whole solar system become nothing more than a dot in a much larger field. Such screen moments as these, entirely hypothetical though they are, do not seem more stunningly "real" to audiences watching them now than the parting of the Red Sea in Cecil B. DeMille's *The Ten Commandments* seemed stunningly real to audiences in 1956. As technology for achieving a "reality effect" moves forward, the viewer's own historical involvements can fade, finally evaporate in time. What prevents this process is only the viewer's wholehearted commitment to a particular "reality effect" as a present experience; a commitment not to the principle of such effects in general, not to their ongoingness and urgent development, but to a particular moment of viewing situated in historical time.

Further, the "reality effect" that is the fruit of our watching we believe is owed ultimately to experts, so that it is in accession to the supreme (often mechanized) skill of unknown others that viewers' imaginations come alive. Since we live in a culture of professionalization, with work fragmented and isolated, with specialists in one field hardly relating to specialists in another, we have elevated our regard for those who perform arcane technical work, turned effects experts and trick photographers into gods whose capacities seem unlimited and unconstrained and whose skills and methods, claiming a space and time all their own, rest above reproach and beyond critique. The film viewer has become a sort of professional, too.

Brooking no critique of his opinion, since his opinion is not only grounded in his individuality—protected bastion of late capitalism—but also founded in a kind of committed and focused devotion, the new "professional" viewer takes himself very seriously when he watches film. And since he is permitting them to command and seduce his loyalty and attention, he accords to those who make films—the writers, the producers, the performers, the technical personnel—a strength and clarity of purpose, a level of competence, that are simply not to be questioned. From the viewer's pious point of view, it is exactly the skill and competence of the filmmakers that should be credited with the making of the sacred object that merits his skillful and competent concentration. Just as the viewer's perception and opinion of a motion picture spring directly from an intensity of involvement and concentration, from a biographical history of being a viewer, so does the film spring from the capacities of those who make it—capacities which are taken for granted, because filmmakers are become our new repositories of knowledge and wisdom. Filled to the brim with cultural knowledge the viewer presumes himself not to have—the viewer already so worthy of self-congratulation—these experts can be relied upon to exercise their capacities methodically and consistently. To exercise their capacities, and not to fail.

So it is that when the viewer catches a technical glitch, the very fabric of professionalism can seem to have been rent. The men behind the camera—Pirandello's Gubbio and his brethren—have failed execrably in their task, which is to utilize and also hide their ability and the mechanisms they employ. Writing about *A Victorian Lady in Her Boudoir* (1896), Nead points out a particular vulnerability to collapse: "At one point in the film someone behind the camera seems to tell the woman to keep moving, to keep it going, keep it professional. To stop is to introduce a fatal hiatus in the fantasy being played out on the screen with its own rhythm of revelation and deferral" (*Gallery* 190). When behind-the-scenes professionalism has fallen down, everything that underpins a film goes with it; everything that has been brought together and organized to attract the viewer is dissolved. And then there is nothing further to look at, although the audience finds itself (now inexplicably, thus with embarrassment) trapped into the condition of looking.

A sad case: several years ago, I screened for an undergraduate audience a film that, up to a certain peculiar narrative moment, they were able to appreciate wholeheartedly. It was Anthony Harvey's *They Might Be Giants* (1971), an anodyne vehicle for George C. Scott and Joanne Woodward (from a play by James Goldman) about a psychiatric patient in modern-day Manhattan who is convinced that he is Sherlock Holmes. Students could follow the somewhat self-reflexive story—an actor (Scott) playing the role of a man (Justin Playfair) playing a role (Sherlock Holmes) and accepting it as the truth—until a scene with Scott and Woodward confabulating in her apartment one evening. As they sit on the couch together, feelingfully chatting, it suddenly becomes possible to see—possible to see and also impossible not to see—at the very top center of the screen a boom microphone dangling down into the frame: indubitably a lapse on the part of a technician who was drowsy or distracted or unhappy or just unconscious of what he was doing in relation to the camera's frame. Perhaps no one saw this until the set had been struck or one of the actors was sent home from the production, so that no retake was possible. The prepossessing object, at any rate, hung there, hung there dumbly, it must be said, quite as though unconscious of itself and its "noisy" interruption of the scene, and my students began to become uncomfortable and to guffaw. That was the end of *They Might Be Giants* as any kind of absorbing substance. Now it was merely a piece of celluloid that had been manufactured by a team of *so-called* "professionals," people who had, sloppily and in a way that could mobilize an audience's resentment, given up their ghost.

Here is produced a catastrophic collapse of the diegesis, the sudden dissolution, even assassination, of Justin Playfair and his psychiatrist Dr. Mildred Watson, through the spectacular intrusion of elements from the several other worlds of reality imbricated with the fabular one (and that I have detailed above). While production, gravity, social circumstances, personal troubles were typically disregarded, indeed made invisible, through viewers' conviction in storytelling "reality," they now stepped in, with or without intent it makes no matter, and with a clumsy and bold movement that inspired no confidence. But rather than accepting illusion in its fullness—that the story, the storyteller, and the storytelling system have their own gracelessness and precariousness to negotiate, and achieve what they achieve against all odds—it was possible for viewers of this scene to expect something no filmic "reality" could ever give, absolute perfection (as judged by the audience's educated powers of observation).

What is it that we can say results from such a collapse? As Playfair and Watson no longer exist, we are now—and apparently always have been—gazing at only the actors Scott and Woodward, going through their dance like a pair of trained beasts in a circus. They are in not an apartment, just a set that looks like an apartment (or perhaps an actual non-diegetic apartment that belonged to somebody who rented it out to a producer for temporary use as an "apartment" [the film was shot at unspecified locations in New York]). That they are talking not to us, through some magic whereby we can be "present" in the room and hear their every murmur, but only to this dumb microphone, this bold prosthesis, which has now so indecorously shown its phallic little head and lacks the grace to retreat.

Yes, they are talking into a mere microphone and their voices are being
etched onto that quintessence of crudeness, magnetic tape, later to be converted to a sound track embedded in flimsy celluloid, the reduction that is all this motion picture ultimately is. Also gone forever (at least until the next movie) is the fact that the fictional bubble in which they breathed the ethers of entrancement is now altogether blown, along with the belief that fictional bubbles such as this are mounted by sophisticated, gifted specialists who "really" know what they are doing. The experts are replaced by a bunch of hacks working together to produce a complete failure at illusion. These hacks, further, most likely work for what Orwell aptly named "great monopoly companies which are actively interested in maintaining the status quo and therefore in preventing the common man from becoming too intelligent" ("Poetry" 351).

The shock of our deflowering in the presence of this horrid little microphone is profound and stunning.

The experience brings jittery silence, then chortles, then dismissive laughter, then howls of protest. And it shows us a reality we do not wish to see lying in wait beneath a "reality" that we do, much as the hapless narrator of Stanislaw Lem's *The Futurological Congress*, reveling in a "magnificent hall, covered with carpets, filled with palms, the ornamented majolica walls, the elegance of the sparkling tables, and the orchestra in the back that played exquisite chamber music while we dined" finds himself, after the ingestion of a drug called Up 'n' atem, staring at only "a concrete bunker, . . . a rough wooden table, a straw mat—badly frayed—beneath our feet. The music was still there, but I saw now that it came from a loudspeaker hung on a rusted wire. And the rainbow-crystal chandelier was now a dusty, naked light bulb" (114). Of *They Might Be Giants* we may secretly believe, along with my students, that just because the shimmering mask is indeed vulnerable to dropping away, therefore it should have been properly bolstered and protected to prevent this from happening, since if and when the screen reality fails as a reality, what our naked senses are left with is a world deeply contaminated with the sort of coarseness and ugliness that properly belong to an existence beneath our dignity. The supporting framework not only waits inside or beneath a fiction, but waits there repugnantly. It must be denied, eradicated, covered over. That microphone committed a major infraction.

It may well be guilt about pleasure that makes viewers fall to such a nadir, else they might feel gratitude at the sudden revelation of a mechanism that has helped produce their enchantment. Beyond the direct thrill of "reality," after all, is the more profound, even sublime realization of the interconnectedness of people and things, life and light. Once the microphone has come into view, one may be prompted to think about the many instances here and elsewhere where it doesn't, and thus to wonder about what accident or miracle might have happened to cause this particular lapse. Beyond imagining or envisioning the production itself, we may see it as a complex and fraught collaboration between—not experts manqué but—seriously committed workers who face interwoven challenges as they struggle together through take after take. The microphone as a tool for drawing up sound, after all, points not only to itself but also to Scott and Woodward as human beings hard at work producing the sound being drawn, and so it is humanizing, and shows us that people, not figments, make films like this one. (Again, that reality we evacuate from our cherished "reality.") Instead of denying the production per se, one can estimate it intensively as work, seeing that none of what must transpire here happens either naturally or effortlessly. (In *The Golden Coach*, the actors in the little commedia troupe talk about the fact that when they are not experiencing their two-hours' delight upon the stage, they have less glamorous lives to lead.) The maintenance of expressive facial tone by Scott and Woodward, through take after take, and this whether they are feeling up to working or not. The skillful reproduction of vocalization—whether it is picked up magically or by a microphone. The elaborate construction of the scenario, not to mention the work of the assistant directors in plotting out shooting schedules to take the most efficient advantage of the multifaceted labor of dozens of workers each of whom must be contracted to this job. For the cinematographer, the choice of film stock and lighting so as to balance the need for focal clarity with the need for movement inside a shot. The designer's problems working out spatial details in a small space, and matching the look of the apartment with the look of the costumer's clothing. The legal complexities of insurance. The director's vision and how it does or does not match what he is able to coax from his actors and crew at a given moment. And so on. All this is a wonder, not a shame. But we shun it in our demand for the gloss that will hide it all. We know, but we wish to see.

In the end there is no particular reason for believing anything visible onscreen is not precisely what the "author"—writer, director, actor, producer, cameraman, designer, assistant director, script girl, editor—wanted. To see with new eyes that everything made available to us is worth taking seriously and wondering about is to appreciate that at each of its moments film has been achieved as some kind of extension of true capabilities in the face of weakness, debility, flaw, limit, or boundary that can cut work short, and then to see the screen image as a flowering of devotion. In the moment of collapse, then, film becomes alive. "Reality" is a commitment— even an affirmation—in our way of seeing. And the "reality effects" we have learned to love are our own techniques of loving cinema.

Is it indeed a crime in itself for two people
to be as alike as two drops of blood?

—Vladimir Nabokov, *Despair*

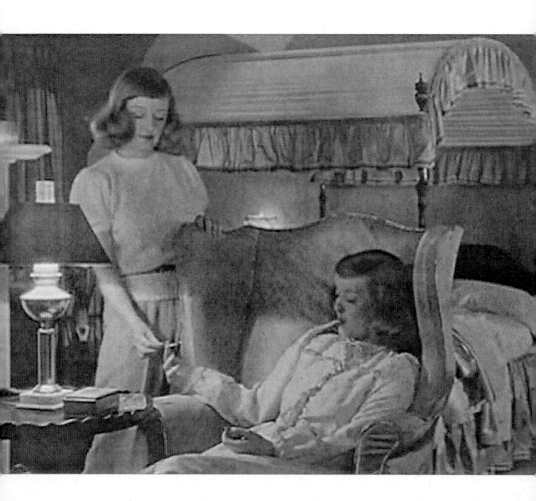

2

The Two of Us

The leap of mortality, the *salto mortale*, an old acrobatic trick and crowd pleaser, goes all the way back to a primitive doubling and replacement ritual in which the priest and his priesthood are simultaneously overcome and renewed through an act of extremity. Nietzsche plays upon it in the Prologue to his *Also Sprach Zarathustra*:

> The tight-rope walker had begun his work: he had emerged from a little door and was proceeding across the rope, which was stretched between two towers and thus hung over the people and the market square. Just as he had reached the middle of his course the little door opened again and a brightly-dressed fellow like a buffoon sprang out and followed the former with rapid steps. "Forward, lame-foot!" cried his fearsome voice. . . . With each word he came nearer and nearer to him: but when he was only a single pace behind him, there occurred the dreadful thing that silenced every mouth and fixed every eye: he emitted a cry like a devil and sprang over the man standing in his path. But the latter, when he saw his rival thus triumph, lost his head and the rope; he threw away his pole and fell. . . . (Ansell-Pearson and Large 259–60)

The primitive rite upon which this celebrated description stands was familiar in the earliest days of recorded history, and is set forth in Frazer's *The Golden Bough*:

> In the sacred grove [of Nemi] there grew a certain tree round which at any time of the day, and probably far into the night, a grim figure might be seen

to prowl. In his hand he carried a drawn sword, and he kept peering warily about him as if at every instant he expected to be set upon by an enemy. He was a priest and a murderer; and the man for whom he looked was sooner or later to murder him and hold the priesthood in his stead. Such was the rule of the sanctuary. A candidate for the priesthood could only succeed to office by slaying the priest, and having slain him, he retained office till he was himself slain by a stronger or a craftier. (Frazer I: 8–9)

The leaping buffoon in Nietzsche transcends both time and space through the power of his excellent gesture: he triumphs by being both behind and ahead of his competitor at once, by exemplifying both the past and the future. And similarly at Nemi, the prowling priest is both alive and dead, both himself and the negation of himself (by a successor who will slay him), just as this successor is seeker and victor at once, and also not-priest and priest, now, and for eternity.

The ritual of the *salto mortale* is recapitulated, revised, modernized, and itself overcome in the "Circus" ballet of Gene Kelly's *Invitation to the Dance* (1956; music by Jacques Ibert). Here, in an eighteenth-century French public square done up in magnificent pastels by Alfred Junge and photographed in London in Technicolor by Freddie Young,[1] a forlorn Pierrot (Kelly), caught up in an impossible love-fascination for the ballerina "Columbine" (Claire Sombert), is vanquished in his efforts by the dark and cunning lover (Igor Youskévitch), who slyly out-woos him. In a particular gesture that references both the Grove of Nemi and the Nietzschean acrobat, the lover shows off by doing an elaborate tightrope routine in which he somersaults both forward and backward while balanced high above the crowd. At twilight, when the mournful Pierrot realizes that there is little hope for him, he climbs up to the rope and tries to walk it himself, tottering pathetically at its center before plummeting to his death. Here, then, the (somewhat callous) lover represents novelty, youth, and the future while Pierrot is the delicate and vulnerable past; and while one body does not exactly leap over the other, there is still a tightrope competition invoking the dangerous flip (it being evident that the lover is merely showing off his virile capacity), and a final unequivocal triumph imbricated with the pathos of lost love. It may be that the unfamiliarity of contemporary audiences with both the form of the commedia dell'arte, in which the ballet is set, and the legendary background of the leaping competition which climaxes the "narrative" led to the extremely cautious reception that the film—or at least this brilliant routine in it—received. (*Variety* noted merely that the film had "skillful photography" and that the circus number "is similar to the Pagliacci theme" [December 31, 1955, online at variety. com]). But quite as unimpressed as were industry and lay viewers, critics, too, stood back a little from *Invitation*. The *New York Times's* Bosley Crowther crowed that the film "throws a heap of hoofing of a rather gaudy sort into one show" and, somewhat synchronically pointing to Kelly's Pierrot as reminiscent of Marcel Marceau, describes the routine as a "formal, postured ballet" (May 23, 1956, online at movies.nytimes.com), entirely eliding the stunning camera and color effects. More recently, Adrienne McLean notes a critical reception that decried what she summarizes as its "paucity of choreographic ideas and invention" (168). Even without invention, and in a profoundly beautiful way, "Circus" tells a very old tale again and indelibly, a tale, indeed, much predating Pagliacci and centering on not only love but circulation, the replacement of the past, and thus our double experience of being young in memory and old in futurity at once. The circle, the priesthood, the dance, and then: our twofold lives.

The *Salto Mortale* Revisited

As the acrobat jumps over himself and becomes his own future the human figure is, in effect, temporally doubled. Could it "really" be possible to be in two places at the same time? To move so quickly between a "here" and a "there" that one seems to be omnipresent? "Speed has conquered space," Hannah Arendt observes, although not only of cinema; "this conquering process finds its limit at the unconquerable boundary of the simultaneous presence of one body at two different places" (250). For breaking through this "limit," an act of desire if not of physics, one would have to exist in double bodies, bodies independent in space; or else space would have to be warped in a way unaccounted for in the present understanding of earthly topography.[2]

This is the idea that centers the narrative in Christopher Nolan's *The Prestige* (2006) (a film based on the 1995 novel of the same name by a second Christopher, Christopher Priest). Toward the end of the nineteenth century, as the story goes, a performing magician, Alfred Borden, whose career is by this point virtually in ruins, invents the trick of "The Transported Man," in which a gentleman standing in a cabinet on one side of a stage instantly and inexplicably disappears, showing up—the perfect metaphor—half a breath later in a cabinet on the other side. (In his novel

Priest had called the trick "The New Transported Man" and had neatly positioned his character Borden as both a protégé of the real stage illusionists John Henry Anderson [1814–74] and John Nevil Maskelyne [1839–1917] and a contemporary of Harry Houdini [Erik Weisz, 1874–1926], David Devant [1868–1941], Chung Ling Soo [William Ellsworth Robinson, 1861–1918], and Buatier de Kolta [Joseph Buatier, 1845–1903], all famous and principal masters of stage illusion in the latter part of the nineteenth century and the first years of the twentieth.) There are inexact antecedents to the "Transported Man" in nineteenth-century magic lore and popular culture. Albert Hopkins describes a disappearing and materializing caliph and odalisk, for instance: "The swinging cage appears to be empty and apparently the odalisk has passed through the air to the other cage" (38–39); Laurent Mannoni describes a complex projection technique through which "the audience would see onstage the diaphanous living image of a real actor, with all his or her natural gestures" when no actor was physically present there (248–49). And discussing the Davenport Brothers and their critics, Simon During notes not only the way stage illusions (such as those of disappearing and appearing personae) were yoked to Spiritualist tenets but also how such performer-critics as Maskelyne, at his Home of Mysteries in London, could unmask Spiritualism by explicitly advertising his own performances as "difficult and wonderful stage illusions" and thus pointing directly to the Davenports' work as a mere orchestration of tricks (155ff.).

The "trick" in *The Prestige* remains unelucidated through most of the film, less because it is allied with Spiritualist principles than because it is rooted in certain utterly incredible facts, facts, indeed, which even the film audience may find it deeply distressing to assimilate when the narrative draws to a close. But regardless of the overall plot in which the trick is embedded, with whatever narrative logic, the stunning effect of watching "The Transported Man" is a sharp vision in which the inhabitant of one cabinet clearly dematerializes and then rematerializes thirty feet away, in a fraction of a second. Again, Priest has his narrator describe the thrill of the business as resting in "a short, humorous preamble . . . about *the desirability of being in two places at once*" (77).

For example, that I could be here writing this sentence, dear Reader, and also looking over your shoulder as you read it . . .

Subtly implicit here is the Galvanic idea of electric life—not merely that integument and fiber can be usefully charged by electricity but that flesh is an electromagnetic essence—an idea linked to experimental work that was undertaken early in the 1890s by the theorist Nikola Tesla (1856–1943), using the earth and the atmosphere as media by which electrical current could be transmitted. Tesla (embodied by the "galvanic" David Bowie) also appears in Nolan's film. In the mid-1960s, of course, this same basic conceit had been usurped and elaborated by Gene Roddenberry for the "beam-up/beam-down" maneuver in his "Star Trek" universe.

Taking the problem to a new level is Doug Liman's *Jumper* (2008).[3] It tells the story of young David Rice (Max Thieriot as a child, Hayden Christensen later), who is afflicted with a strange and unaccountable "malady": he can jump through space, shifting from one location to another—even a destination halfway around the world—so rapidly, in even less than the blink of an eye, that it seems no time has gone by and he exists in both places at once. In fact, Liman presents a scene where David shifts from one end of his sofa to the other, just to try out his powers: the trace of him in the first location lingers while he is visible settling in at the second. At the beginning of the film, David is a high school student. He gifts the girl of his heart with a snow globe, which the school bully immediately steals and tosses into the middle of an ice-covered river. Against the girl's emotional warnings, the boy bravely walks over to retrieve it, but once he has it in his hand the ice collapses beneath him and he is trapped in the freezing water, groping frantically beneath the solid surface and unable to find an escape (in homage to an asphyxiating sequence in George Marshall's *Houdini* [1953]). Just at the point of expiration, David finds himself sopping wet on the floor of the stacks of the Ann Arbor Public Library. This sequence suggests how cinema can place and re-place a person, in a flash.

The *Jumper* sequence is exciting and attention-grabbing as drama, but what is more deeply fascinating about it is that the doubling of placement also illustrates what can happen in any cinematic splice between any two frames, to any character who is first here and then there, yet moving with such stunning rapidity that viewers cannot perceive the motion and are left with only the double trace of a body situated, as it were, in two spots at once. *Jumper* is a metaphor for cinema itself, then, and David's "medical" problem in it is that he is a living splice. The working grammar for watching movies, as every watcher knows, is that one reads edits as signals of transition: if there are two shots joined, each with a different location, the story (along with its character) has "moved" from one to the other; and if both locations appear the same, whether or not a character onscreen seems to be the same in both shots, it is to be concluded that "time has passed."[4] With Liman's film the cutaway comes in the middle of David's struggling gestures under the ice, however, apparently occurring within one gasping breath and offering no resolution of his gestures. That is, we cut before the initial action comes to its apotheosis; and the edit moves from a position of danger to one of blissful safety; so that it seems no time has passed between the two shots. David simply exists (sopping wet) in a new, safe space at the same time and in the same way that he existed previously in a perilous one, and because the film does not return to the trauma of the river the safe space dominates the narrative unfolding. Is it a dream to which he has traveled in his death throes? Has he been in the library always, and did he only dream of freezing in the river? In coming up with the strategy of interrupting the struggle beneath the ice for the cut, as his way of illustrating the "jumping" that is the centerpiece of his film, Liman is also finding a good way to solve the more general aesthetic problem of performing a standard jump cut in such a way as to offer audiences a new way of interpreting it. Given the fact that this jump cut is conventional in form it is historically remarkable for its narraturgical power in this film, where the fact of a moment's "swift becoming" is the be-all and end-all of the story itself.

Step by Step: Narrative Procedure and Presence

In her book *The Art of Taking a Walk*, Anke Gleber invokes the German writer Franz Hessel, whose flâneur experiences the streets of the city not only as an atmosphere but as a "text": "Naming the relays between walking and seeing, reading and writing, Hessel has recourse to an analogy between the street and the text, a trope that had first appeared in the early modern period." The modern world, in other words, has become "legible," and every phenomenon of experience is read as part of a continuous textual flow. More than read: read casually, which is to say, soon enough by habit and not by intent. The idea and image of "reading the street," as had been introduced to contemporary thought by Ludwig Börne, implied that Paris, for example, was "an unfolded book" and that "wandering through its streets means *reading*" (in Gleber 10; hilariously in Christopher Nolan's *Inception* [2010] the "book" of Paris is folded up again while the reader [Ellen Page] watches in astonishment along with the audience). Hessel took this diffuse idea of reading the city and adapted it to the particular streets of Berlin, where "people's faces, displays, shop windows, café terraces, cars, tracks, trees turn into an entire series of equivalent letters, which together

form words, sentences, and pages of a book that is always new" (65–66),
a book, indeed, whose novelty might seem to be spontaneous. A little of
this easy "reading" of a city can be seen in Fritz Lang's *M* (see Pomerance,
Horse 86–109).

Implicit in both Börne and Hessel, and also in Walter Benjamin's reflection upon them (which is Gleber's pretext for writing), is an even more
primary notion of presence that inflects considerable theorizing of the
modern experience. While the world pulsates electrically and mechanically around, nevertheless as he strolls through its exciting territories the
flâneur is always inexorably *here*: this because as one moves through any
text, pulsing forward on cement or on parchment, perching upon the word
is inevitable. If the flâneur is like a reader, so be it: making way through
a sentence the eye moves in a line, pausing on this word, recycling on
that one, but is always to be located at some definitive point inside the
bounded field of some definitive textual space. Peter Wollen notes how
"architecture and cinema both provide sets of places and spaces which
the user must learn how to *travel through*—a kind of knowledge which,
in our culture, is acquired from a very early age" (201; my emphasis). And
walking down the pavement is equally a matter of taking placements and
occupying locations, as high-tech surveillance films like *Patriot Games*
(1992), *Enemy of the State* (1997), *Minority Report* (2002), *The Bourne Ul-
timatum* (2007), or *Green Zone* (2010) make clear by their sequences in
which individual strollers, creepers, or runners can (apparently always) be
pegged and mapped, using satellite or other surveillance techniques, inside
some bounded and knowable space—all this furious location deriving, of
course, from Hitchcock's *The Lodger* (1927) and Lang's later *M*, where the
mapping of a criminal's activity is a central figuration (for more on diegesis
and mapping, see Conley).

If we are always multiply positioned, modernity has it that our positions can always be seen and known. Traces are left, and can be followed.

Green Zone reaches a new apogee of surveillance and thus excites
a new awareness and produces a new tremor in the viewer. The fugitive
is a U.S. Army platoon chief, Miller (Matt Damon), who has chosen to
flee using his regular jeep (with driver). So it is that the pursuing American helicopter and its team (led by Briggs [Jason Isaac]) can easily call
his transponder up on a screen and follow his every move through the
winding labyrinth of Baghdad at night. Miller is visible to Briggs and to
the audience as a colored blip. An Iraqi general he is himself chasing is
visible, too, as a blip of another color, and the men in the helicopter have

no trouble keeping Miller and his general in "sight" no matter what moves they make—although they do not know who or what that second blip really is. Thus, at the same time Miller is so visible he is invisible, because his pursuers do not know what it is that he is trying to do, why he is racing, who precisely it is that he has in his sights, what plan he is trying to effect that will perhaps uncover the falsities underpinning the American military engagement in Iraq. The fanatic Briggs and his men see everything and nothing at once—they read and are stymied in reading; just as Miller at each moment is on display and in hiding—legible and illegible. In the end, Miller corners his prey before Briggs can stop him but it is all for nothing, since someone else has been in on the chase, another hunter, with a premodern consciousness that works through secrecy and darkness. This one isn't on any monitor screen, isn't mappable or mapping, and in practice it is he who is running the game.

To read, if reading is walking, is always to be *here* before one is *there*, and to move as a way of direction, no matter how lazy or serendipitous the project might turn out to be. One never lacks for a sense of the *here* coupled with a memory trace of where one has been and a projection of one's target. Seen in this way, reading is purposive and tactical, and is linked to orientation. "In the wonderful days of speechless cinema," wrote James Card, "there was no problem about young people learning to read. We were seeing movies two or three times a week, and we *had* to know what Tom Mix and Doug Fairbanks were saying" (55)—which is to say, what they were doing, what they had done, what they were going to do next.

The sense of presence—a full sense of being embedded in a manifest and direct "here"ness—is very often taken for granted as a given, what Flaubert would have called a "received" aspect of experience, principally, no doubt, because we have it through an infusion of sensations and because our senses are both delicate in reach, powerful in effect, indiscernable in operation, and immediate. Siegfried Kracauer points to cinema's ability to reveal "things normally unseen; phenomena overwhelming consciousness" (46). And Richard Shiff, meditating on his own history of perception, goes a little further in noting the considerable role that is played in the reception of modern art by the history of technology:

> Like many people my age, I frequently experienced not only photography but also some of the first television broadcast images well before I was interested in the techniques that had been developed in design and painting, with which I had no previous familiarity. . . . I tended to view older forms

of representation in terms of newer mechanical and electronic forms. If I was struck by Jean-François Millet's *Plaine au soleil couchant* (*Plain at Sunset,* 1865–1870), a drawing without much detail but really accomplished from the point of view of its conception and technical execution, it's because of its strange resemblance to television. (227; translation mine)

Whatever the surround is that stretches ahead, whatever circumscribes the sense of presence, is taken as *merely being*, given that its capacity to stimulate overtakes notice of the fact that it is there at all.

Far more than a natural occurrence, the sense of presence in the here and now is a complex achievement, one that is learned, then taken for granted, even disregarded, yet an achievement nevertheless. Consider again William James's observation about the importance of vividness and pungency in the perception of presence (301), or his dictum as regards the status of perceptions that "each subworld while it is attended to is real after its own fashion" (293). The caveat "while it is attended to" presents no slight issue. The production of attention involves a relatively sharp concentration of the mental faculties, a framing of relevant features of a space and a moment, a concomitant rejection of what is secondary, a persistence of sensibility such that a perceiver does not lose her grasp by briefly engaging in one of the many turns that are always available: daydreaming, change of focus, peripheral gaze or attentiveness, calculation, inquiry. The sense of presence requires that all these distracting possibilities be relegated to what Goffman calls a "back channel" (on this and the structuring of disattention see *Frame Analysis,* chap. 7), so that the immediate surround can dominate consciousness and take on the character of the *here.* In the movie theater, one is further confronted by a constant and haranguing division and choice, since there are two co-present *here*s, which can interfere with one another: the *here* of the screen world (which is, of course, a representation of elsewhere!); and the *here* of the theater world, containing the screen and its dark commercial envelope (the speakers, the electrical grid, the air conditioning, the heater, the box office, that incandescent white rectangle Michel Chion called a *toile trouée,* a "holey canvas," and the popcorn machine . . .). To have a sense of presence while watching a film is to engage a considerable energy toward rejection and disattention, to actively deny the theater space in order that the diegetic world can ascend.

Sartre—who writes that as a child, after seeing a film, "in the street I found myself superfluous" (*Words* 125)—concluded, comparing film with theater, that in watching a movie, I am "shown what someone wants me to see: our perception of the images is *directed*," while in the theater, "one looks at whatever one wants" ("Theatre" 200). But it makes little sense to posit that while one watches a film the eye does not move about the screen. There is always more than one thing to see and the eye must engage in the competition, moving about and making critical decisions about how and when to flit from foreground to telling background material. A good example of competition and freedom in our view of the organized visual array is given by a critical scene in Alfred Hitchcock's *The Man Who Knew Too Much* (1956), when an underling who has been paid to organize the assassination of a foreign prime minister is called on the carpet by his employer because the project failed. In a gilded private study in the sanctum of a London embassy, the diminutive and withdrawn Drayton (Bernard Miles) cowers in front of the ambassador (Mogens Wieth), a portly, peachy, now glowering man in a tuxedo and sash, all of this shot in such a way that the camera, looking up at the inflamed diplomat, cannot help but see upon the wall behind the man's head a massive portrait of his prime minister, the assassination target and thus now, unfortunately for him, his living guest. This man in the painting—any viewer might note, if instead of being "shown what someone wants [her] to see" she allowed herself to focus upon him—is also clad in a tuxedo and sash, and with his florid and stupid-looking expression bears not a little resemblance to the angry bureaucrat who is hosting him. We must choose in this scene where to focus our gaze, upon the ambassador or upon the subject of the canvas hanging behind him, or, in rapid alternation, upon both. If in some manner the viewer looks at both, she may find it difficult not to grasp with some immediacy that the prime minister (Alexei Bobrinskoy) and the ambassador are father and son. In this shot there are no special effects used, beyond the artful construction and placement of the portrait and the very effective light that bathes both it and the ambassador at the same time. This "straight" shot raises an interesting optical and philosophical problem that impinges upon a reading of the entire film: the criminal mastermind is an intended patricide, not merely a killer, all this in the context of a father-son story of great complexity. The script never brings this issue to light, but the shot does—for viewers who bring forward into attentive focus what might otherwise have been disattended. Any complex shot might work in much this way, if the narrative and the design are interwoven. But here, it is crucial to note, there is no seam between foreground and background except that provided by the viewer through the act of concentration. The portrait hangs on the wall of a room (a set) in which the angry man is standing. The interpretive task is to acknowledge that the portrait is not simple decoration, to let the eye be its own "jumper" and hop from the front to the back of the frame as it reads.

Rear projection turns the screws on this problem, offering to viewers a shot in which foreground and background did not originate in the same space but are conjoined through an actual seam. To shift attention to the background, to examine it carefully, is to threaten the integrity of the screen construction unless very great care has been taken by filmmakers to make it impossible for us to recognize what we are looking at, just at the moment that we are looking. In looking at rear projections, one accomplishes the same "jumps" as in edits, but all inside a single shot.

Rear Windows: Process Photography and "Reality"

Rear projection was used, if ineffectively, as early as 1913 for *The Drifter* (Fielding, "Dawn" 148). "Process shots," as they came generally to be known (with some ambiguity, since there are other "processes" in cinematic production), found regular use before and during the 1920s, in particular with such films as Arthur Rosson's *Sahara* (1919). An even more substantial incarnation was David Butler's *Just Imagine* (1930). By 1932—at a time when theaters across North America had not yet all been rewired for sound— the number of composite shots used at Paramount studios alone increased from 146 to more than 600 in a year (Rickitt 82). Along with other major studios, Paramount created a special effects photography team, principally devoted to the challenges of process photography. Farciot Edouart (1894– 1980) was its head.

Although there are numerous taxing complications that come up in execution, the principles of rear projection are simple. Sometimes it is necessary to dramatize an action or interaction in a setting where it would be difficult, if even possible, actually to film. As Hal Wallis told a seminar at the American Film Institute, "Locations are quite expensive. You travel with an army—any number of trucks, station wagons, cars, eighty to a hundred people on a crew. You have to transport them, you have to house them, and it's a *very* expensive operation" (qtd. in McBride 23).

Perhaps location shooting is just visually impractical. For example, with all films made during the studio era the principal characters of the film had to be shot in such a way that the commercial identities of the actors who were playing them got special illumination, this partly because actors' continuing work before the movie camera depended on their being seen in a noteworthy fashion in the work they did before; but more importantly because the star system operated by marketing cinema to a paying public on the basis of star identification, recognition, and sighting. Close-ups were effected and lit so as to round the star's face, sculpt its shadowing, and in other ways architect the indelible star image (about which, see Dyer, especially 63–85). One often-used technique was to increase the illumination on the star's face by comparison with that on all the other performers in a scene. Subtle and thorough control of lighting for these purposes can be achieved only in the studio. Beyond the star close-up, occasionally medium shots must be set up this way as well. Rear projection makes it possible to achieve all these ends in one move, since the studio space allows for control of lighting and the production of an ideal number of takes regardless of the weather, and the rear projection provides a topical sense of dramatic space. Thus, even when a scene is shot on location, producers will move the company into the rear-projection stage for the star close-ups.

We can see this mobility in George Cukor's *Born Yesterday* (1950), where the hilariously uneducated "Billie" Dawn (Judy Holliday) and the writer Paul Verrall (William Holden) flirt with one another at the Library of Congress. A number of setups are done on location with the performers in medium shot: here they are just people, realistic enough but hardly worth the price of admission to a movie only because of that. As many other tourists are also doing, they stare together at the Constitution and the Declaration of Independence; she proudly leads him over to see the Bill of Rights (now that, with his tutelage—"This whole country is practically founded on these three pieces of paper"—she is slowly learning to frame her own such Bill). Outside, he buys her ice cream—"Anything but tutti-frutti!"—and she comments that she likes him better with "them" on: "What?" "Yer glasses!" Now that the issue of what he looks like has been invoked, however, and, by implication, what she looks like, too, it is necessary to get a more serious—that is to say, movie-style—*look* at them. For this, star close-ups are done in the studio with the Capitol building woven into the background through rear projection. She is shot on location looking at the Capitol over a parapet; then on location he gets the ice cream; but when he walks up in medium-close shot to hand it to her, and then when she informs him in closer focus that "chocolate's the most popula,'" we are in the studio, able to take advantage of hair lights, key spots in the eyes, and Renaissance framing of the delicate shadows on Holliday's face.

"It's interesting," says she, "how many interesting things a person could learn . . . if they read." In a brief moment she will ham it up with horn-rimmed spectacles turning her into a raccoon, and Holden will grin with affection, telling her they make her look "lovelier than ever" and at the same time having an opportunity to show us his trademark gleamy smile.

There are still other reasons for using rear projections. Possibly an actual setting is a source of potential danger to performers, and thus poses an insurance nightmare: Cary Grant and Eva Marie Saint are not really dangling "high above real earth" in *North by Northwest* (1959), nor are Norman Lloyd in *Saboteur* (1942), Milla Jovovich in *The Fifth Element* (1997), Maureen O'Sullivan in *Tarzan the Ape-Man* (1932), Matt Damon in *The Bourne Identity* (2003), and many other adventurers, comic and serious, played by performers whose lives could not have been placed at risk in the way that the "lives" of their characters were. In *Postcards from the Edge* (1990), Meryl Streep mocks up the Hollywood strategy of artificial dangling, in a shot that begins by seeming precarious and ends by seeming flatly comic.

A more frequently recurring problem involves controlling the nuances of sound recording: location shooting makes it impossible to get high-quality close-ups and high-fidelity sound. Keith Fulton and Louis Pepe's *Lost in La Mancha* dramatizes this problem diegetically as for the film-within-the-film, *Don Quixote*, filmmaker Terry Gilliam (Gilliam) tries to get a useful take with Johnny Depp while Spanish Air Force jets keep passing thunderously overhead: the pilots all want to catch a glimpse of Johnny! It can also occur that some aspect of a scene cannot be shot at the same time as other action because materials necessary to the photography do not exist in our world: Grant Williams fighting off a "giant" spider in the basement of his home, after he has shrunk to the size of a kernel of popcorn, in Jack Arnold's *The Incredible Shrinking Man* (1957); mercifully for arachnophobes like me, spiders that huge do not exist (not, at least, as far as I care to know). Nor do playful orange kitties the size of elephants, one of which would have been needed to film a challenging and delightful earlier scene in which, after he has shrunk to the extent that a doll's house is an appropriate apartment for him, Williams meets his pet cat under trying circumstances. Since the actor could not be miniaturized in truth, the cat would have had to be expanded somehow—an equally impossible resolution.

Similarly, a shot might be impossible because it depicts a catastrophe that cannot be simulated before the camera: Cecil B. DeMille's *The*

Greatest Show on Earth (1952) has a train wreck scene (done with miniatures) prefaced by a shot of the oncoming train heading down the tracks at night and viewed from an automobile blocking the right of way. Or, in *North by Northwest* again, Grant's Roger O. Thornhill wraps up the famous cropduster scene by standing in the middle of the highway while a massive sixteen-wheeler comes barreling down upon him, and we must share his perspective of the oncoming vehicle. Sometimes just getting a camera and lighting crew into a situation would be physically impossible: the typical shot made inside a moving vehicle as the landscape flies past outside—Robert Cummings chatting with truck driver Murray Alper in *Saboteur* (1942), or villainous Joseph Cotten trapped in a little vessel that is heading for the lip of the falls in Henry Hathaway's *Niagara* (1953). The thrills provided for audiences who watch films like these couldn't have been possible if filmmakers had subjected themselves to the dangers their characters faced. Frequently with train shots, a rear projection is used so that the framing and lighting can properly concentrate on a passenger going for a ride: Bette Davis's Charlotte Vale traversing the countryside immediately after the death of her mother in *Now, Voyager* (1942); Cornel Wilde gliding down to Arizona at the beginning of *Leave Her to Heaven* (1945). Or still again in *North by Northwest*, that celebrated sequence in the dining car, as the Hudson River slides past outside and Cary Grant doesn't make love to Eva Marie Saint on an empty stomach. The rear-projection composites in all these circumstances combine a background that has been shot on location with foreground action that is shot in studio. The two elements are brought together in the process of principal photography, and if this is done meticulously enough viewers will have the sense, as the story unspools, that they are watching a coherent event in a single coherent space.

The view of this coherence need not be untrammeled or uninquisitive. There is often, after all, some perceivable distinction between the quality of the rear-projected image and that of the studio characters working before it. Many critical observers young enough to have been reared on artfully composited animation effects since 1990 complain more or less bitterly about, or at least find "problematic," "unbelievable" or "unrealistic" rear projections of the 1950s and earlier (see, for one example, Turnock), forgetting in their analysis that producers were not usually interested in the viewer holding both foreground and background realities in attention *with equal strength*. The stars in the foreground were always more important, and during the days of classical filmmaking audiences understood

Carvell

this as implicit to the very process of watching movies. People went to the cinema to see certain personae behaving in varying circumstances, not to see the down-to-earth "reality" of circumstances themselves. Thus, Bette Davis was the focus of attention in *The Letter* (1940), not the Chinese community in Singapore; and in the numerous rear projections that work to frame the opening sequence of *Love Is a Many-Splendored Thing* (1955), it was Jennifer Jones and William Holden that audiences had flocked to see, not the "reality" of Hong Kong as a topical support for love.

is it exclusive? Do sp's desires determine text?

If in rear projection the sense of an audience's presence to the image is the result of careful technical arrangements that blend foreground and background action seamlessly, the seamlessness itself is only partly a technical production and partly involves structuring of the audience's gaze so that attention does not fall upon the spatial division implicit in the sequence. Foreground action is staged, lit, and finally photographed on a large soundstage (in the bigger studios, a stage routinely dedicated to rear-projection composition) where the available space is divided by a screen. The actors stand only on one side of this screen, and the lighting must be done with great skill so that no beams fall upon the screen itself, lest there be fall-off or glare in the background image that is projected there. Further, the foreground lighting must not cast shadows of the foreground performers or pieces of scenery onto the screen in any way that will show up in the composite, yet must be sufficient to give the impression that the foreground action is taking place at the same time of day or night as what will be projected behind it.

The background is thrown upon the screen from a projector situated on the other side of it and at some distance, sometimes as great as a hundred and fifty feet away, so that the image will be large enough in proportion to the foreground action to seem like "a world." (A much more recent technique, front projection, uses a projector positioned on the same side of the screen as the actors and a screen made of a special material that is exceedingly sensitive to light; for this the projected image can be rather dim and still it will be picked up and reflected brightly into the recording camera.) In 1933, Kodak developed a special "Background" negative film for the purpose of rear projection, its notable characteristic being relatively fine grain. This made for the possibility of blowing up the image on a large background screen without the grain showing. "Fineness of grain" refers to the size of the silver particles converted by light on the film's emulsion, and ultimately affects the crispness of an image produced from a negative of this film, once it is magnified through projection on a screen. The larger the grain, the more a projected image looks like photography and not like the unphotographed world out of which it originates. Our ontological fascination with images as originating in the world of our experience has received diligent attention from such scholars as André Bazin and Vivian Sobchack, among others.

The background "plate," as the image is called when it is moving rather than still (a "stereo"), has been shot in advance of principal photography by a second-unit team who worked independently of the principal actors but with a very precise plan as to what (or who) should be included, how the camera should move, and so on. Shooting process plates is an expertise. By the time work is ready to be done on the projection stage, the plate is already a final product to which corrections cannot be made; thus, plates must be perfectly executed in advance. Any angle between the filming camera and the soundstage screen would result in warping and fall-off in the studio shot of the projected plate, thus a loss of verisimilitude, and so it is typically necessary for the studio camera to be locked down at precisely ninety degrees to the screen for composite photography. The same holds true for the projector at the other end of the studio. This means that any angles that are to appear in the composite shot must have been produced in the plate in advance, and in reverse; with the live actors adjusting their positions vis-à-vis the camera in studio. Obviously, the plate must have been lit in a way that can flawlessly match what is to be accomplished later in the studio.

For background plates to be photographed with proper exposure and contrast, considerable light was necessary. If the special photographic effects teams that made these plates were shooting in broad daylight on a sunny day, such plate photography was a straightforward enough matter (and, correspondingly, lighting actors strongly enough later in the studio was demanding, and unpleasant for them). Early plate photography worked best in situations where the script called for sunny exteriors, and this fact did something to narrow the range of story situations that could usefully be included in films. Any alteration of lighting conditions through the addition of studio-style lighting on location required a source of power, transportation of the equipment and technicians, and insurance, all of which increased the budget (and to some degree negated the advantages of using the rear projection process at all). In the case of color films, further complicating this problem were requirements of the early three-strip Technicolor camera for exceptionally high lighting levels, levels that couldn't be matched by the transmission properties of early background screen materials when very large images were in use. Unless the screens were relatively small, this otherwise first-class process for color rendition didn't work in rear projection. If we look at some of the principal Technicolor productions of the mid- to late 1930s—Richard Boleslawski's *The Garden of Allah* (1936), William Wellman's *A Star Is Born* (1937), or Victor Fleming's *The Wizard of Oz* (1939)—we see very little use of rear projection, especially large rear-projected images. As long as the rear-projection image indicated a view through a window or something similarly restricted, a small (five- to seven-foot) screen would work and Technicolor plates could be used. By the mid- to late 1940s, the Technicolor recording film had a considerably higher ASA (American Standards Association) rating, and so less light was required and consequently larger rear-projection color images could come into play, as by the 1950s they did.[5]

In early background projections, technicians noticed a number of problems that led to fall-off or fringing in the photographed image. Fall-off is a radical degradation of the brightness of the background image from the center of the screen, where the projector beam hits, outward toward the margins. Such unevenness of illumination cued viewers to the photographic nature of the background image and threw off the illusion of unity between (previously shot) background and (studio-shot) foreground space. Fall-off was due to screen materials with very low internal diffusion, so that light traveled only straight through them. Light moving from the projector to the edges of a screen has further to travel than light aimed at the center, and so some fall-off is natural (Fielding 274). The woven silk screens that had been in use during the 1920s worked unsatisfactorily to diffuse light, nor did the ground glass screens used in *Metropolis* (1927) or the twelve-foot-wide translucent celluloid screens used in *King Kong* (1933) fare much better. During the 1940s and 1950s, new experimental materials were used for background projection screens, and screens were produced with "both diffused surfaces and internal diffusion" (272), with the result that light would diffuse laterally through the screen in a more uniform way. Raymond Fielding notes that the more light that can be made to diffuse through the background screen the brighter the background image can be, *up to a certain point*, at which the diffusion ceases to have a positive effect. In general, since the lighting of the rear-projected image must match studio lighting, with a brighter screen image more light can be used to illuminate the foreground objects and personnel in the studio and thus the finer can be the film grain and the smaller the aperture on the photographing camera, a condition that can lead to increased depth of field and a sense of startlingly sharp presentation of all materials at hand.

Fringing is a tendency of the background image to flicker on and off rapidly as the scene progresses, caused in much early rear-projection work because the camera aperture and the projector aperture were not perfectly synchronized in their opening and closing. (Fringing has long been a bane of film producers' working lives. Joshua Yumibe notes [43–44] how in early hand-colored cinematic images, the virtual impossibility of matching brushstrokes and paint intensity in successive frames made for what one source regards as bulging and contracting of color, or for fringing as the film was screened.) Fringing was eliminated when a way was found to power the front camera and the rear projector—both of which normally operate at twenty-four frames per second—on a single source, so that the apertures of both mechanisms would open and close in perfect synchronization. This system was a modification of what had been devised for sound-picture synchronization in the late 1920s: the Warner Bros. Vitaphone sound system was based on a sixteen-inch vinyl disc that played in the projection booth in linkage with the picture, since "the projector and record player were operated by the same driveshaft" and "would remain in interlock" (Eyman 77). With rear projection it was a marriage of projector and camera, not unlike the more confined arrangement in the device known as the optical printer (discussed below).

That rear projections had to be as bright as possible was yet another problem for some time, since the distance of the projector from the screen, required in order that an image might be sufficiently large, mitigated against the brightness of the image that could be thrown. Thanks principally to the work of Edouart, a triple-head projector was invented and put into operation that would screen, at one moment, three distinct but identical copies of the background plate. The Paramount Triple-Head Projector (1938) used a lamp of unusually high intensity. In order that the heat produced during projection might not kindle the celluloid passing in front of the bulb the light source had to be cooled by an air-blower and set behind a water filter, not to mention that the noise of the operation could be dampened only if the entire projector apparatus was blimped. As to the three identical plates (made from the same negative but each printed with as much contrast as necessary to achieve the overall effect required), they were fed into the projector in a way analogous to the feed of black-and-white recording film in the Technicolor three-strip camera—through a pin and roller system that brought them synchronously inside the device, where one would advance in front of the bulb while the other two passed next to a pair of gold-plated forty-five-degree mirrors that would reflect the images in a forward direction (see Edouart "Paramount"). The three images were adjustable individually and were lined up by technicians patiently using plumb lines in a laborious and time-consuming operation before each shot onstage, this obviously cutting down the number of finished shots possible per day and thus lengthening the shooting schedule. Once the three plates were aligned, it was possible to throw an immense and exceedingly bright image—as bright as 125,000 lumens—onto the screen from behind. By March of 1952, MGM had acquired a triple-head projector as well and planned to use it on Stages 30, 14, and 12. "It is imperative," wrote special effects chief A. Arnold Gillespie there, "that all departments concerned make every effort towards smooth and speedy operation of this new piece of equipment to avoid shooting delays during production" (Inter-Office Communication).

Further, from the early 1950s Paramount was using its new VistaVision process for shooting background plates: passing 35 mm film through the camera laterally rather than vertically, this process permitted the conjunction of two frames at a time, and thus a negative size virtually twice what it would otherwise have been and a projected screen ratio of 1.85:1 (rather than the academy ratio of 1.33:1 which had prevailed). Beyond being immense, the VistaVision image is almost grain free. Once it became possible to use VistaVision plates with the triple-head projector, rear projection composites could be obtained that were both enormous and crisp and brilliant, virtually indistinguishable from straight, unmanipulated cinematography.

It is possible for an astute and technically aware filmmaker to modify the background projection technique in order to achieve distinct effects, such as the separation (alienation) of a character from her surround and a corresponding distancing of the audience from the character's experience. For instance, Adrian Danks has perceptively suggested how in a sequence in Hitchcock's *Marnie*, where Mark Rutland (Sean Connery) is driving Marnie Edgar ('Tippi' Hedren) to her mother's home in Baltimore, the fact that the transparency plate is somewhat identifiable as such creates a withdrawal of the figures from their ground, puts them, as it were, in a bounded-off space removed from the world through which they move. I would suggest that Hitchcock had a motive, however. The eye is easily distracted; and keeping the background plate slightly out of focus in straight shots where Mark and Marnie sit before us in rapt concentration assisted in gluing the viewer's attention to them. Further, what is not so obvious in this sequence is something else: a variation between the speed of motion apparent in the plate, depending on whether we are looking at Mark behind the wheel with his world cascading in leisurely fashion past his shoulder, or at Marnie in the passenger's seat, with her world tumbling behind swiftly, swiftly, swiftly, so that she seems to be rushing into the future. When one is shooting plates for a "moving vehicle" effect, one normally drives the camera car at full speed for any shot made through the rear window; at 60 percent of full speed for any shot looking out perpendicularly through the driver's or passenger's window; and at 80 percent of full speed for shots to the rear corners. In shooting these plates for *Marnie*, alterations would have been made to the formulaic speeds for the camera car, so that the shots made to appear behind Connery were likely done at 60 or 70 percent while the shots for Hedren were made at 80 or 85. The outside world is indeed cut off, but differentially for two conflicted characters. Mark's apparently easy dominance over the shrinking, nervous Marnie in this sequence is thus partly due to the way the backgrounds move behind them. The eye of the viewer leaps back and forth from each figure to the background, reading Mark's experience and Marnie's in relation to one another. Danks is interested specifically in the way rear projection can allow for explorations of a "bifurcated sense of space (both enclosed and open), form (both documentary and fiction), place (both here and there), time (both now and then) and mobility (both stationary and moving)." While the "bifurcation" of space is a serious and interesting concern, equally revealing is Hitchcock's full awareness that this bifurcation is a *materiel* in itself—a feature of the composite shot that is open to his manipulation.

Neither Here Nor There:
Rear Projection and the Critical Eye

Laura Mulvey wishes to argue that "rear projection introduces a . . . kind of dual temporality: two diverse registration times are 'montaged' into a single image." She would draw our attention to the fact that in rear projections, the camera is in two time zones, speaking historically. Does this mean that in actually experiencing rear projections viewers are inevitably spatially or temporally split?

To address this fascinating possibility, let me begin by considering an obverse question—if *not* watching rear projections are viewers *not* split?—with a sequence from Woody Allen's celebrated *Annie Hall* (1977). Our schlemiel protagonist Alvie Singer (Allen) has been courting the goofy and alluring über-WASP Annie Hall (Diane Keaton) and one day finds himself cooking lobster for her at a nice little beach house in the Hamptons. There is a stove with a mammoth lobster pot, there are lots of writhing green lobsters that both Alvie (the New York Jew) and Annie (the Midwestern Protestant) consider alien, there is a nice white floor, there is a window looking out upon the dunes, there is a sink, a captain's table with some chairs, pleasant light, and great comedy as our poor pathetic (Jewish) hero ends up with (goyisch) lobsters scuttling around his feet. We may be reminded of Kracauer's observation that "the film actor is not necessarily the hub of the narrative, the carrier of all its meanings. Cinematic action is always likely to pass through regions which, should they contain human beings at all, yet involve them only in an accessory, unspecified way" (97). Most viewers who have seen this film tend to recollect this scene as unforgettably comic. Alvie and Annie appear to be *in* this kitchen, although it is only in one shot—where we see them scrambling to catch the lobsters—that we see their full bodies in what might be this space. Given that Alvie appears to be here; and that Annie appears to be here; given that the dunes appear to be outside this very window over this very sink, the presence of the characters and their action are unified with the topography of the place, and one reasonably *thinks of* this as a coherent scene.

What is it that makes all the components of the lobster scene seem to originate in the same place (even while, actually, they do)?

There is a uniform lighting scheme, with "sunlight" touching the bodies and objects in the scene rationally, consistently, uniformly. There is a balance between the indoor lighting (accomplished through particular fixtures appropriate to filmmaking) and the light streaming through the window from the dunes outside. The space is designed in such a way that the stove, the steamer pot, the table, and the floor all seem to fit in harmoniously. And finally, most emphatically, conventions for reading drama lead to the perception of action in place, and to the unification of understanding action with an understanding of place. In short, one has no predispositions toward seeing the space as independent of the action that fills it, no cue for thinking this scene, and our viewing, split—that, for instance, the dunes outside the window are seen in a rear projection. All that need happen here is that no clue should be presented to the viewer that might instigate suspicion about this harmonious relation. If the scene outside—the dunes, the dune grass, the blue sky—is in fact a rear projection, it need only *not look as though it does not fit*. If most of the kitchen is a rear projection for most of the shots, the place need only seem crisp, well lit, and well designed to hold the action. For all these very good reasons, the suspicion that this scene is artificially guyed does not raise itself; the place and the action seem to fit directly and tightly; one doesn't imagine the self being tricked, or the time, as Mulvey would have it, being "doubled."

In historical fact, this entire scene was shot on location, and everything about it, save the white floor, was not only actually present to the camera at the same time as everything else but also authentic to the house that had been rented for the filming; the floor, in short, is the only element of scenic design in play here (the actual red brick floor of that kitchen didn't show the lobsters well enough, and had to disappear swiftly underneath some whitewashed pieces of plywood). My point, however, isn't that this location is intrinsically coherent for film; it's that it might very well have been used only in fractions to integrate a composite shot, had any of the elements been difficult to achieve. It *could have been achieved* through rear projection, had there been a need (and in that event, it would have looked just as it does). Cinematic scenes that are not composites in fact look like scenes that are composites: that is the point with composites. Every scene in cinema, then, is *conceivable as* a puzzle put together from film shot in different locations at different times, whether it has been made this way or not. We may always imagine ourselves as having been split (in the way that Mulvey proposes). When, therefore, is this imagination, this rhetoric, invoked? When do audiences claim to see a split, regardless of whether there is one?

Wherever it is that Allen and Keaton are standing, after all, is a space from which the viewer is practically absent. The same goes for the background exterior. Viewers instead inhabit a cinematic space that is composed on film by the joining of actors, action, setting, and motive (as, in *A Grammar of Motives*, Kenneth Burke suggested happens generally). If the lobster scene was shot on location in a beach house; if outside the window were real dunes; if the stove was a real stove, the lobster pot a real lobster pot (in which many lobsters had previously been cooked, some by me), still none of these (historically accurate) facts matter cinematically, since there is no way to verify them in watching. Alvie could have freaked out with Annie on a soundstage in Los Angeles with rear projections and set design (Henry Bumstead, for example, specialized in domestic interiors, as can be seen with his stunning work in *Mystic River* [2003]); and the same crew that was filming this scene directly could have come earlier to shoot transparency plates. Had it been done that way, designers and cinematographer would have worked to cover the seams of production, and to withhold from audiences all substantial reason for suspecting the scene was anything but natural, and the fact that it *was* mostly natural only means that producers did not need to employ a covering artifice in this case. Given the amazing capacity of artists to cover seams in cinema, how can one tell the difference between a rear projection that has been artfully done and a scene that has been shot integrally? How can one tell, and when *do* viewers trouble to tell? Much of the apparently "fake" rear projection of classical cinema is just rear projection below what we would now consider the supreme level of technical accomplishment. The really expert cases do not stand out at all.

Examine a piece of the Marrakech marketplace sequence from *The Man Who Knew Too Much* for its resonances and implications regarding the dualism of rear projection. The setup: Louis Bernard (Daniel Gélin), a French gentleman whom Ben and Jo McKenna (James Stewart, Doris Day) met on the bus coming into town in the film's opening, has stood them up for dinner and engendered some middle-American pique (seeing the man arrive with a date, Ben, in fact, wants to go up and punch him). Now, the following morning, in the jam-packed market of the Place Djemaa el Fna, around noontime on a bright summer's day, with the sun high overhead, and disguised in an Arab burnoose, the same "fellah" is stabbed in the back and staggers forward to die in Ben's arms, first identifying himself as Bernard and then whispering a secret that will lead the McKennas on an adventurous chase that is the principal driver of the plot henceforward. As Ben squats over Bernard's body, these two framed neatly in the lower center of the screen by a camera cranked down near the ground, the shot displays curious passers-by in burnooses of every description shifting and standing around them, and behind these people the adobe walls of buildings reflecting the hot yellow sunshine.

An argument could be made about this sequence that in seeing it, one is positioned in both the Paramount soundstage and the Marrakech marketplace simultaneously—in short, that viewers are "jumpers" shifting rapidly

from one location to another—since McKenna and the dead man are photographed at Paramount, along with two or three of the extras, while the
bulk of the extras and the background are photographed in Marrakech.
But can one really say—even if the rear projection can be discerned in operation (which it cannot, in this and many other shots of the sequence)—
that here are two distinct and disparate spaces? The delicate and profound
reality as one actually watches the film is subtly different: the viewer is
neither alerted nor is she split; neither fully in Los Angeles nor fully in
the real Marrakech. One lingers and gazes instead in the cinematic "Marrakech," which is made through composition but in a way to which viewers
have no direct access. The sophistication of rear projection technique had
by 1955 made it possible to do combinations like this in such a way that
evidence of them was quite erased. Some of these shots were filmed on
location with the principal performers—on May 18, 1955—and some are
composites made from plates shot in Marrakech (between May 13 and 21)
and studio photography done months later at Paramount's Stage 2 (June
30, July 1, and July 2). The exceedingly intense illumination in Edouart's
VistaVision plates is beautifully matched by Robert Burks's studio lighting. Crowds milling to and fro intermingle with Ben and Jo, and even with
Alfred Hitchcock making his cameo appearance. For almost every one of
the crowd shots, only Ben and Jo and the two or three people standing
nearest them are actually live in front of the camera; all the others are in
the street background photographed in advance. But the matching lighting and constant crowd motion cover the join between projected and un-
projected realities, giving the effect of one single event in one unified space.
Hitchcock, more than a narrative impresario with a sharp eye and a taste
for the macabre and the absurd, more even than a brilliant social observer,
was a man who knew and prized cinematic technique. He had a particular
fondness for the transparency plate and what could be achieved with it,
and this sequence from *The Man Who Knew Too Much* is one of the real
masterpieces of plate photography in Hollywood history.[6]

To distill the separate components of this construction, and to argue
that the viewer is torn somehow between them, is to deny the moment
of cinematic art. A further step: to be in "Marrakech" in just this way is
something one can do only in cinema. "Just this way": with James Stewart
evincing the production value of the star presence co-extensive with Ben
McKenna in his rather shapeless characterological form and his handsome tweed sport coat; with the swarthy dying face of Gélin, from which

the swarthy makeup has partially come off in McKenna's hands (in fact, Stewart "wiped" white makeup onto Gélin); with the nosy crowd in brown and white and blue burnooses all mingling in front of the tawny buildings in the crisp, intense, saturating mountain light of Morocco; and with this gnawing sense in which as viewers we happen to capture only the most pungent moments of the action, and see them from only the most superior point of vantage, while also hearing every murmur and every whisper. To answer the question, "Are we in two places at once," one must say, "We are in a single place that is itself a composite of places, a cinema that is made up of multiple visions all handsomely integrated." To see division as separation is to divorce oneself from cinema. Division is unity.

If we return to *Marnie*, it is possible to understand at least the source of a certain objection many viewers have brought forward after seeing this film, namely that at some striking moments the rear projection is so "sloppily" done—as I would paraphrase their comments—that we are sharply aware of the technique and not the drama. With delicious skepticism, Robin Wood synopsizes this (as he finds it, unintelligent) complaint as asserting Hitchcock's presumptive "technical naiveté": "The film is full of absurdly clumsy, lazy, crude devices, used with a blatant disregard for realism" (173). The scene most often cited is Marnie's horseback ride on sleek black Forio, where she seems to be on a studio mounting device while a rear projection of flashing trees and fields unspools rather unceremoniously behind her: behind her and also in a curious distance, just a little less in focus than she is, with just a little less light. "Because of the back-projection," Wood offers sagaciously, "she doesn't look released at all, though her face tells us that she *thinks* she is. And, of course, that is the point" (175).

By late 1963, when *Marnie* was shot, there was plenty of process camera expertise at Universal; plenty of skill; plenty of technical capacity for rendering rear-projection composites to be absolutely seamless onscreen. It is far more logical to assume in this scene, where one has the distinct feeling, for a moment, that the girl on the horse is not really traveling through that Pennsylvania countryside; where one senses not only disunity but outright fragmentation in the experience; where, indeed, her presence seems fake and contrived by comparison with the natural setting through which she rides; where that setting pales away and blurs to some extent—in short, where the horseback ride is a mess, and Marnie a mess, and for Marnie the countryside an unfocussed mess—that one is seeing and experiencing precisely what the filmmaker intends. There are plenty of ways to aver that Marnie is discomposed and broken, but here Hitchcock has found a way to show it. There are times when we are psychologically wounded, set apart from the physical world in an interior zone of trauma and distress, and this scene beautifully portrays such a condition, literally distancing the audience from Marnie and from the countryside in two different ways, to two different degrees, one identified by Wood and the other by Mulvey (both of whom seem to neglect that in a shot of Marnie riding Forio after her robbery at Rutlands, Hitchcock shoots her without a cut, thus indicating that the actor can ride and that he can photograph her doing so). "The back-projection gives a dream-like quality to the ride, but no sense of genuine release," concludes Wood, one of a very small number of observers for whom *Marnie* is a major masterpiece. Unable to lose her sense of discordance in rear projection, Laura Mulvey flags this particular "fault," and does not view it as a way of showing—*showing*, not telling—something otherwise very difficult for audiences to see or imagine: "The intensity of movement is reduced to static studio gesturing. As the star appears in this strange, disorienting space, her emotion trumps her parody of movement. In fact, Marnie herself loses all sense of time and place just when the discordance of time and place characteristic of rear projection is most evident. This paradoxical, impossible space, detached from either an approximation to reality or the verisimilitude of fiction, allows the audience to see the dream space of the cinema." "Dream space," for Mulvey, must be a fracture between negations. But does not our lively viewing actually prove that Marnie's space is possible, and unique?

It is not really true that watching this scene—and other rear projections of greater or lesser fidelity—audiences sense with definite clarity that there are two worlds represented (in the way that both the appreciative Wood and the less appreciative Mulvey imply); or that they *lack* one or the other of reality and fictionality. Rather, I would say audiences are charged with both reality and fictionality together. The rear projection thus places viewers, not in a null, deficient space that is neither one thing nor the other, that somewhat equivocal "dream space of the cinema," but in a space that is purely cinematic because it is so replete and so disturbingly doubled. Everything one could desire is there at once—fakery along with accuracy; removal in space and time along with excessive and spontaneous presence ("Musicality always comes across as spontaneity," wrote Joan Acocella); technical achievement along with the grace of human presence.

Cinema always involves multiple placement.

"Slice of Life": Cinema and Verisimilitude

As to verisimilitude, of which in every cinematic scene there seems to be either not quite enough (Marnie on her horse) or far too much (perhaps Harry Lime disappearing into the echoey—and rather overbearing—sewers of Vienna in *The Third Man* [1949]), or just the right amount (Gregory Peck visiting Lauren Bacall in her apartment in *Designing Woman* [1957] at the moment when her precocious black poodle makes an appearance from the bedroom with the wrong shoe in its mouth!), it involves the source of a viewer's commitment to an authentic sense of presence, and the structure of a taste for a scene's plenitude and precision. This taste is exercised with variance and play, but however and whenever it operates there results a certain sense of contiguity between image and viewer feeling.

Consider that people's everyday lives are lived in what could be called "present reality," a locale and a substance that is tasted and moved in without much consideration being paid: "How real!" One simply treats what is "real" as absolutely and perfunctorily given in that way, the world into which the consciousness emerges. This world is "of course" already there to receive the visitor and supports his continuing and unfolding presence. To claim that an image has verisimilitude is to mean that it resembles this "present reality" so closely that—aside from the sometimes intrusive edges of the screen that frame it—it is indistinguishable from what is labeled the "real." At worst, reality is offered second-hand, through the eyes of someone (the sacred filmmaker) who received and devoured it directly before passing it along. Even though in watching cinema one sees easily enough that the image is generally very large (by comparison with the always present standard of the viewer's own body) and generally ideally achieved, even though viewers can sense themselves moving toward and away from it with the editor's sweeping and deft gestures, nevertheless that image seems to encapsulate in an unaffected and direct way some part of a world already taken for granted. And seeing verisimilitudinous imagery, viewers do not remark upon it as being what it actually is: exceptionally related to, derivative from, or modeled after and affecting to imitate the "presently real." It seems, more or less, simply to *be* the presently real, if it has enough verisimilitude, and if awareness is suspended of the cinematic process through which the imagery is being mobilized. Very often, indeed, realities are presented that we have no power to judge: in *Hook* (1991), Peter Banning (Robin Williams) caught up by Tinker dust and flying away over the rooftops of moonlit London: is this actually what

London looked like at some historical (early twentieth-century) moment, from the air, or are we watching an image of a publicly received imagination of London, replicated yet once again for delectation?

The cult of verisimilitude has fixed upon the valuation of what it calls "realism," at all costs. Things apparently *should* seem to be real, like everyday life. Thus, what is "wrong" with Marnie riding her horse (in the conventional realist critique) is that as she rides she doesn't enough seem to be doing it in present reality—verisimilitude is lacking. And those sewers of Vienna, found by Vincent Korda and John Hawkesworth for Carol Reed and lit and photographed (from every imaginable angle) by Robert Krasker, are just too fantastic, too engagingly Piranesian: if they are real and only real, they are like no reality we have ever known, and so they feel hyper-real, exaggerated, effected, not quite "presently real": the realism is overdone. Perfect verisimilitude is a kind of invisibility, in that it leads to recognition but not really to looking; to acknowledgment but not really to sense; to acceptance but not to engagement. Speaking bluntly against verisimilitude as a value in itself, Hitchcock told Truffaut: "Let's be logical if you're going to analyze everything in terms of plausibility or credibility, then no fiction script can stand up to that approach, and you wind up doing a documentary. . . . We should have total freedom to do as we like, just so long as it's not dull. A critic who talks to me about plausibility is a dull fellow" (102).

With cinema, as Hitchcock said, verisimilitude is not so desirable for its own sake: it's certainly not the treasure that viewers most deeply want. It can be argued that viewers want to be carried away from, not into, the "present everyday," to transform the personae of routine life—wherever possible—into emissaries from the world of myth: myth, perhaps, that illumines the everyday. Tom Wolfe writes about two doyennes of the bourgeoisie, encountering an actor named Cary Grant while he lunched at the Plaza Hotel and instantly transmogrifying him into the movie star they adored:

"Cary Grant!" says the first one, coming right up and putting one hand on his shoulder. "Look at you! I just had to come over here and touch you!"

Cary Grant plays a wonderful Cary Grant. He cocks his head and gives her the Cary Grant mock-quizzical look—just like he does in the movies—the look that says, "I don't know what's happening, but we're not going to take it very seriously, are we? Or are we?" (168)

What is ultimately offered in cinema is cinematic realities, not real realities. A setting that looks plausible but visually exciting is one thing; a setting with all the shabby tedium of the worn tried-and-true is another. Cinematic realities, such as they are, pop out in vivid colorations, striking compositions, and dramatic forms; and are peopled with stunning, glorious types (fabulous to look at, whether they are famous or not), not to speak of their cultural embedding, emphasized many times over by Bordwell (see for example Bordwell and Thompson, *Art* 120, 123, 132, 198). An excess of verisimilitude can ruin a cinematic experience, much as Cary Grant could have ruined an experience for his two fans at the Plaza if he had behaved more like a man eating his lunch, which is what he also was.

Mortal Twins

A few days before his funeral in the evening of September 3, 2009, and clad in a white shirt, dark slacks, and a scarf wrapped around his face, Michael Jackson, who had died June 25 of heart failure induced by a drug reaction, was reported by the Cable News Network as possibly hiding in Los Angeles. In a brief clip could be seen what might well have been Jackson hopping out of the back of a van parked at what was described as a police station. Entirely notwithstanding the issue of whether the death of this media superstar might have been faked—the covered body on the gurney at UCLA Medical Center, the LAPD investigation (not to mention the global media frenzy), the memorial in front of twenty thousand living fans (and "untold millions watching around the world" [msnbc.com]) on August 12 at Los Angeles's Staples Center, the prolonged forensic investigation of his blood chemistry, and so on—faked perhaps in order to afford him an opportunity of finally escaping the public personality that had been tormenting him of late, like a hairshirt or iron mask, what was essentially fascinating about this little news clip, far more than the fact that it questioned Jackson's decease, was its suggestion that there could be something utterly possible, not to say current, in believing that a person might be dead and alive at the same time.[7] The news clip played to an audience that, producers were aware, thought Jackson was dead yet could have been seized by the intriguing idea that he was, at the same time, still living. Why not, it "happened" to Elvis. Whether or not Jackson was alive, then, he might be thought to be. A curious form of doubling thus permeates the popular imagination, one in which a funeral both is and is not happening; in which a death both did and did not occur; in which a career both is and is not terminated; and, further, as regards Jackson himself, a doubling in which a kind and generous human benefactor is simultaneously an alleged pedophilic aggressor, a charitable soul at once a cupidinous addicted shopper whose money has run out, an African American of great prominence become something of a tacky white man. The idea that one might live a double life, or that anyone's life might be riddled with doublings, is what intrigues about the Jackson news clip. That any one might be two people, and two people at once: in the most extreme iteration, one twin alive and the other dead.[8]

The film frame is one in which the dead may live again, as Bazin reflected and as has been obvious to those who, addicted to films of the golden age, again and again watch the living movements of persons long gone. Stephen Sprague wrote about this phenomenal and enchanting duplicity in an essay on photographic practices among the Yoruba. In a culture devoted to photographic representations of the dead, problems arise sometimes when a twin deceases without ever having been photographed. Put on display then might well be a photograph of the twins as they were in life, where the deceased one is performed by the survivor, whose photograph in his sibling's clothing is printed into another photograph of himself in his own. The surviving twin is both alive and dead at the same time.

In the Hollywood canon, doubling as such sometimes occurs blatantly onscreen. It is most frequently treated through the trope of the split personality, an obvious archetype being Robert Louis Stevenson's twin specters, Dr. Jekyll and Mr. Hyde as embodied variously by such luminaries as John Barrymore (1920), Fredric March (1931), Spencer Tracy (1941), and, of course, Jerry Lewis (1963). One discerns a similar doubling in the shifts into and out of paranoiac fear displayed by Paula (Ingrid Bergman) in George Cukor's *Gaslight* (1944), as her monomaniacal husband torments her with schemes to drive her into genuine madness. Johnny Depp doubles himself in Rand Ravich's *The Astronaut's Wife* (1999), as do Dustin Hoffman in Arthur Penn's *Little Big Man* (1970) and all of the central performers excepting Kevin McCarthy in Don Siegel's *Invasion of the Body Snatchers* (1956). The typical dramatic form is that a conventional personality is shown to exhibit remarkable and outstanding sensitivity of one kind or another, so that when subjected to certain vibrations, perturbations, chemicals, or other specific influences it is helplessly morphed or melted into something alien and frightening, the very furthest sort of manifestation from the normal and a creature that busily engages itself with grisly anti-social acts almost always ending in a hideous murder. Guile can replace chemical or spiritual agencies, as in Hitchcock's *Stage Fright* (1950) and other films with double narratives, double tellings, double intentions, and double entendres. Reduced to its most simplistic formula, the double-personality film demonstrates how the most mild-mannered and civilized among us cloaks within his educated and sociable veneer the corpse of a deformed, animalistic, and voraciously blood-thirsty criminal who will—who can—stop at nothing until his lusts have been sated (sated, indeed, at night, either in the chilling light of the moon or in the provocative, dense, brooding darkness that signals its absence). The hero's task—but he almost always arrives too late to accomplish it!—is to save the cultured soul from his barbaric doppelgänger *alter*. The monster perishes at the good man's hands, reconverting to a shining exemplar of sweetness and light just as, with the girl he craves gazing tragically on, he takes his final breath. In cases where the bad and good selves inhabit a single body, the virtuous hero must die in order that his darker side will be extinguished, and this is, of course, very sad but the way things are. The *Superman* stories (1978; 1980; 1983; 1987; 2006) are inversions, but not rule breakers: the "monster" is heroic and the civilized man a monstrosity of banality in a world of debasing evil.

There has surely never been a more melodic treatment of this theme than John Brahm's *Hangover Square* (1945),[9] where an eccentric pianist-composer, George Bone (Laird Cregar), thrown off at random moments by sounds that he hears as shrilly dissonant, slides into a sort of hypnotic fit in which, ostensibly unbeknownst to himself, he commits murder. Bone is at work composing a virtuoso concerto, which he intends to perform under the distinguished baton of Sir Henry Chapman (Alan Napier), a philanthropic conductor-neighbor (whose daughter Barbara [Faye Marlowe] is interested in him), but his intensive bouts of concentration and passionate labor are interrupted by the persistent demands of Netta Longdon, a morally vacuous dance-hall singer (Linda Darnell). Netta wants him to write popular melodies for her and, completely smitten, he complies. But tensions come to a head one night when, catching him at work on his concerto, she demands one of the themes for herself. "You can't have it!" he protests, "It's for the concerto!" But Netta will have her way, until, at least, Bone goes into another fit, strangles her with a curtain sash, and places her body atop a Guy Fawkes bonfire to be incinerated. Finally, he is performing the concerto at Chapman's house as the police close in. He collapses at the keyboard, begging Barbara to take over, then proceeds to set the house afire. In the mad scramble, the police, the audience, and the musicians in the orchestra all flee, notwithstanding his protests that they must sit to hear the ending of the concerto. With blazing beams crashing all round him, Bone sits at the keyboard again and performs the concluding coda—written by Bernard Herrmann as a somber and magnificent solo for piano. We see all this from a towering crane shot looking down from the chandeliers, as with the concerto's final, brooding, sumptuous, depressive chords, Bone disappears in flames and the house comes down.

As with *Gaslight*, the doubling in *Hangover Square* is an effect achieved principally through use and manipulation of what Raymond Durgnat calls "primary" elements, comprising the set, the performers, the script, and those elements of direction addressed to them (32–33). One might consider as well the possibility—perhaps far more striking and certainly, as the history of motion picture production goes, more contemporary—of "secondary" effects, these having to do with the camera and any construction or adjustment of profilmic elements that is intended (more than merely expressing itself) to address what the camera can do and see. As to primary elements, *Gaslight* depends on Bergman's ability to present radically discontinuous exemplifications of contrasting emotional states, sweet and demure, and hysterically fearful; while *Hangover* requires Cregar to slide in and out of his "trance" condition and thus to simulate "normal" and "affected" mental states, which have distinctly different patterns of perception, movement, and control. As to secondary elements, rear projection and matte photography are notable techniques by which the audience is led to see two worlds that appear conjoined as one. Or only one manifestation, when in fact two exist.

In both rear projection and matte work, but with extreme finesse in the case of mattes, the camera's regard constructs a harmonic unity from fragmented multiplicity, indeed both fashions and examines the duplicity of a scene. An exemplary use of mattes to confound our detective abilities, to stun us with the doubled personality, can be seen in a film where Bette Davis plays each of two twin sisters. This film is indeed one of the absolutely primary cases of skilled matte photography lending credence to the utterly impossible.

Curtis Bernhardt's *A Stolen Life* (1946) is a relatively strange melodrama—perhaps one should say moral tale, since justice, not happiness, seems to be its fulcrum—in which then-thirty-seven-year-old Bette Davis, fulfilling what the *New York Times* called the "ambition" of "every actress" to "play dual roles in a movie, thus multiplying her presence by two," plays the Bosworth sisters, Kate and Patricia, each of whom, in her peculiar way, falls in love with the handsome leading man (Glenn Ford). Possibly it is unnecessary to add that one of these sisters is good—very very good— and the other bad—very very very very bad—or that, principally in order that the blithe young man should be suitably gulled at a critical point in the narrative, they are so identical a pair of twins as to be quite indistin- guishable. It is one of the ploys of such dramas that of course one must always be able to tell the apple from the orange, while the relevant charac- ters with whom these figures interact must not. Kate is a lonely artist, of no extremely remarkable talent but deeply convicted and pure. She would like to paint with truth, and to see with truth, and to feel truth, and she has a fresh, almost oxygenated spirit. Pat is a manipulative flirt, the sort of girl who must have everything she sets her eyes upon no matter who must be stepped on for getting it.

In the (somewhat thin and confounding) story,[10] Kate comes to Mar- tha's Vineyard, befriends and falls in love with Ford's Bill Emerson (a lighthouse inspector), then proceeds to lose him to her twin, also present but taken by Bill for the same girl he has been seeing. Bill, who comes to learn the truth, marries Pat! Kate, meanwhile, returns to the big city, en- dures an unsuccessful affaire de coeur, and decides that the thing for her is to go back to the island in New England and think about her life. She dis- covers Pat there, running away from a bad marriage to Bill. The two young women go out in a sailboat. There is a virulent storm at sea. As Pat slips overboard, her wedding ring is miraculously left behind,[11] so that now the utterly distraught Kate can pretend to be her own sister and in this way pick up the traces of her own torn life. Bill finds his way to her, but sees through the deception. Now it comes to light that he still loves her, and always has, and the film can happily end.

The mid-1940s was a time ripe for such a story, with women now con- fronted by a postwar reality that made them question who they were in life, buttresses of the economy or mindless domesticated consumers. Lucy Fischer notes how "during the World War II years, as part of the broad category of woman's melodrama, a particular genre emerged focusing on female identical twins played by the same actress" (25). Before war's end, the theme of the hopelessly neurotic split female, a perfect icon for *noir*, had been struck as well in Robert Siodmak's *The Dark Mirror* (filmed February-March 1942; released 1946). Here Olivia de Havilland is a pair of twin sisters, one an epitome of evil, the other a sweet innocent. Involved are insanity and murder, secrecy and revelation. If character doubling through emotional leaps or transcendental transformation held implicit the idea of the one being two, movies about twins made all the essential thrill of doubling embodied and explicit in a way that no plot could cover or substantiate. "Jumping" between the onscreen twins, the *this* and the *that*, viewers are confounded to know which is which, especially when seeing two identical creatures side by side. Even more pressing is the urgent will to know how the human identity can be, at once and maybe forever, both here and there.

Much of the more pedestrian material in *A Stolen Life* illustrates the most fundamental—and completely taken-for-granted—way in which doubling occurs in Hollywood, namely, with one location or object standing in for another: that the "Martha's Vineyard" of the story was really sometimes the Warner Bros. backlot and studio space, for example, and sometimes the town of Laguna Beach: location doubling. The misanthropic artist "Karnock" was the actor Dane Clark: doubling through standard characterization. But these "doublings" are inconsequential most of the time in viewing film, since one easily and unselfconsciously accepts these transformations of production by virtue of which actors become characters and geographical places become fictional ones. Far more complex and astonishing is a stunning doubling that left audiences inside and outside of the film business agape and that remains remarkable today, given its achievement in the absence of digital manipulation: the production of Bette Davis as the twins Kate and Patricia, not merely because the actor had to modulate her performance in tune with two diametrically contradictory personalities yet without ever being so extreme in rendition that Bill Emerson would seem incredible to us in his belief that the girls are one and the same, but far beyond this, since at various moments in the film Kate and Patricia actually appear onscreen interacting with one another at a single instant of dramatic time and in a single coherently unified dramatic space. While the trick of doubling an actor's performance has been performed many times in cinema, such as by James Whale with Louis Hayward, or Randall Wallace with Leonardo DiCaprio, in *The Man in the Iron Mask* (1939; 1998); David Swift with Hayley Mills in *The Parent Trap* (1961); and David Cronenberg with Jeremy Irons in *Dead Ringers* (1988), it is very frequently achieved using costume, makeup, and performance technique alone and without having the twins appearing together onscreen. Of the above examples, only the 1998 *Iron Mask* and

the Cronenberg *Dead Ringers* achieve this effect of simultaneous presence.
Stolen Life represents a real turning point in Hollywood's ability to offer
viewers a particularly enchanting, and chilling, twin vision of reality.

Bette Davis Bette Davis

Stationary mattes had been used in some of the very earliest filmmaking.
There is a noteworthy case in the station scene that begins *The Great Train
Robbery* (1903) in which we see, through a large window, a train passing by
"outside." The challenge of "traveling mattes" was not taken up until the
1920s and not mastered until considerably later. In the traveling matte, to
quote Richard Rickitt, who gives one of the more lambent explanations
of a process that has oddly defied simple and straightforward elucidation,
a foreground actor, or other element, could "move in front of a separately
filmed background with absolute freedom. Such a system would allow
characters filmed in a studio to appear to inhabit places that were located
on the other side of the world" (57), or for that matter, since matte shots
are very frequently used in science fiction and fantasy film, located on the
other side of the universe as we dream it. I should stress that in a traveling
matte this "inhabiting" would involve motion, as in flying over mountain
ranges on the back of a *djinn* (*The Thief of Bagdad* [1940]) or a massive
puppy (*The NeverEnding Story* [*Die Unendliche geschichte*, 1984]) or a Hip-
pogriff (*Harry Potter and the Prisoner of Azkaban* [2004]).

To make a traveling matte, the cinematographer began by filming a (I)
background scene in a straightforward manner. Then he filmed (II) an
actor in motion—not inside that scene but against a large flat background
painted black or lit so as to show up black on film. The piece of film on
which this was recorded was developed and then re-photographed onto a
high-contrast stock that when all of the middle tones were reduced away
would make the background thoroughly transparent and the foreground
actor(s) completely black. This (III) "male matte" was sandwiched against
(I) the full background in a contact printer, also loaded with blank film
stock, so that the combined "image" as recorded on that stock would show
a background that was completely defined (because seen through the
completely transparent parts of the male matte) with the moving figure,
appearing in frame after frame, always represented by a perfectly shaped
black silhouette. The new piece of film (IV) showed the scene as it would
finally appear in structure, with the only omission being the body of the

moving foreground actor, now replaced consistently by that correspond-ing—perfectly corresponding—negative space. Now, the female matte, a second high-contrast print of the actor (V)—this time reducing the back-ground to black and exposing the performer's figure properly—could be sandwiched with this printed composite to make (VI) the matte compos-ite: the black background would prevent any light in the optical printer (the device being used for all this sandwiching and re-photography) from reaching the background area of the film, which was already perfectly ex-posed, and the well-exposed actor figure could be inserted into the black "hole" that was awaiting her in each frame of the film. Obviously, any number of moving performers or objects could move simultaneously in one or more mattes (as we see, for example, in the *Harry Potter* films): if on a set a number of actors could with reasonable ease be choreographed together, a single matte could be shot with all of them; otherwise a succes-sion of mattes could be made.

This elementary process was later refined by C. Dodge Dunning and thereafter by Roy J. Pomeroy, who invented a way for the matte to be con-structed not on a separate piece of film but in the camera itself using a particular lighting setup on the soundstage: the film in the camera needed only to be rewound and shot multiple times. Eventually the Dunning-Pomeroy process was redeveloped as bluescreen cinematography (Rickitt 60ff.). But in all these ways of filmmaking the essential process remained the same—a foreground figure was isolated through some exposure tech-nique; a negative matte was achieved where this figure's motion appeared against a background as a "hole"; and then a full exposure of the isolated foreground figure was printed into that "hole" to make the composite shot.

To render the matte composite, filmmakers used a complex device called an optical printer. This is essentially an interconnected camera-projector array, with the camera's lens in effect positioned directly in front of the projector's. Film is projected directly into the camera and re-filmed there. The projector has multiple feeds, so that numerous pieces of film can be input simultaneously into a gate system where in some predeter-mined registration with one another they can be manipulated in front of a light source. Any light emitted from the projector is exposed to raw film stock at the camera end. An optical printer makes a movie of a movie. For this photography of film, the incoming image components must be of the highest quality, thus the optical printer's projection apparatus must be ca-pable of precise registration and a perfect alignment of multiple images in relation to one another. One frequent (and easily recognized) possibility in optical printing is the performance of fades and dissolves, and various forms of the optical "wipe." In a classic dissolve—for example, at Midway Airport in *North by Northwest*, Roger Thornhill stands on the tarmac while a TWA plane taxis gently toward him; its brilliant lights shine into our eyes as the scene changes to the monument at Mount Rushmore— one scene is put through the optical projector, the aperture of which is closed down frame by frame as the film moves, until there is no more light. Now the film in the camera, on which this has been recorded, is rewound back to the start, and the second scene is projected with the aperture closed at the start and gradually opening. In the composite, the first scene will "dissolve" into the second. When we see a scene "fade to black," only the first part of the above procedure is used.

In making matte shots, the various phases of production can all be achieved in the optical printer. This occurs, for instance, when the background scene is contact-printed against the strip of film containing the blacked-out moving foreground figure (the male matte): the two pieces of film are fed into the optical printer's projector simultaneously from separate reels and through a pin registration system that keeps them in perfect sync frame by frame as they are sandwiched together and pass through the gate in front of the light. The resultant image is captured at the camera end on a new piece of film. This piece can now be run through the projector in tandem with the female matte (the fully exposed figure against a black ground) and the resultant image will be a complete matte composition. All of the mechanisms of the optical printer have independent speed adjustments, so that the frame rate of the projected film can be matched with that of the film moving through the camera (or not, as the particular case may require). To get a slow-motion effect onscreen, one can use the optical printer, running the gate of the projector end at a speed slower (by a definite fraction) than the mechanism at the camera end. The optical printer is designed so as to optimize the quality of reproduction at every level, since in photography every generation of picture that is made from another picture loses a little in quality. To maintain the highest possibly quality, then, foreign substances such as dust or skivings (sliverings-off) from the celluloid are all excluded; and the abutment of two pieces of incoming film in contact as they move through the gate minimizes any maladjustment of the image that could occur without perfect alignment.

If to a lay reader an obsessive concern with an image's alignment, perfection, and synchronization may seem incongruous or strange, it would be well to consider what was written (in 1943) in reflection about the rear

projection process—another projector-camera conjunction—by its greatest pioneer, Farciot Edouart. Edouart's worries apply to all big screen effects work:

> When you magnify a single-frame motion picture image 1 × 1 ½-inches in
> size to fill a screen 27 × 36 feet, you are at the same time magnifying every
> mechanical and optical imperfection in the equipment that projects it. More-
> over, when you consider that in effect this enormously magnified picture is at
> the long end of a lever arm 100 feet or more in length, you will see that any
> irregularity of film registration and the like in the original film or its passage
> through the projector will be disproportionately enlarged on the screen. It
> will show up as doubly defective in comparison with the steadiness of the
> actual foreground action as photographed by a modern studio camera. With
> the foreground steady, and the projected background portion of the scene
> badly unsteady, all illusion of reality would be lost in the composite scene.
> ("History" 114)

It need hardly be said that the traveling matte technique found vast
and extensive use in Hollywood filmmaking, freeing actors from the tra-
vails of perilous and uncomfortable location work and freeing writers to
envision character/setting formulae that had been unimaginably bizarre
and inconceivable for production until now. In 1939, for example, Dorothy's bedroom could spin in the tornado while outside her window frame
horrible Miss Gulch pedaled by in thin air. By the 1980s, Indiana Jones
could flee from a giant concrete ball. Superman could swoop down into
Niagara Falls. In the early 2000s, teeny-weeny Harry Potter could play
quidditch. The technique works well enough in situations where a single
foreground actor or form—or a collection of disconnected forms—must
move through a space in which direct shooting is impossible. There remained a slight black line around the moving form—called the "minus"—
that made it possible for keen observers to discern the effect in operation;
much of the technical progress in matte production was aimed at reducing
and then eliminating this "minus" but even into the 1970s and 1980s one
will still find it. We can note Vladimir Nabokov's arch observation about
effects technique that "a film actor in a double part can hardly deceive anyone, for even if he does appear in both impersonations at once, the eye
cannot help tracing a line down the middle where the halves of the picture
have been joined" (15–16).

Nabokov is invoking a technique that had been developed for the efficient production of "twin" shots by the mid-1930s, split-screen. Some
clear examples can be seen in Roy William Neill's Columbia production
The Black Room (1935) with Boris Karloff as both Anton and Gregor de
Berghman confronting one another stentoriously over matters of dignity
and morality; or, in John Ford's *The Whole Town's Talking* (1935), with
meek reporter Edward G. Robinson being told by his snarling Public
Enemy No. 1 lookalike, "Remember, one more word outa you and yer out
like a light!"[12] By 1945, Danny Kaye had filmed *Wonder Man* at the Goldwyn Studios, where special effects photographer John P. Fulton executed
an optical split-screen process so that the actor could be onscreen with
himself. Two cardinal rules had to apply to action that would be effected
through the split-screen technique: first the two performances had to occupy discrete portions of the scene, and secondly crossing over the axis
was beyond the capability of the technique. Similarly problematic was a
shot in which any piece of prop or scenery was interposed between the
actor and the lens. To make the split-screen shot, the camera had to be
securely locked into position, and the set entirely secured physically. The
actor worked first on one side of the set, then for a second take on the
other. The first piece of film is fed into an optical printer and advanced
frame by frame, while the operator moves a matting device inside the apparatus (a dividing card, like a wipe blade, placed "next to the intermittent movement of the printer head" [Fielding 168]) in order to cover one
side of the picture. The film is rewound and exposed a second time with a
reverse matte in operation, now printing from light exposed through the
second shot made on set, this time with the actor on the other side of the
scene. In order that the composite might look unmanipulated and normal,
especially if, as in the case of *Wonder Man*, it had been produced from
filmic materials shot and processed by Technicolor, extreme care had to
be taken in the lighting of the set and action for both takes of each scene,
so that the colorations—especially of the background—would perfectly
match. (Again, the smallest deviations of color would be magnified on the
big screen.)

But:

Neither conventional rear projection nor matte composites would be
sufficient to meet the challenge of *A Stolen Life*. For this film, regardless
of the costume changes and affectations of manner that were required of
Davis, and completely beyond the fact that as both producer and star of

the film she was already living a "double life," a cinematographic technique had to be devised that would permit her two Bosworth sisters to appear onscreen simultaneously—indeed, to interact physically with one another in front of the camera. To have an actor appearing twice on the screen at the same moment—as, say, twins—was straightforward enough if the action was minimal: Kaye on one side of the screen playing to Kaye on the other in *Wonder Man*. But to have twins moving around one another and even touching was a completely different matter.

Before *A Stolen Life*, no film had been exhibited that showed matted figures *moving against one another, face to camera* in the same shot: no matted-in character had touched another visibly identical matted-in character, or passed in front of her, or lit her cigarette. A problem for this film, and one that became a potential tax upon realism every time Pat and Kate got together, involved realizing the shadows their bodies would naturalistically cast inside the rooms where they interacted. If in action or adventure cinema the very existence of a character in a strange setting so entranced an audience that no one would question the minor issue of an absent shadow, in *A Stolen Life* the action would be comparatively protracted and embedded in a conventional situation. For realism's sake, the characters had to seem to be flesh and blood, fully three-dimensional, fully present in a single place.

Part of the solution involved the use of stand-in doubles. Fascinating in their own right, indeed, were the contractual arrangements that underpinned this aspect of split-screening:

When Bette was Kate, she "played to" her twin sister Pat, portrayed by Sally Sage, who for ten years was her stand-in.

When Bette portrayed Pat, she had to emote to the other twin, Kate, played by Elizabeth Wright.

Both Sally Sage and Elizabeth Wright had their own stand-ins, so at this point the count was up to five Bettes. Bette's own stand-in brought the total up to six. (*Stolen Life* British Pressbook)

With a methodical and obsessive attentiveness to their challenge, the filmmaking team employed not one but two stand-ins for the ostensibly twin sisters. After all, Sally Sage, who had been working with Davis "for ten years," could have managed on her $150-per-week stipend to offer both a pretend Pat for Kate and a pretend Kate for Pat, yet not without compromising the sense of duplicity and reflection that was apparently inherent

not only in the script but also on the set. And the publicity that gushed
out, bizarre in its own way, was calculated to stimulate the audience's curiosity no more than to bolster its admiration for the principal player, but
hardly to draw attention to the techniques behind the phenomenon:

> I pull up a chair and Bernhardt does a rave about Bette's characterizations.
> "There are no makeup tricks," he says. "And she doesn't even change her voice
> for the different girls. She does it all with the eyes. But she creates two dis-
> tinct individuals."
>
> On the set, Bette even talks about herself as two different people.
>
> "I'm the nice girl in the next scene," she says. "My sister, Pat, is off dancing
> with my beau, the so-and-so."
>
> "Sounds very confusing," I observe. "Aren't you afraid this picture will give
> you a split personality?"
>
> Bette laughs gaily.
>
> "Oh, I've always had that," she says. (*Herald Express*)

Let us examine one particular sequence from *A Stolen Life*, rendering
one of the most difficult technical scenes in the film, a bedroom conversation between two far-from-mutually adoring sisters. The doubling of
Davis's two performances here is accomplished, as Herb Lightman notes,
"with incredible smoothness and a complete atmosphere of reality" (196).[13]
This is a technical solution to the philosophical problem of being in two
places at the same time.

The scene opens with Kate in long shot turning out the light in the
hallway and walking into a large and well-furnished bedroom. She closes
the door behind her, turns to the camera, walks forward (as the camera
dollies backward with her steps), drops a few items on the dressing table
(right). She perches on a tiny padded seat, then swivels a little, crossing
her legs under her with a smile on her face. Kate is now just off-center,
screen right, with the canopied four-poster bed about twelve feet behind
her, lit by a bedside table lamp that matches in brightness the white short-
sleeved cashmere crew-neck she is wearing. At screen left and to the left
of the bed in a shadowed area stands a tall, upholstered wing chair. Suddenly we see movement on this chair, two arms stretching upward in a
yawn, and hear the rather sharp words, "Hello, Sis!" Kate turns to look
over her shoulder: "Pat, what are you doing here?" Sitting forward a little
in the shady distance, Pat says she couldn't sleep and thought they would
chew the fat for a while. We see her dark mass of curled hair, her flannel

nightgown flecked with lines of shadow. "Got a match, Kate?" Obligingly, Kate gets up from her perch and heads to the back of the room.

This shot makes use of a double for Pat, ensconced throughout in shadow and thus somewhat indiscernable. Pat's voice is pre-recorded by Davis and looped into the shot, since we do not see the double in close-up and cannot detect her lips moving. The sound of this voice cues the viewer to an immediate acoustic doubling, that the "sound of Bette Davis" is in two places in this room at once, and prepares her for the visual doubling that will follow: without this preparation, stunned shock on seeing Bette Davis replicated in the next shot could produce a sustained moment of disengagement—disengagement, further, that could develop on its own and shatter any possibility of belief in the action that ensues.

The editing now jumps to a medium shot looking directly at the wing chair with Pat sitting back in it and fitting a pale cigarette into her mouth—and a truly astonishing filmmaking accomplishment. The four-poster is now in the background. Enshadowed, Kate marches from screen right to left behind the armchair until she is standing to the left side of it, where she reaches forward and turns on a table lamp. Her doing this fully lights the foreground of the shot. One can see with unmistakable clarity that the girl sitting in the chair, extending her right hand leftward on the screen for the match, and the girl standing beside the chair, striking a match upon her shoe, are both Bette Davis. Bantering a little, the standing Kate reaches down with the lit match, the flame of which is distinctively flickering, and places it in her sister's fingers. "Not trying to get rid of me, are you?" asks Pat snidely, lifting the match toward the cigarette that is between her lips, while Kate takes a step to fold her arms comfortably on the back of the chair. Throughout this shot, Pat in her chair moves her head slightly, but does not move her body.

This shot exemplifies one of the most difficult effects challenges in cinema, often attempted and only half-achieved but here mastered by Ernest Haller (1896–1970),[14] working in careful collaboration with his art director Robert Haas (1889–1962) and the man who would ultimately achieve the illusion through optical printing, Russell Collings (1902–1967). This shot is among a small number of triumphs in this film that represented, at the time, the acme of cinematic effects "magic." Even today, by a contemporary standard that has been substantially raised thanks to the efficiencies of a motion-control system for cameras—invented at Lucasfilm for the original *Star Wars* production (1977) and then further elaborated at Universal for *Back to the Future Part II* (1989) and by David Cronenberg in

Toronto for his *Dead Ringers*—and thanks to blue- and greenscreen traveling matte work, this shot in *A Stolen Life* remains coherent and incalculably smooth, indeed utterly enigmatic (because of its apparent "realness") for the lay viewer. How, after all, with a celebrated star whose publicity had never leaked even a hint of a hint that she had an identical twin who could act as well as she did, was it possible to show Davis standing next to Davis, and in such a complex way that her hand could extend itself and pass a lit match—the flame of which is never interrupted in the maneuver—to the hand of her "sister"? This is a shot effected not in the camera, as had been typical previously—with the actor on two sides of a set and a matte card blocking half the picture, as I detailed above—but after principal photography, in the laboratory.

What is required for a shot like this is two pieces of film, A and B, that can be "combined" in an optical printer to make a single image.[15] When A (say, Davis in the chair) is projected in the printer into the lens of the printer's camera apparatus, a ("male") matte device is inserted into the printer and manipulated to obscure part of the picture area. The film is rewound and strip B (Davis walking and standing) is projected into the camera, with a corresponding ("female") matte device in operation to block out the other part of the picture. The trick in this shot was to matte out Davis in the chair in shot B successfully enough that the wrist and hand of her double, who was filmed there in this shot, would fit onto Davis's arm from shot A, at the matte join. The matte had a vertical line running up from the bottom of the frame, through the seated "Davis'"s wrist (where she wore a nightgown with a frill at that spot) and up the side of the chair—yet only to the top of the chair, since the standing Davis's hand had to rest easily at the top corner—then along the chair top to the other side, and down. This irregular matte and its match would have been made out of dark card or blackened tin, some material easily cut to a very specific shape.

Given the difficulty of making the match, it is very likely that a number of takes of shot B would have been made, so that Collings could have had his choice in doing the optical printing. He could have advanced the film frame by frame in the optical printer, moving the matte cut-out arbitrarily with each frame, had that been necessary. To further assist in optical printing, shots created to be subjected to this process were done on a special material, Kodak "lavender" duping stock,[16] that had extra and very precisely punched sprocket holes. Regular film stock had sprocket holes that were slightly oblong in order that the camera's intermittent claw, in seizing and pulling down the film before the aperture twenty-four times a second, could be effective even if it were not absolutely 100% accurate in its grasp. Larger holes work perfectly well for normal shooting, but in an optical printer, film with such sprockets can jiggle slightly, and even the slightest jiggle of a piece of film there is magnified intensively on the screen later on. Both shot A and shot B must be in absolutely perfect registration.[17]

Film editor Rudi Fehr was exceptionally pleased with this particular shot. "An editor's *dream* to get it right," he said (Bell 246).

As to the "magical" flaming match. Only by watching this shot proceed in freeze-frame, split-second by split-second, can we see that the match goes out as the standing figure hands it over, but is alight again when the seated one, having snatched, it, moves the flame toward her face. One or two frames of film—taking up less than a tenth of a second onscreen—move too quickly to be seen.[18]

The sequence continues with a number of more straightforward split-screen shots, in which the matte cut-outs needed for optical printing are more regularly shaped. There is also a medium-close profile shot of Pat standing up from the chair, turning toward the camera, then pacing over toward the door—"I knew something was happening to you. You were singing like mad in the shower this morning"—accomplished with Pat walking in front of a small rear-projection screen showing a plate of the seated Kate, the bed, and all of Kate's shadowing (Fehr, qtd. in Bell 246). A normal shot with an offscreen model projecting a shadow is followed by a second rear-projection of Kate at the bedside, doing up the buttons on her pajamas. She moves right, swiftly crossing in front of Pat, going through a door to a closet. The plate in this case is a "double," or "twin," of the plate from the earlier shot, since it is Pat who is included in it and Kate who is moving on the soundstage in front of the screen. Again, with rear projection under any circumstances it is lighting that is the major challenge, both in the plate and on the soundstage. Here, with a room essentially dark and the difficult challenge of matching images of twins, the lighting nuances are spectacular.

Following is a normal medium shot of Pat, looking screen right after Kate, folding her arms, then a traveling matte split-screen medium shot of Kate at the closet door, looking left toward Pat. She closes the closet and walks back left, again crossing in front of Pat, to the bed, where she stretches across and makes to get under the coverlet on the far side. "Pat, I'm dead." Now we are treated to a conventional split-screen long shot with two doubles, from the foot of the bed on Kate's side, showing her under at the head of the bed on the far side. Pat puts herself on the other side of the bed and stretches out. She and Kate converse, the former leaning her head on one hand and the latter reaching up to put a hand behind her own head. Here, with a slightly diagonal matte manipulated in the optical printer, a shot with Davis lying on one side of the bed and conversing with her acting double is joined to a second shot with Davis on the other side (and the other acting double). In these split-screen shots, Lightman informs us, "dialogue was keyed by means of a playback recording so that all of the action of both twins could be synchronized" (197).

In this sequence, as was common practice among special effects teams at the Hollywood studios through the 1940s, 1950s, 1960s, 1970s, and beyond, a variety of effects techniques are utilized to create a fluid and continuously developing scene, and often shots that have been made in entirely different ways are intercut with one another. The viewer's ability to detect a matte shot as such, for example, is handily compromised when it is juxtaposed against unmanipulated shots lined up on either side of it; and, further, when the matte is onscreen for only a short while. In the sequence from *A Stolen Life*, the split-screen shots are interlinked with normal shots to subtract attention from them. An editing technique roughly similar to Fehr's here is used by George Tomasini for Hitchcock's Mount Rushmore sequence of *North by Northwest* (1959), where mattes, rear projections, dramatic close-ups, and shots with painted backdrops are interconnected in a powerful sequence that pulses forward, thanks to the urgently beating fandango theme of Bernard Herrmann on the sound track. In all such camouflaging of effects, it is true—as John Belton describes a contention of Jean-Louis Baudry—that the camera "transforms what is set before it but conceals the *work* of that transformation by effacing all traces of it" (Belton 63, referring to Baudry 40); and yet here, too, even emphatically, one's deep knowledge that the doubling in view is impossible makes for a state of wonder and engagement that superficial cynical dismissal would dissipate.

Nor was the bedroom scene the only technical marvel of twinning in this film. For another sequence in broad daylight, as the twins walk together in conversation upon a local dock, rear projection was used behind them to depict village life. But this was a *split-screen* shot, made out of elements that had been shot so that matte cut-outs could block parts of them in the optical printer. What had to be organized in this case was an absolutely precise interlinkage of camera operation with that of the rear projector, so that in the two parts of the shot finally being combined, the material in the background was exactly the same. As Lightman has it, "The blending had to be synchronized down to the last frame" (197).

The skill involved in *Stolen Life* was not only that of the director, Curtis Bernhardt. Quite as fruitful in working out the staging for camera was the meticulous labor, both hiding and intensely present, of a significant number of creative artists, since filmmaking is never a solo process. As Alan J. Pakula once said, "I am working with endless, endless numbers of people. It is enraging at times and it is also the most exciting part of it at times. In the end, if the film is successful, it is a synthesis of so many people that it is impossible to remember who did what and when" (qtd. in McBride [vi]). In appreciating a sequence like this one must acknowledge the knowing labor of Collings in the optical printing; Haller in photographing Davis and her doubles; the decorator (Fred MacLean) and his team in carefully matching the arrangement of the coverlet under the bodies; the wardrobe team (Marguerite Royce and L. Ryde Loshak) in carefully duplicating the precise fit of the nightgowns; the makeup artist (Joe Stinton) in matching the facial tones; the hairdresser (Agnes Flannagin) in working the coiffures for twinny match and twinny differentiation; the propmen (G. W. Berntsen and Sam Mendelson) getting that cigarette right take after take; Haller's assistants (William Schurr and James Cairns, as well as gaffer James Goldenhar and best boy Rene Steffen) precisely maintaining the illumination levels at every point in the shot; the grip (S. E. Young) in ensuring the precise immobility of the camera; and finally the editor (Fehr), whose delicate assembly of the pieces, establishment of their rhythm, and feeling for visual continuity truly "stitches" the sequence. Ironically, while Davis's work carrying out the two halves of the performance is exacting of its own nature, as is all acting before the camera, what makes it most difficult for setups like this is the ideal that as few takes as possible should be executed, since every retake involves the probabilities of new errors of one kind or another. Beyond that, her acting is the least complicated and least vulnerable part of what is going on.

As to Davis herself, she had to be two people in many ways, well beyond producing and acting simultaneously. She had to split herself rather mechanically during the performance, acting in one body but keeping a tight mental record of the double's positions and alignments so that she could later come to take them up. She had to play all the doubles scenes, in short, doubly, being inside her own body for one take, while at the same time projecting herself outward into her listening (and thinking) "twin," and then in the ensuing take occupying the "body" of that twin. Not only this, but she had to duplicate her personality, because the twins are entirely unalike in mood, attitude, and intent: "One sister is good and the other is evil, and the audience's sympathies are directed toward the former" (Fischer 27). Like Jeremy Irons in *Dead Ringers*, like Danny Kaye in *The Wonder Man*, like Hayley Mills in *The Parent Trap*, and so many others, Davis appeared onscreen in this film by being twice—as Blake wrote, "Twofold always. May God us keep / From single vision and Newton's sleep"—that is, by being there at the same time as she was here: not in succession, as though one might grow from one personality into another, but at the same time, always in the light and always, too, a shadow of herself.

Is it necessary to say that these prodigies are nothing more than effects of optics? They are the playthings of an artist skilled in benefiting from the contrast of light and shadow; the rays of a torch directed and concentrated onto a single object.

—*La Feuille Villageoise* (February 28, 1793), 508, qtd. in Laurent Mannoni, *The Great Art of Light and Shadow* 143

3

Being There

Paul Philidor, who had been projecting moving images of the dead to the astonished eyes of their friends and relatives (having obtained beforehand images that he could have copied in paint onto slides), applied his art by playing to, and with, the properties of light and the imagination, *La Feuille Villageoise* reported. Thanks to his phantasmagoria, one could enter a dark room, be addressed by a figure of light, and "see" someone who "really" wasn't there (or who was really "somewhere else"). This was in 1792, a little more than a hundred years before screen acting began to establish a new reality of personality and presence in the modern imagination. In their wonderful *Stairway to Heaven* (1946), Michael Powell and Emeric Pressburger assign Philidor's name to an emissary from heaven (Marius Goring) who escorts people to the other world and intercedes on their behalf if by some divine miscalculation they have "died too soon."

What does it come to, to act in front of a movie camera, and in doing this to *seem real* in one's character? Roberta Pearson has suggested a dichotomy in early screen performance between histrionic and verisimilar styles and notes a "transformation of performance style" that is "inextricably linked with the shift from the pure melodrama to the realist psychological narrative" (57). Early film was not essentially about getting "into" characters. Histrionic acting is full of exaggerated gestures and broadly contorted facial expressions, aimed to come through at a distance, as, for example, when players on a stage needed to be read by spectators sitting very far away. In Jean Renoir's glorious film *The Golden Coach* (1952), Anna Magnani, incarnating a lead member of a commedia dell'arte troupe, had to render histrionic work in many scenes where her character was "on stage"; she bows, she flails, she gesticulates, she stands archly, she prances. The same year, MGM produced *Scaramouche*, in which Stewart Granger had to do likewise. Verisimilar acting, by contrast, is a response to the close-up and works as an imitation of the everyday behavior one might see at close range. Rhett Butler (Clark Gable) sweeping Scarlett O'Hara (Vivien Leigh) into his arms is histrionic, but Roy Scheider wryly suggesting that Robert Shaw is "going to need a bigger boat" in *Jaws* (1975) is doing purely verisimilar acting, knowing he is being seen chest-up in a medium close-up. In Pinter's *Betrayal* at New York's Trafalgar Theater in 1980, Scheider's performance was, and needed to be, a distinctly more histrionic one since in the theater there is no close-up. A more recent example of verisimilar performance can be seen in Jason Bourne (Matt Damon) calmly telling Pamela Landy (Joan Allen) on the telephone that she looks tired, thus revealing that he's been watching through a scope from a neighboring skyscraper.

As to modern performance, logical as verisimilar technique may seem as a theoretical account of it, acting style must vary according to circumstance, and audiences can have a vacillating sense of "realness" from moment to moment. Consider in *Modern Times* (1936) how Charlie Chaplin seems histrionic when he is slaving like a rhythmically twitching human mechanism at the assembly line or acrobatically taking his "lunch" from the feeding machine, yet verisimilar as he tries to have a quiet smoke in the bathroom or as he talks in confidence to his girl (Paulette Goddard). Even more importantly, as James Naremore acknowledges, extra-diegetic issues can have bearing on a viewer's experience of screen action: "Viewers . . . lose sight of [Cary] Grant's craft [in *North by Northwest*] because his image, like that of most of the major stars, overshadows the technique that helped to create it. It is common to hear his admiring critics and even his fellow players speak of him as if he were a relatively natural phenomenon" (*Acting* 234).[1]

From Siegfried Kracauer, Konstantin Stanislavsky, and André Bazin to Richard Dyer, Pearson, Richard DeCordova, Naremore, Nicholas Ray, and, more recently, Lesley Stern, much has been written by scholars and teachers about the problem of fostering an illusion of reality through gestures, hesitations, vocalizations, postures, and muscular exertions. Stanislavsky and Ray both worked on the assumption that a young actor might not recognize the power of a behavior, and both worked to show their students their own accomplishments by a kind of stop-action technique.

However the elusive properties of screen performance, the nuances of experience that actors commit to presentation and recording, their experience of being in front of the lens, the duplicity of the self ... all these are lingering riddles that betray any simplistic or single-minded analysis and linger to provoke, no matter how many exquisite or challenging performances one has seen (see Pomerance *Depp*). Screen performance can be easy to watch and enjoy, but cantankerously difficult to talk or write about ... or do. The articulate doing of performance is indeed something that many who critique and dissect it do not comprehend, since they are adept at watching but have no idea what it is to make action flow out of the self in front of the camera eye.

To participate in, even generate, one of the legion moments of profound presence that can be found in screen history: what is that? And since, with cinema, every moment visible on the screen betrays simultaneously an opening into an actor's actual life (lived, while the camera turns, before the camera), we must seek to wonder not only what an actor *does* in making performance but also who an actor *is*. Not that performance is exclusively contained in the actor's moving and articulating body (as we shall see further below). In Arnold Glassman, Todd McCarthy, and Stuart Samuels's engaging documentary *Visions of Light*, we are told that Louis B. Mayer dictated to cinematographers that his actresses should always look good, no matter what they were doing, this evidenced through a shot of the glamorous Jean Harlow radiant in a storm in *Red Dust* (1932): the performance inheres to some degree in the image of it. In *Dinner at Eight* (1933), Harlow is costumed and lit with a chilling radiance that actually makes her seem horrible, and the horror of her is what makes her come alive. Cornel Wilde, mortified with disgust at his possessive (and similarly horrible) wife, Gene Tierney, in *Leave Her to Heaven* (1946), as slowly he begins to register the magnitude and depth of her desperate possessiveness: how did he work to reshape the closure of his face in order that his character's personality might also appear to be receding? Some of that magic is in the lighting of Leon Shamroy, some in the colorations of Ben Nye's makeup and Maurice Ransford and Lyle Wheeler's sets, but much has to do with the shaping of his mouth and the extent to which Wilde opens his eyes — tiny operations of the facial muscles that he worked with expertise. The supreme Judy Holliday, apparently incapable of putting two sentences together in *Born Yesterday* (1950) but as smart as a whip: how, where, when could she have learned that comic timing, that unmistakable, perfect rhythm of delivery, that vocal dance? Peter O'Toole, fawning upon his own face reflected in the blade of his knife, in *Lawrence of Arabia* (1962): was this not his spontaneous idea, just something he came up with in the mid-day heat? (David Lean confessed it was.) That in a supreme moment, this Lawrence would want only to see how pretty he looked, to gauge the effect of the sun shining upon him! Scheider, frozen in a rictus of fear in *Jaws*, improvising that celebrated tag line out of the clear blue sky. Gaunt—much too gaunt—Sandra Bernhard, obscenely stripping while she croons "You're Gonna Love Me" to Jerry Lewis in *The King of Comedy* (1982): what guide told her that the quality of her voice should be totally sincere at that moment, that she should be singing love from the depths of her heart, a young comedian to her mentor? Obese Marlon Brando, cuddling in bed with Faye Dunaway in *Don Juan DeMarco* (1994): how do these two seem so very faithfully married? Not only well matched but "really" matched, matched in a coupling that is embedded in the "real"? They had never worked together before. Had each of them, for some time, been "married" to the other in the imagination?

Further, what is it to watch and believe an actor's performance, to see a hollow character transformed into a person, yet not merely a person but someone who can be followed and spied upon, whose every move and gesture the viewer drinks in? "What you have done is so much more than mere acting," Joseph Stefano wrote to Janet Leigh about her indelible performance in *Psycho*. "You've created a person, a live and touching and extremely moving person, and I believe it is your interpretation of Marion Crane that gives the picture a dimension which extends it somewhat outside the bounds of the usual motion picture" (Stefano to Leigh). Leigh's work is one of the elements of *Psycho* that raises it beyond the macabre thriller and makes us feel touched. How is the special mode of relationship established that permits intimacy without commitment, revelation without implication? What surrender of the viewer's self is implicit in every acceptance of acted reality?

Nicholas Ray wrote of "probing" and "doing a little surgery" in order "to find out how actors arrive at that state beyond their own personalities, that state of being able to convince people they are who they are and yet not who they are within a situation" (73). Following are, perhaps, a different kind of probing and surgery, some reflections on the actor's achievement—not a systematic theory of film acting or a catalogue of all those delicious contrivances and gestures our best actors have put together in constructing their performances, but a way of trying to come to terms with

Performance and Body Etiquette

A wonderful anecdote is shared by François Truffaut, who in the spring of
1966 was shooting his *Fahrenheit 451* at Pinewood Studios. During spare
moments, his habit was to watch old films in an editing room, sometimes
frame by frame. In his diary entry for May 3, he reflects on how when
cutting a film one looks back on the actors, with whom one worked intensively but for whom one no longer has any need; "One can see if they
were happy or sad one day, if they made love or were too busy." Again, the
personhood of the performer, present as a surround to the characterization but also, perhaps, as a substrate for it, since the actor's person and
personality never really go away (whither could they go?). Suddenly, from
Truffaut, this:

> In the three thousand films that I have seen, the most beautiful shot is in
> *Singin' in the Rain*. In the middle of the film, Gene Kelly, Donald O'Connor,
> and Debbie Reynolds, after a moment of discouragement, get their taste
> for life back and throw themselves into singing and dancing in their apart-
> ment. The dance brings them to jump over a couch on which they are to
> find themselves seated, all three of them side by side. In the process of her
> jumping over the couch, Debbie Reynolds makes a rapid intentional gesture,
> with one hand folding back the little pink pleated skirt on her knees in such
> a way that her underpants won't be visible when she lands in a seated posi-
> tion. This gesture, as quick as a flash, is beautiful because in one shot we have
> cinematic convention (people who sing and dance instead of walking and
> talking) and the height of truth, a little girl being careful not to show her
> ass. All of this happened once, fifteen years ago. It lasted less than a second.
> But it was printed on film as definitively as the arrival of a train at the La
> Ciotat station. These sixteen frames of *Singin' in the Rain*, this pretty gesture
> of Debbie Reynolds's, almost invisible, nicely illustrate a secondary action of
> film, a secondary life. (Truffaut, "Journal" 23; translation mine)

The idea of the "secondary life" suggests that after all, if living is not always acting acting is surely always living, that between the character's

breath and the actor's there never is a separation. Film performances are constructed and fake, but at the same time they are actual and real. Actual and real and seductive. . . . Seductive, perhaps, exactly because what is seen onscreen really did, once before a lens and some light, happen just in this way. In Arthur Hiller's *The Hospital* (1971) an exceedingly depressed George C. Scott is to stand at an open window after a number of patients have been murdered in his hospital and hiss "Jesus Christ!" to the New York streets. Take after take, he merely muttered the line. Finally, Hiller snatched it from the sound track of another scene and looped it in. The filmmaker told me that Scott saw the scene and walked out without a word (and didn't speak to him again).

An especially beautiful and revealing verisimilar performance is given by Frank Sinatra, working with Janet Leigh in a scene for John Frankenheimer's *The Manchurian Candidate* (1962). In many ways, and in terms of the image he projected in his film work from the 1940s (*On the Town*) to *The First Deadly Sin* in 1980, Sinatra already represented a pointed, solitary, and elemental Americanness. Like other stars, but in a distinct and inimitable way, he "was" the American personality, sensitive, progressive at the same time as traditional, articulate but also emotive. Screen acting, however, isn't set in a vacuum; the scene—here a train hurtling forward from Washington to New York—not only backs it up but fleshes it through, has the capacity to imbue every breath with both realism and moment.

I digress only to note that it was not a haphazard choice to place this action aboard a train. In his extended essay on railway travel, Wolfgang Schivelbusch adduces some remarks of the nineteenth-century engineer and cultural observer Michel Chevalier as to how quintessentially American it was—and remains—to enjoy voyaging, especially on trains. "One may assume," writes Schivelbusch, "that the 'passion for locomotion' that Michel Chevalier and countless other European visitors observed in the nineteenth century applied not only to general commercial and technological dynamics in America but was also characteristic of individual American bodies" (*Journey* 112). The American body had always to be going places. Even home life could be filled with motion according to David Nye, who observes of streamlining that "it made [domestic appliances] appear temporarily arrested in flight, as if toasters and refrigerators were by nature in motion, rushing from the present into the future" (354). Schivelbusch goes on to quote Chevalier's 1903 report about "the American": "When his feet are not in motion, his fingers must be in action; he must be whittling a piece of wood, cutting the back of his chair, or notching the

edge of the table, or his jaws must be at work grinding tobacco. . . . He
always has something to do, he is always in a terrible hurry. He is fit for all
sorts of work except those which require a careful slowness" (270, qtd. in
Schivelbusch, *Journey* 112).

Of course, this interesting description was never meant to apply to an
"American" of the mid-twentieth century, the sort of modern neurotic
represented by Sinatra's Major Bennett Marco, nor was *The Manchurian
Candidate* intended in any way as an illustration of the keen observations
of Chevalier. But all Chevalier's observations of the American personality
seem in retrospect to have been correct and appropriate when we watch
this film. Generally speaking, Marco is a nervous wreck, unable to bring
a "careful slowness" to his work and indeed being embroiled in a chase—
perhaps, as far as he is aware, a chase after phantoms—that leaves him
sweating with anxiety and perturbation, this to some large extent because
of his recent participation and experience in the Korean War, that broadly
conceived American "movement" or "movement against": David Halberstam notes that "its value was psychological rather than strategic—the
enemy had crossed a border" (62).

Smoking, especially, is important to Ben. The camera finds him seated
in the club car, clutching what looks like a Scotch on the rocks (but is
probably a rye old-fashioned [Condon 164]) and reaching tremulously for
a cigarette from a pack of Kents. Because of recurring nightmares, Ben
has been placed on medical leave. His face is bathed in perspiration that
makes him seem entirely out of place in the tidy and gleamy train environment, unmanaged, even disembodied to some degree. (Sinatra's 1955
performance as a junkie in Otto Preminger's landmark *The Man with
the Golden Arm* was preparation for this.) As he goes for the matches,
his mouth spontaneously relaxes and the cigarette drops from between
his lips and into his drink. Resigned, defeated, he sets the glass down. A
young woman has been watching from an adjacent seat, her eyes dark and
sharp with concern for him. The countryside is skimming past in broad
daylight through the window behind her. Ben has another cigarette in his
mouth now and is trying to light it, but his hands are shaking too much.
He gestures toward her with the cigarette: "Do you mind if I smoke?"

It is a plea for help, nothing else, since clearly he's getting nowhere—
either in his career or with this cigarette. In a "culture permeated by ner-
vousness," Schivelbusch writes in *Tastes of Paradise*, is found "the primacy
of mental labor" (149; 110), Ben being without doubt a paragon of the diligent mental worker who has been taken beyond his bounds. The young

woman goes back to her reading, but his next match flickers out entirely. Angry that his nervous condition has got the better of him, he gets up and moves off, stumbling down the corridor and into the connecting vestibule between cars. As the countryside races past outside the metal door, he leans back and closes his eyes. (It is worth noting that for railway travelers this vestibule was a liminal space in the 1950s and 1960s, sacred in its way since trainmen permitted people to stand between cars and yet made clear that safe conduct was a more precarious business there than anywhere else on the train. This was certainly the spot where one could have the great-est sense of rattling motion and also the greatest sense of stasis.) Marco is in limbo, a space between redemption and damnation that is ill defined, tenuous, shifting, and horrid.

The young woman has followed him, and now stands calmly looking at his profile. He does not turn to reciprocate her regard. Gracefully, she puts a cigarette into her mouth, uses a lighter on it, and then, gently tap-ping him on the shoulder so that he will open his eyes, turns the cigarette and places it into his hand, looking off (respectfully) at the scenery be-hind the camera as he manages to get the thing into his mouth and in-hale. "Maryland's a beautiful state," she tries, and he responds, a little flatly, "This is Delaware."

What I want to point to in this scene (written by George Axelrod, with some dialogue taken from Richard Condon's original text) is a certain em-phatic repose, a measuring of tone and stance, conveyed in the soft and eloquent conversation these two now hold. Ben is looking out the same window she is, offscreen right, while she lights her own cigarette. Thus, they are both looking past the camera, but not at one another: no doubt he doesn't feel the need to watch her (perhaps because it's "known" that an audience is watching; perhaps because he has brought her entirely into himself already). He remains, at any rate, wrapped in some inner torment and fracture. She knows it's Delaware, but Maryland *is* a beautiful state and so's Ohio, for that matter. He guesses so; Columbus is a tremendous football town. (In *Forms of Talk*, Goffman teaches that there is really no such thing as small talk.) A brief pause. "You in the railroad business?" He asks this—it cannot be more evident—not because he cares what busi-ness she is in, if she is in any business, but because he senses the need for this encounter to go on, perhaps so that they can finish their cigarettes but more likely because he has felt her reassuring presence, her bedrock nature, and he knows that his ship is foundering.

Not anymore, says she, but—if he will permit her to point out—when he asks that question he really should say, "Are you in a railroad *line?*" (This I take to be a cue for better recognition of her deftness with words, and deftness with words in general here; that one should listen very carefully to every syllable of these utterances, just as one attends very carefully to every nuance of facial expression and posture.) She's right, nods he, his face etched with pain, the perspiration still glowing on his forehead. Where's your home, she wants to know, and without any particular pride he says he's in the army, he's a major: looks up, eyes bright; looks off; looks anywhere but at her, this sweet, even gentle avoidance being a very bold statement that he desires to look at her very much. "I've been in the army most of my life," a rote voice, as though programmed to answer questions like these, "We move a good deal"—a big sigh—"I was born in New Hampshire." Her eyes are fixed on his face, and still he cannot look at her. She comes in now as though accompanying a soloist in a sonata: "I went to a girls' camp once on Lake Frances." His head down, nodding, loosening a little: "It's pretty far north." She smiles warmly, looks away, turns her eyes to see him again while he continues to stare off into the distance. His question comes directly but without energy: "What's your name?"

How long this scene has wound on before this telltale moment, this meeting!

"Eugènie."

Slowly he turns his head and looks into her face. She is gazing at him, open, unpretentious, smiling a little. "I really mean it, crazy French pronunciation and all." (This is the Janet Leigh who only months before had taken a shower for Alfred Hitchcock, dried off now, healthy, at ease.)

He turns away again, still not comfortable, closes his eyes as though safety is inside. "I guess your friends call you Jenny."

"Not yet they haven't, for which I am deeply grateful."

Now the director cuts to a close shot looking directly at Marco biting his lip, his eyes focused forward and on nothing in particular. He is entirely the embodiment of Frank Sinatra, yet not Sinatra in any way at all. He is somewhere else, yet here—that beautiful contradiction; wounded, yet healing. He is caught in a terrible confusion and mystery, yet at this moment life is clear and simple and true. "But . . . ," her soft voice beckons, "you may call me Jenny." He opens his eyes: "What do your friends call you?" (Does he wish to be her friend?)

A close shot reveals she's a little surprised. "Rosie." (This is the Janet

Leigh who, when she has finished this shoot, will go on to make *Bye Bye Birdie* for George Sidney, playing the role of Rosie with a jet black wig.)

Now he's turned his eyes to her. "Why?"

She smiles politely. "My full name is Eugènie Rose. Of the two names, I've always favored Rosie, because it smells of brown soap and beer." A pleading smile.

He is looking away again, nervous, defensive, tentative, awkward, wounded, lost.

"Eugènie is somehow more . . . fragile," says she, catching him again, watching him intently.

He lowers his head, takes a drag, then speaks in a voice broken and sharp. "Still, when I asked you what it was you said it was Eugènie." The train is passing a crossing, the bell at which can be heard advancing and then fading away (as if to prompt a recall that Ben Marco is fundamentally an investigator, a prober, and that he is on an investigation now—even as he is on leave—looking for something deeply dark and strange far away in New York. Yet, too, the fading of that bell brings us back to sweet, unaffected Rosie). "It's quite possible," says she, smiling with twinkly eyes; "I was feeling more or less fragile at that instant."

He shakes his head and says softly, "I could never figure out what that phrase meant, 'more or less.' " He waits and then looks her way. "You are Arabic?"

"No."

Back to the two-shot as he extends his hand. "My name is Ben. Really Bennett. I was named after Arnold Bennett."

She moves around to face him directly. "The writer?"

"No, a lieutenant-colonel. He was my father's commanding officer at the time." He is looking up and off again, but she is now eased into conversational proximity and is looking at him with frank interest. "What's your last name?" He tells her. "Major Marco," she smiles. And then, not quite preposterously: "Are *you* Arabic?"

"No," he shakes his head and looks down, "no." But of course he really means something else, just as every line of this conversation has really meant something else. "Let me put it another way." He is looking directly down and away from her face as he asks, "Are you married?"

"No, you?"

"No." Biting his lip again, he nods—nods what? Understanding? Relief? He looks at her with a new directness. "What's your last name?"

"Chaney. I'm production assistant for a man named Justin, who had two hits last season. I live on 54th Street, a few doors from the Modern Museum of Art, of which I'm a Tea Privileges member. No cream." He is looking away from her again, chewing his lip, his eyes on the verge of tears. "I live at 53 West 54th Street. Apartment 3B. Can you remember that?"

A painful silence. He closes his eyes. "Yes."

"EL Dorado 5-9970. Can you remember that?"

"Yes."

"Are you stationed in New York? Or is stationed the right word?" He turns his head further away from her. His profile is etched in shadow on the wall behind him. "I'm not exactly stationed in New York, I was stationed in Washington, but I got sick and now I'm on leave and I'm going to spend it in New York." His eyes are open again, hopeless, desperate, flat, weary, stale.

"EL Dorado 5-9970."

For readers who have not seen this galvanizing film, let me reveal at once that Ben Marco will turn out to have need of that telephone number; but that Ben and Rosie do not really become lovers as this scene elapses or in the audience's view. She is his friend, exactly as demonstrated here. They could certainly be lovers, and perhaps they will be when the film is done. Nothing in the story obstructs the imagination of a happy future for them, except that at the end, when he is standing with Rosie in delicious, domestic privacy, happiness is a long way off. This scene, then, is not really a love scene. Nor is it a prelude to love. Nor a setup for relationship, since Eugènie Rose will hardly be seen again.

It's a scene about perturbation, movement, racing, displacement, being lost, trying to find comfort and stability, trying to hold on, getting that cigarette between one's lips, trying to look somebody in the face without fear. And the scene moves forward with a really delicious slowness, with a kind of breathing, with thought. There are dozens of shots here in which neither character moves and the countryside speeds past outside. While their faces—eyes, cheeks, lips—show that they are alive and sensitive; sensuous; aware; desirous; wanting, still Ben and Rosie do not twitch, do not stutter. One has the comforting sense with both Leigh and Sinatra that they feel perfectly confident merely standing in front of the camera and breathing, that for long moments no real "business" is necessary. Indeed, any action at all could disturb this calm. A less experienced actor, or an actor in the hands of a director with less assurance, makes certain at each instant to do something that will legitimize his presence before the lens. In such cases, it is as though the cast members play at making a movie, trying to give the best possible impression of movie acting. Here, nobody is giving an impression of anything. Sinatra is with Leigh in a vestibule between two railway cars, smoking. The filmmaker will get whatever he wants, use it in whatever way he wants, but neither actor need be concerned. This scene, which provides a palpable moment of "reality," of really watching two people standing on a train, was shot in one take.[2]

"Did You Ever Kill Anybody?": Performance, Silence, Light

A tranquility and direct presentation of self in performance similar to what Sinatra and Leigh achieve can be seen in two much more recent films, made in an era when concentration, development, and perspective have been less important to the cinematic moment than shock, disorientation, and jittery propulsion. Since there is less and less of this kind of relaxed assuredness to be seen onscreen nowadays, performances like these stand out. In Daniel Barber's *Harry Brown* (2009), Michael Caine is an elderly widower living in a South London housing project full of anxious and violent drug-abusing teenagers. His only friend Len (Daniel Ramsay) comforts him at the death of his wife, while also admitting a pervasive fear because the kids have been attacking and threatening him. Len will be murdered and the film will follow Harry as he sets out to avenge that death, but an early and remarkable scene has the two men playing chess in a shaft of blinding sunlight in a local pub. With their half-finished pints, and sitting wrapped in modest working-class British clothing, the two old gents are studies in social position, economic hardship, loneliness, and fidelity (such as had been rendered on canvas during the 1930s, 1940s, and 1950s by Stanley Spencer). By virtue of his softened posture, the way he cocks his head a fraction of an angle to one side, the way he turns the corners of his mouth, and the steady gray gaze of his moist eyes, Caine gives a masterful portrait of a broken but dignified man. Ramsay matches him perfectly, his voice breaking as he enunciates his fear. In the matching one-shots that make up the conversation scene, there is hardly any movement at all—of character or of the camera—merely the easeful, measured, pensive drawing out of the moments by both men as, trading numerous silences, they relate to one another. Len pulls out a bayonet at one point to suggest he is ready to fight back, this a direct comment on his early life in the army. Harry, it turns out, had been in the marines. "In the marines, Harry, did you ever kill anybody?" Len asks. It is a question quiet and measured and abrupt.

Harry gives him a somewhat withdrawn look, still relaxed, unpressured, unfazed, yet also purposive and lethally still. "You can't ask me that, Len." There is no emphasis in Caine's delivery, no affectation. He has merely brought his gravitas to the moment and is allowing it full play. Nor can it be doubted for a moment that when Harry was in the marines he absolutely did kill, again and again. He says now that with his marriage he gave all that up, gave that person up, became someone else; but through his stillness, his directness, it is clear that the killer is still present behind his eyes.

Not long later, Harry is accosted one night by a thug who points a knife at him and demands his money. Harry seems to twitch, to twitch as an old man with creaky joints might do—his movement is so deft and so shockingly quick—and in a gasp the knife is embedded in the assailant's chest. How in a blur Harry managed to reach out, seize it by the handle, turn it around, and stab the thug—all in less than a quarter of a second—is imperceptible and unknowable, except by virtue of a military training still present and real, never to evaporate, a kind of ghost trace that will haunt him for the rest of his life. The action of the scene, then, is a blurring and almost instantaneous turnaround; but Caine's performance remains calm, wholly at rest in the heart of the movement. He does not thrust himself, does not change his position on the screen. Harry Brown is merely an old man standing there, a man with a presence and a place. And the breathing of the scene is regular and continuous, as though without thinking, on an inspiration, and in the same way he might turn his eyes to cast a quick glance at a hair upon his comrade's shoulder, he has turned life into death, mobilized himself a little and then retreated again to tranquility, to the overwhelming rest and stability that characterize his every move in this film.

Harry Brown is something of a retelling of the psychological and historical conditions, if not the actual social setting, of Clint Eastwood's *Gran Torino* (2008), in which there is another overpowering conversation. Walt Kowalski (Eastwood) has retired from the Ford plant where he worked on the line for fifty years building, among other things, the Gran Torino. Father Janovich (Christopher Carley) is fresh out of the seminary, shiny as a new apple, and does not understand Walt's extreme Republican values or the abysmal depth of his grief at the recent death of his wife. At a key moment in the film the two men sit in Walt's living room to converse about faith, life, action, commitment, and what is for Walt the hopeless hollowness of the Church. Eastwood brings a more expressive face—the thundercloud brows darkening the ruddy cheeks—to his work here than Caine will do in *Harry Brown* the following year, but as filmmaker he sets the scene by placing large swaths of darkness beside each of the characters in their portrait shots. Further, this darkness—lit with spectacular skill by cinematographer Tom Stern—is not just relative, in the sense that in almost any shot there will be shadow areas where the light falls off by comparison with the highlights and thus allows for a three-dimensional molding of the narrative space, but a darkness absolutely and formlessly black, a Black Darkness, produced by a lighting scheme that falls far below the minimal requirements for exposure so that each character, and particularly Walt, seems to sit at the edge of an abyss. For each part of the man-to-man conversation, then, the camera shows a person occupying half a frame with virtually unexposed film beside him, a space that is a perfect nullity. Walt needs to make the priest see that he does not believe in a force or world beyond life, that for him it's all here, all now. As he sits and speaks, he is margined, then, not by a shady and suggestive periphery but by a completely obscure and uninformative void.

As an actor in this scene, Eastwood's main accomplishment is to avoid moving in such a way as to disturb this lighting design, either by partly falling off into the darkness or by being too animated in the face of it. His sense of stillness, confidence, poise, and presence are here compromised not by another actor's work but by something definitive and limiting in the optical field. The shine from his eyes, the taut mouth, the unflinching muscles of the face all work to give a portrait of a man who has made his peace, defined his cosmos, brought himself to the cusp of pure existential action.

Performance and Self-Reference

Given the availability today of what, as late as the 1970s, was undreamed of—DVDs and home playing units, download capabilities, hand-held screening devices, not to mention the more sophisticated media players now embedded in aircraft that make possible the screening of all or part of dozens of films while floating five miles off the ground (standing in the aisle to stretch your legs you can spy twenty or more movies at the same time); the relative omnipresence of visual dramatic material on screens in public bars, public facilities like libraries and meeting halls, and on gigantic superscreens such as can be found at Times Square in New York and other venues; not to mention the possibility of interrupting, replaying, freezing, fast-forwarding, and otherwise altering the images that are available—the screen performance has become something that can be manipulated and possessed rather than a larger-than-life experience that possessed and manipulated the watcher. Commentary tracks even permit the film worker to discourse upon the very actions viewers are watching from the point of view of an ultimate expert (the writer, the director, the star), who details motive, working conditions, arrangements, difficulties, pleasures, challenges, and secrets audiences not only did not know in their previous mode of watching film but also did not trouble to imagine. As to performance: in general it is not unfair to say that while audiences once watched characters onscreen, they now watch actors. For the actor today to bring a character to life, and to disappear beneath or inside that character, is a far greater challenge than it was before 1990. In 1977, for instance, we met Han Solo; and four years later, Indiana Jones. Thanks to fore- and backstage publicity, it is now impossible not to see Harrison Ford.[3]

A particular feature of the mediated environment has spurred and exacerbated this distancing effect, and that is the presence—since the birth of *People* magazine (1974); and "Entertainment Tonight" (1981) and its myriad competitive tabloid "backstage" exposés on television—of a climate of performance deconstruction that pervades all of visual entertainment. Since the early 1960s, late-night talk-show hosts, such as Jack Paar and Johnny Carson, had been habituated to entertaining celebrity "guests," but their producers had tended astutely to select stars who could centralize a display of flamboyant personality and raconteurism (such as Alexander King or Shelley Winters or Phyllis Diller), foreign accent and culture (such as Zsa Zsa Gabor or Peter Lawford or, in his many storytelling modes, Orson Welles), or manic emotional trouble, real or presumptive (such as Oscar Levant or, after he became known for his antics on "Mork and Mindy" [1978], the young and terminally unpredictable Robin Williams). It was the celebrity as "self" or as "person" who framed the structure of the on-air "conversation" that was the essence of the talk-show "visit." The fiction was that each night the host was having a "party" and viewers could tune in to see how crazy the guests were and how outrageously they might behave. These guests did not, by and large, spend their time in front of the TV camera talking about work. By the 1980s, however, this narrational structure was incontrovertibly altered, so that the centerpiece of the celebrity appearance was a promotional discussion about some current project being worked on, its challenges, and the ostensibly "true" nature of the working relationships the guest had with co-workers, relationships that now, here, "privately," could be revealed. While the talk show had always functioned to showcase talent, its existence as a venue soon enough became a part of producers' advertising plans for films and TV shows. Early talk shows held their audience so that advertisers could pounce upon them in commercial breaks; later, talk shows competed with their own sponsors, by luring viewers for sales during the program content.

What such "backstage journalism" of various sorts taught viewers, no matter what any particular celebrity said about any particular project in any particular circumstance, was that there was more to performance than one could see onscreen, and, further, that *this fact was noteworthy of its own accord.* Earlier audiences knew that characters were performed by actors, but did not treat the actors as though their unseen work in creating characters was itself worthy of being staged. In short, the fact of there being something backstage—and indeed the very existence of the backstage area—had invoked disregard, even disavowal, while one was being entranced by performance. The exception that proves the rule was so-called "backstage" musicals, in which the lives of performers off-stage centered the drama: but in these, there was no hint given that the performers playing the "performers" had lives one might come to know, beyond what was touted about them in such fan magazines as *Photoplay* (in which the writing style betrayed a thick veneer of constructedness). Nowadays, very often, actorly performance is nothing more than a glib and perfunctory marker of a palpable and fundamentally fascinating backstage world, a continual index of the more urgent and exciting backstage "reality" that is our most cherished prize. The link between this backstage consciousness and the critique of consumerism that identifies postmodernism is not so very clear, since there has long been a vast market of hungry consumers eager to buy into screened imagery and ready for what would come to be postmodernist dissection. Backstage consciousness treats filmic production, when it is screened as part of an arrangement outside of itself, as a play-within-a-play, bringing heightened reality to the off-realm in which the screen image is constructed and depleting our reserves of commitment to the screen image itself. As, more and more, production companies made actors available to television if they could be permitted to bring along teaser clips from work to be sold, the clips containing a guest's performance came to highlight the guest's on-air persona, to become the *raison d'être* for the appearance itself, and thus to be material worth interrogating. And the interrogation of performance became the single overridingly public feature of contemporary visual drama, an actor's performance existing merely, it seemed, so that discussions could be based upon it. In these discussions performances could be dissected, reinitiated, reimagined, and reconfigured in terms accessible to a global audience that knew little about acting method and problems. Conversations of this sort could easily be scripted, since actors' publicity agents could provide "stories," "events," and "private secrets"—notably spicier than the sorts of stories studio publicity departments would place about stars in fan magazines in the 1930s, 1940s, and 1950s—in addition to the clip materials supplied by movie producers. So it is that most deconstructions of screen performance are carried on in terms of personality, relationships, and comic anecdotes—material that reveals a world beyond characterization but that does not depend upon technical expertise for its decoding.

Whereas in cinema of the golden age the poster shot or rendered pose was intended to refer both to a performance and an unfolding interior dramatic world of the story, nowadays the poster shot *is* the story. The film exists to subtend the poster shot—which will be the central decorative principle in sales campaigns for the DVD and Blu-ray disk—rather than the other way round.

Actors Not Met: Performance and Worker Residue

Part of the problem for any actor intending to self-effacingly mobilize a character is to find a particular route into the character's "self" in such a way that traces of the actor's persona are dissolved for the audience—the actor's persona, not his personality, since the persona is a known entity, while the true personality of the actor, except to his closest friends, and perhaps even to them, is a mere speculation. The actor's persona is a cluster of perceivable traits that emerge again and again in appearances with which the actor is associated publicly, much beyond what is called for in any one film. Emma Recchi in *I Am Love* (2009), Elizabeth Abbott in *The Curious Case of Benjamin Button* (2008), Karen Crowder in *Michael Clayton* (2007), Penny in *Broken Flowers* (2005), Audrey Cobb in *Thumbsucker* (2005), Margaret Hall in *The Deep End* (2001), the White Witch in *The*

Chronicles of Narnia (2005, 2008, 2010)—all these are "Tilda Swinton," which is to say, all flow from and center upon the common germ or residue that is the real person Swinton's persona. No one of these characters is fully Swinton while in motion, yet our conviction is that a repeatable "Swinton" underlies them all, a repeatable "Swinton" who returns again and again under this persona, this residue, to do actorly work.

For an especially fascinating case involving the actorly residue, consider the rendition of a girl named Hortense Cumberbatch (in Mike Leigh's *Secrets & Lies* [1996]) that is accomplished by an actor named Marianne Jean-Baptiste. She had three screen credits to her name previously, one for a single episode of a poorly circulated British series, "Cracker"; and two for bit parts in lesser-known films. Jean-Baptiste had little public persona to hide—Hortense thus carried but a tiny residue—and she was able to more or less walk into the role. Given that she was not known, viewers were unable to tell anything about the actor "lying beneath" the character they were watching—this being a debility, once again, quite distinct from not being able to tell anything about the person mounting the actorly persona. The well-knownness of a performer is one of the tools or agencies of her performance. By contrast with Jean-Baptiste, Renée Zellweger had several memorable screen credits by the time she created the role of Bridget Jones in 2001: her work in *Dazed and Confused* (1993) and *Reality Bites* (1994), marginal to the stories yet memorable, had been widely circulated; her work in *Jerry Maguire* (1996) made a splash. In watching Bridget, since one was able to recollect other versions of Zellweger, one had to imaginatively subtract them from the current performance, and for her part the actor had to be conscious of those earlier performances and of various ways in which her other characters might obstruct an audience's attempts to grasp the present Bridget clearly and directly. She makes distinctive and exaggerated use of clothing, for example, as a way of repositioning herself in a fresh "garb" before the audience's gaze, while Jean-Baptiste has no similar need to play with her costume or performative history. The stardom of a movie star inheres in a magnified performance residue, one that becomes the center of commercially calculated attentiveness just as the performances the person gives become pretexts for the residue's appearance.

The more unfamiliar a performer, the more everything about her can emerge in appeal to the audience's interest, whereas with a well-known figure certain features of anatomy, gesture, and poise are quickly recognized (known again, because they have been repetitively exhibited) and thus, in a way, deductible from the presentation of self. Jean-Baptiste plays a long scene with Penny, a social worker (Lesley Manville), in which she must explain why, as an adoptee, she wishes at this point in her life to search for her birth mother. Penny politely, and with professional slickness, explains a "catch" in the process, that while it is now legal for the twenty-eight year old to be searching out information about her origins, it is possible that her mother—"out there" somewhere, "we don't know where"—might very well *not* want to see her. The camera is shooting Hortense, who is seated in the social worker's pale green cubicle (all plastered over with posters for various forms of social aid), roughly from waist level upward. When these words come from Penny's lips off-camera, Jean-Baptiste makes a trio of the tiniest possible gestures, each readable on its own terms as an indication of fear and discomfort, anticipation and foreboding, yet also vulnerability to the mechanisms of the official process. First, she raises her head just a little, as if to say, "I am alert to what you are about to say; I am attending," but also as if to say, in a completely defensive and deferential way: "Please don't wound me!" Secondly, she gives the smallest possible cant to her head, emphasizing auricular access but also demonstrating a reticence and withdrawal from the situation and its possible horrors. Finally, and most tellingly, she silently gulps, a frank statement of relative weakness and impotence. These tiny indicators become large onscreen in part because of the directness and unselfconsciousness in which they are put forth, and in part because the actor is opening herself to the closest inspection: opening herself because she is not already known; and she knows this as she works.

Performance to and with Camera

Screen performance is always *for* the camera, that trembling entity: "Already my eyes and my ears, too, from force of habit," says Pirandello's Serafino Gubbio, "are beginning to see and hear everything in the guise of this rapid, quivering, ticking mechanical reproduction" (8). But there is a fascinating illustration of the ways in which screen performance, beyond being *to* it, is also *with* the camera, that is, not only accompanied by and in the name of the camera but also with the loving collaboration of the device (and its operators), a collaboration that has passed into the lingo of filmmaking: of a successful screen actor, producers and directors say in Hollywood, "The camera loves him." Performing *to* a camera, an actor will want to know the lens that the cinematographer is using, since it will dictate certain adjustments of posture, certain limitations of movement, and preferential angles for holding the body and the head (so as to help produce images that will be flattering to the conceit the actor wishes to favor). Acting *with* camera can be something else entirely, however.

Consider the bizarre and oblique comedy *40 Days and 40 Nights* (2002), in which an anxious and depressed young man, Matt Sullivan (Josh Hartnett), starts to see his ceiling opening up into a black hole whenever he is in the throes of making love (it apparently being impossible for him to have an orgasm unless he is lying on his back—that is, able to look skyward—and *in extremis*). Finally reaching a point of sufficient desperation about his condition to consult with his brother, a priest-in-training, he happens to meet the father superior himself, a man who happily (and quite out of the blue) confesses that for Lent he's going to give up his favorite thing in the world, Starbucks lattes. This makes Matt realize that Religion Might Save Him, and on the spot he decides to give up *his* favorite thing in the world, which is obviously sex (what else could a twenty-something who looks like Josh Hartnett prize above all?). One day soon later, at the advertising agency where (where else?) he works, he learns that his ex-girlfriend Nicole, upon whom he cannot cease fixing his desire, is engaged to be married to someone else! He lapses into a kind of quasi-paralytic trance, and as he leaves the building there is a cut to a medium close-up of him, head and torso, moving toward the lens, with a co-worker at his side asking solicitously, "You all right?"

But the director, Michael Lehmann, has pulled a little trick. The camera, conventionally enough, is on a dolly, and the dolly is on a dolly track, so that as Matt moves we feel ourselves smoothly backing away from his every step. Hartnett, however, *is standing on the dolly*, so that as he advances away from the building there are no telltale bumps of his shoulders or shudders of his frame. He is gliding through space exactly as the camera is; exactly as the camera, in film after film, normally does. He has become a kind of train, sliding on rails. Also, he has become a camera.[4]

Had Hartnett been walking on a treadmill one would have been able to discern a different effect. Often, an actor will walk on a treadmill in front of a rear-projection screen, thus creating the impression of perambulating through a territory when in fact she is going nowhere. Doris Day performs this magic quite effortlessly, along with James Stewart, in a number of shots for Hitchcock's *The Man Who Knew Too Much* (1956), where she must appear to be walking in Marrakech but is in fact on a Paramount soundstage. In *40 Days*, Hartnett's body does not exhibit the telltale muscular movements associated with walking, but seems to fly through space. A tranquility and grace envelop him, and seem to suffuse his body and desire. His tensions about Nicole are eliminated not only through narrative explanation but through direct visualization, as he is freed to travel outside the laws of gravity. This shot lasts only a second or two onscreen. But it is surprising, refreshing, and strange, and one does not forget it. Indeed it is possible to extract this shot from its narrative context altogether and see a portrait of human motion and composure elevated to an unanticipated level. Here is a person who suddenly and shockingly no longer moves as people move, but instead picks up the characteristic movement of a buffered mechanism. As a record of performance, and brief as it is, this shot even supersedes Fred Astaire dancing in the gazebo with Ginger Rogers, during a pounding rainstorm, in *Top Hat* (1935) ("Isn't This a Lovely Day?"), a sequence in which the human motion is quintessentially graceful but the camera does not join it; or Robert Duvall leaning outside the door of the helicopter as it glides in for the kill in *Apocalypse Now* (1979), where the helicopter does the work, enslaving Duvall's character; or John Travolta swinging Karen Lynn Gorney around the floor of a rehearsal studio in *Saturday Night Fever* (1977), where if the camera is seduced to revolve along with them it finally dominates their movement. With Hartnett in *40 Days*, there is a deeply feelingful—but also casual and, it seems, unconscious—marriage between the actor and the lens-camera-dolly combination. They have joined, merged, interpenetrated, unified, in a wink.

I mention this moment, narratively and narratologically trivial as it is, in order to suggest that sometimes the power and effect of screen performance is coming from outside the body of the performer altogether. What the actor must do is trustingly yield to the process. In *Funny Girl* (1968), during the "Don't Rain on My Parade" number, directed by Herbert Ross—an impeccably lit (by Harry Stradling) and edited (by William Sands and Maury Winetrobe) visual sequence with a profoundly pulsing rhythm and a galvanizing vocal performance by Barbra Streisand—many of the shots gain their power not from the singer's emphatic gesticulations and postures but from positions and moves of the camera, especially, for instance, when in mid-phrase the editor cuts to an aerial shot (made in a helicopter piloted by J. David Jones) of Streisand riding in a train through the countryside—starting in long focus with the train a mere thread woven in the greenery and zooming in . . . in . . . in . . . in . . . in, until she is seen filling the screen and moving her lips exactly to match the beat; or when there is a shot of her standing in the prow of a tugboat steaming out of the harbor to intercept Nicky Arnstein ("Mr. Arnstein:——Here . . . I . . . am!!") on his departing ship. While it is true that through the sequence, as through the film, it is always Streisand who occupies attention, Streisand of the screen is frequently a singer working in tandem with a mobile visual system. In live stage performance, choreography may simulate movement like this, but there are strict gravitational limits beyond which a performer cannot go (even if she is Mary Martin singing and flying in *Peter Pan* in 1955): the stage is a confine that the performance transcends, while the screen represents a repository of techniques that enrich performance.[5]

Even more fundamental than its ability to move (along with an actor), the camera has the power to frame. Thence the ease in seeing performance-with-camera in static shots, as Orson Welles realized in composing that celebrated vision of Kane stumbling slowly from left to right in front of the lens, after his wife Susan (Dorothy Comingore) has left Xanadu, and passing between two ornate floor-to-ceiling mirrors. The visual effect is to have Kane in his jerky movement momentarily produce a chain of baroque reflections of himself that extends away toward infinity.[6] Here is Kane the impresario and magnate multiplied without limit, his puissance extended as far as the eye can see, yet all this at a moment when he has been defeated by the one person on earth who can dominate him. "You can't do this to me, Susan," he had said to her. "I can't?" she shrilled, and strode out. Now he is only an echo of himself, and this shot conveys that directly.

In virtually all moments of screen performance some transform is accomplished by the camera so as to augment, modify, complete, or embellish what the actor does with his body and voice: most frequently viewers are unaware of the slight magnifications, exaggerations, distensions, shrinkages, reductions, approximations, withdrawals, obscurations, and detailings that are embedded in a moment of acting work by virtue of the way a camera "sees" it, and the few cases I have pointed to merely reference a broader realm in which performance is visibly and explicitly aided through cinematography. If all screen performance is performance-with-camera in some way, some screen performance is more directly, openly, and clearly so. These special cases thus explicitly identify what is essentially and normatively cinematic in screen acting. Further, the camera is treated by performers as an invisible, or non-existent, accomplice; they accomplish this by maintaining a respectful distance from the lens, something delightfully violated, for example, in those highly charged nature documentaries when grizzly bears, kangaroos, wombats, pelicans, or other beasts innocently migrate up to a hidden camera position and start sniffing around or nibbling the lens while the film is turning. With human actors and trained beasts, the camera doesn't usually get this kind of treatment. So at specific moments in Mike Nichols's *Who's Afraid of Virginia Woolf?* (1966), Richard Burton can achieve a really potent sharpness in his enunciation and gesture by walking very close to the camera as he speaks, close enough to make one wonder whether he knows that it is there. Again, while this is playing *to* camera unmistakably, it is also playing *with* camera. In *Alfie* (1959), Michael Caine established a reputation by addressing the camera again and again, always producing an increasing cognitive pleasure by hinting that his previous turns to the lens were just as consciously effected as this one, rather than happenstantial. Again and again invoking it, he made the audience his collaborator and friend. In Fellini's *E la nave va . . .* (1983), Freddie Jones does the same thing, but perhaps less memorably: he is no longer as young and insouciant as Caine was in *Alfie*, no longer the charming innocent with cameras and audiences.

These moments of explicit performance with camera all seem stunningly real in the watching, even though it is palpably obvious that they are false and constructed. This odd and delirious *credibly incredible* has been studied in terms of early film (see Bottomore) but most students of the problem have reduced it to a secret manipulation (and suture) of the "apparatus." In short, the impossibility of cinematic vision trumps everything else. For anyone whose search to understand motion pictures is rooted in love, however, the impossibility of cinematic vision is itself ethereal and insignificant, and the "reality" achieved by denying or negating that impossibility is supreme. The nub for film lovers is the feeling of "reality" in the face of clear-cut fakery, this being my principal reason for including a discussion of performance along with analyses of background painting and special effects cinematography in these pages. None of these kinds of cinematic work actually succeed in hiding themselves completely; yet that does not inhibit them from working to stunning effect. I think it far too glib to refer to viewers as "suspending disbelief" because while they are watching, there really is no disbelief to suspend, nor any feeling of accomplishing suspension. Similarly, I do not think it always or even usually true that viewers are seduced, "sutured," or duped by an apparatus. What is happening in watching the screen I would call real, at the watching. "'Real,' you must mean, not real," some will insist, but "real" does become really real when someone is wrapped up in it. A viewer's taking things to be real *is* the reality of things. This "reality effect" is a source of recognition, and thus orientation; a source of self-acknowledgment, since part of what one recognizes is the perduring recognizing self; and at times a source of pleasure—not that pleasure comes always and only from the sense of "reality" nor that the sense of "reality" invariably produces pleasure, but that there is a pleasure to be had in the curious, tentative, suspicious yet yielding sense of finding the "real" onscreen; I would argue that the "reality effect," indeed, can be a principal source of pleasure in cinema—what Jonathan Rosenbaum might call a "new route to pleasure" (53)—far surpassing the thrill of narrative culmination and closure (see also Sperb and Balcerzak; and De Valck and Hagener).

The camera can dominate, shape, control performance. In the very last moment of *Sunset Blvd.* (1950), as Norma Desmond steps toward the camera for her "close-up," and as her face becomes increasingly bloated with distended memory and warped desire, a veil of opacity and whiteness seems to suffuse her so that she vanishes. While this moment is dramatically pungent in the extreme, given this character and what she has meant for viewers, it was technically mandatory, because Gloria Swanson's increasing proximity to the lens and her continuing movement forward would have meant her going out of focus and finally walking into the camera. Some tactic for terminating her daydream had to be employed, and cinematographer John F. Seitz found one that would work narratively and technically at the same time.

Substance and Substantiation:
Inside and Outside of Performance

Screen performance is one thing when reflected upon—reconstituted or analyzed—and quite another thing while it is unfolding before the eyes. Part of screen performance, as actually experienced, is a certain delicate play with its own *substance*, with that which stands beneath. The actor is substantial to the character. While they may be conscious to some degree of the actor's presence—in the case of star performance this consciousness is heightened and sharpened—it remains true for almost all viewers that the actor is an unknown hiding beneath the mask of a public persona. Focus can alternate between a mocked-up characterization and the presence of

an authorial substance in the figure of the actor. But this very alternation
can itself become the subject of concentration in a filmic moment.

Delmer Daves's *Dark Passage* (1947) poses Vincent Parry as a convicted
wife-killer who breaks out of prison to prove his innocence by finding the
real culprit. Afraid he will be too easily recognized as he hunts, Parry sub-
mits to a radical plastic surgery that replaces his face. When the swath
of white bandages comes off—it had rendered Parry a kind of "invisible
man"—we discover not the plain-faced mustachioed nobody represented
in an early newspaper photograph but . . . Humphrey Bogart. It perhaps
needs no elaboration that since his work in *High Sierra* (1941), *The Maltese
Falcon* (1941), *Casablanca* (1942), *Across the Pacific* (1942), *Sahara* (1943),
Passage to Marseille (1944), *To Have and Have Not* (1944), and *The Big
Sleep* (1946), Bogart had achieved a signal stardom and his face was recognized around the world. In a sense, any character he played onscreen
was mounted on a dominating substance, the well-known figure of Bogart
who lived and worked underneath (itself, of course, covering a relatively
unknown Bogart who had, like other citizens of Los Angeles at the time, a
private life). Bogart was never entirely recognizable as Parry anymore than
he had been entirely recognizable as Rick Blaine in *Casablanca*. Yet, *Dark
Passage* presents an interesting twist.

The plot requires of viewers that they engage in a particular reading
of Parry when he appears onscreen in his new "flesh," namely that, once
having looked like that photograph in the newspaper, now through the
"magic" of plastic surgery, he has been transformed into the man portrayed by way of Bogart's face. The individual wearing Bogart's face who
constitutes the substance of his Bogartean Parry is to be understood as
a previous (undoctored) Parry (posed by an uncredited performer). The
doctored being, who looks so much like Bogart that Bogart can play him,
is only a secondary Parry, then, transmuted or reconstituted. To the degree
that the original Parry was changed into the current (Bogartean) Parry, his
unlabeled personifier behind the screen was changed into Bogart; and so,
in a curious way, the actor Bogart and the present character Parry are identical in both being by-products. Both are "upscaled" versions of someone
else, the new Parry a transformation of the old one and Bogart an actor
picking up where another actor left off. By being so organically aligned
with Parry in his condition, Bogart gains a certain innocence or original-
ity: in another dramatic situation, his characterization would stand upon
an acting career produced through the performance system, but here, as it

seems, his Parry stands upon a biological career produced by surgery. Just as his doppelgänger Parry—thought to have murdered his wife but in fact searching for the person who did—is only here by default, in a contingency that results from a plastic surgeon's tricks, so the actor Humphrey Bogart is only here because of the writerly trick of the "changed identity" (a writerly trick that was, of course, the pretext for a film in which Bogart could star).

Still more powerful is another construction. With every glimpse of the new Parry (Bogart) one is to make a truly challenging assumption: that this face did not always look this way, this splendid, broadly recognized face, this Bogartean scheme. People are empowered to make such an assumption all the time, with anybody; but even though visible characteristics can change over time, typically one does not examine the assumption of continuity of appearance or what grounds it. In this particular case, apparently, Bogart's character can effect his presentation only because of plastic surgery. Thus the conceit is fostered that Bogart has no perduring screen persona at all, but appears here merely as a trace of a medical practice. As to Parry, he is two people at once and stands upon two substances: first, an earlier incarnation who submitted himself to the knife (and who looked very much like an actor who looked nothing at all like Humphrey Bogart); and secondly, an incarnation indistinguishable from the actor Humphrey Bogart, who looks nothing much like anybody else. Every screen manifestation of the postsurgical Parry is Bogart-like and utterly not Bogart-like at once: Bogart-like now but not Bogart-like then. The intensive dissonance produced by these conflicting possibilities is most easily resolved through forgetting the face that was printed in the newspaper, that nondescript and certainly unrecognizable face belonging to no known movie star, that face to which the camera was subjected for only a fraction of a second (so that it would be easy to lose), and through concentrating on the simple formula: Bogart = Parry.

But Bogart endured scene after scene early in the film with his face wrapped in white and the dark eyes peering mysteriously out. Or someone did—since until the bandages came off it was impossible to see the face beneath. Someone in bandages became Bogart as Parry. Bogart as Parry is thus one of the results of a procedure that was performed *upon someone*, and is also continually and unendingly Bogart in his every gesture as Parry, since by 1947 no star was more recognizable than he, and he was nothing but recognizable. If Parry is always both Bogart-like and un-Bogart-like, so, too, Bogart onscreen here is always both Parry and not-Parry. The film protests, then, that a nondescript stranger submitted to plastic surgery, then endured for weeks in bandages looking like one-knows-not-what; while at the same time protesting that all along since the surgery, Bogart—that is, this person who so resembles Bogart—has been substantial to Parry, this argument patently flying in the face of the fact that one of the people who could not be substantial to (hide under) any character was, in fact, the much celebrated Bogart. The senses unequivocally inform that it is Bogart in focus, not Parry; that Parry, indeed, is the invisible man. This is a kind of apotheosis of star performance, one in which it is very difficult, if possible at all, to believe in the presence of the character while the actor is visible in his place. In each moment when viewers are asked to believe that the facial structure of Bogart has actually been constructed by a surgeon inside this film, they can only form a denial, since Bogart is accepted as something virtually universal, and surely beyond the bounds of *Dark Passage*. Yet the story rambles on about disguise, recognition, danger, the face, and so on. So the film brilliantly poses a conflict between story and vision, the narrative continuing to make demands that the images refuse to substantiate.

This rather notable case does not guarantee that movie stars are always caught in unstable performance structures, or that stardom can never hide itself. The "performative" is not always and inevitably precarious and unsettled. *Dark Passage* is, on the contrary, an explicit demonstration of how the limits of stardom can work to settle our view, to culture an optical experience and suggest certain situated ambiguities that structure perception toward a musing, an understanding, or a journey of the imagination. Certainly there are cases where stardom absolutely intrudes on the possibilities of fictional characterization: in 1964, for example, when she filmed *Cleopatra* in Rome with Joseph Mankiewicz, Elizabeth Taylor was trapped in her performance by widely distributed publicity about her love affair with Richard Burton and her debilitating illness (that was keeping her off the set and producing an enormous expense for MGM); in short, she became what might be termed "superstantial," entirely dominating the characterization. The film, for which huge efforts had been undertaken to establish its setting authentically ("really") as classical Egypt, could be seen as nothing but a lavish Hollywood production; Cleopatra as nobody but Taylor, and so on. Two years later, however, when she gained weight and slouched to play Martha in *Who's Afraid of Virginia Woolf?* Taylor entirely disappeared in her role. Martha was alive onscreen; Taylor was "really" nowhere.

Kin: Performing the "Reality" of Relationship

The issue of kinship is perhaps always latent in screen performance, in that when a performance seems "real," the actor seems to be related to the character, to share a bloodline; or the character seems to run with the blood of the actor. When the performance fails utterly, or doesn't get off the ground, the character seems bloodless and the actor, wherever he or she is, remains disconnected from the narrative and its embodiments. A case in point of bad performance: Jackson Rathbone hardly trying to infuse himself into the character of Sokka, the heroic young member of the Water Tribe in *The Last Airbender* (2010): he is never other than a callow, if athletically gifted, model standing in front of the camera. At the other extreme, along with many other possibilities, is Taylor in *Virginia Woolf*, giving a performance of complete commitment and engagement, and this to such a degree that she has been "devoured" by the ravenous Martha. Or, again, Janet Leigh in *Psycho*. There is a kinship at stake when an actor begins to "play" a character.

But in a much more explicit way than this, kinship is often realized onscreen as part of the discursive formula of a story. Films are often explicitly about families or family relationships, and actors are cast with one another in so-called "family" affiliations. As absorption in the cinematic moments may rest on absorption with the characters, viewers are dependent on the credibility of these "affiliations." In *Hereafter* (2010), Jay Mohr "is" vulnerable Matt Damon's crass and manipulative brother. In *Mission: Impossible* (1996), sylphlike Emmanuelle Béart "is" the dominating Jon Voight's daughter. In *War of the Worlds* (2005), boisterous Justin Chatwin and timid Dakota Fanning "are" tenacious Tom Cruise's son and daughter. Jessie Royce Landis "is" Grace Kelly's mother in *To Catch a Thief* (1955) and Cary Grant's in *North by Northwest* (1959). Woody Allen "is married to" Mia Farrow in *Husbands and Wives* (1992), while in *Rosemary's Baby* (1968) Farrow "is married to" John Cassavetes, who in *Tempest* (1982) "is married to" Gena Rowlands (and also, is married to Gena Rowlands). William Powell and Myrna Loy "are married" in six *Thin Man* films, and so on. I have elsewhere discussed some of the fascinating difficulties implicit in casting and projecting fictional familiality in film ("Look"). Centrally interesting is that in our social arrangements, and regardless of interpersonal history, invisible and biologically based consanguineous bonds are widely believed to (spontaneously and directly) mount an (externalized and recordable) appearance, such that part of the actor's job, in the absence of consanguinity, is to effect a proper and visible seemliness as spouse, child, parent, etc. People can *look related*, and family members, we think, are supposed to. In *North by Northwest*, Landis seems motherly, not just cast as a mother (while also being younger than Grant); and Grant seems correspondingly filial (Hitchcock was generally tickled by opportunities to exploit the mother-son bond, as with Marion Lorne and Robert Walker in *Strangers on a Train* [1951] or Jessica Tandy and Rod Taylor in *The Birds* [1963]). One can see the mother-child relationship in the structure of the interconnected glances Landis and Grant provide, in the postural angles they take relative to one another, in their vocal tones, in the (familiar) timing that links their comments. As actors, they knew they would be working with such tools to create the effect.

To return in this context to *Secrets & Lies*: in Marianne Jean-Baptiste can be found a delicious hesitation and uncertainty of one kind as she confronts her social worker but an uncertainty of a wholly different kind, warmer, hungrier, yet also flooded with respect, as she meets and gets to know her birth mother (Brenda Blethyn). In the mother, there is a manifest and pervading kindness in spite of her fear of bringing someone new into her life. The conditions specified by the script, in sum, are sufficient to structure the architecture of the actor's performance, yet it takes the actor's imagination and will to support a quality of "reality" that will engender belief. The fact that there are racial (and also—more hidden—class) differences between the two women is covered by the scripted setup, "adoption."

As she plays Albee's Martha, Elizabeth Taylor is already married to Richard Burton, who is playing George (they were wedded on a quick flip to Montreal while residing at Toronto's King Edward Hotel in 1964, when Burton was playing Hamlet in a now legendary production with Alfred Drake as his stepfather Claudius and Eileen Herlie as his mother Gertrude). But the dark love that, in her directionless passion, Martha bears for George is unique to the characters (since at this point Taylor and Burton were simply intoxicated with one another, and quite delirious). Taylor infuses herself and wills herself into an attachment for, not Burton but, George; not the energetic, rowdy man who is her legal husband when the camera is turned off but the timorous, resentful man who "is" her husband when the camera is rolling. It is conceivable that just in the way Martha and George may artfully and accurately represent any real-life married couple, so may they represent Taylor and Burton; yet through publicity (the hydraulic mechanism of star construction) viewers are also encouraged to believe that Taylor and Burton live on another plane, safely removed from the world of tawdry concerns that confines and plagues these characters (for instance, we learn in 2011 that Taylor and the Duchess of Windsor were personal friends ["Elizabeth Taylor Jewelry Auction Sets World Record," online at fashionindie.com]).

A limiting case of cinematic family bonding, and thus of a certain kind of "realistic" performance, is provided in Jonathan Glazer's stunning 2004 film *Birth* (the key to appreciating which, the *New York Times* sourly concluded, "is not so much a suspension of disbelief as an anxious surrender of reason"). Anna (Nicole Kidman) is in mourning for her young husband Sean, who has collapsed and died while jogging in Central Park in the opening credit sequence. She withdraws to the familial bosom of her cultured mother (Lauren Bacall), then becomes engaged to Joseph (Danny Huston), a fellow whose design it is that her past will be dissolved in his sparkling light. But some time later she encounters a young boy, about ten years of age, also named Sean (Cameron Bright). With a certain innocence and straightforwardness, he informs her that he *is* her husband. She of course rejects him (and the very thought as well), but again and again he appears, and slowly, methodically, powerfully, apparently incontrovertibly, she is transformed and comes to believe in him. She brings him to the fancy uptown apartment in which she is living with her mother; shares a bed with him; bonds with him, against everyone's wishes and best advice. What is brilliant and winning about Kidman's work here is the fierceness with which she denies the young Sean at first, and the strength of the self-doubt with which she begins to wonder about him and about herself, all of this racing upon the current of a desperate longing for the husband who has died (characteristic of grief, to be sure) and an unrelenting refusal, once the boy has grown on her, to give up this miraculous rebirth and the opportunities for a reconstitution of the lost love that it offers. No matter what anyone says or does now, she will have this boy/man, who for her can only be the dead husband (in whom all her love was invested), no matter that in some ways he is smooth and untouched and unknowing. Every phrase that comes out of his mouth is either hauntingly wise or else perfectly ambiguous. And, to Glazer's credit, as the film winds on we, too, come to believe in some unnameable miracle that has brought the beloved husband back to life.[7]

Here, then, a husband-wife pairing which is accomplished entirely by the commitments, gestures, expressions, and poses of two actors, Kidman and Bright. And indeed it is Kidman who must activate belief in the end, since the boy is nothing more than the object who invites acceptance. It is her slowly unfolding awareness of him as a full person, her refusal to categorize him (as a mere child), her capacity for tenderness and for receptivity, her thoroughgoing concentration on him—all leading the audience to imitate it—that finally allow for the (frankly outrageous) conviction that the dead live again, and live again here, in the virginal body of this kid. The shocking and deeply touching ending of the film depends entirely on the viewer having accepted Anna's commitment, on sharing her point of view, on believing that this (impossible) relation is "real." A significant part of the work is done by the expert Lauren Bacall, whose denial of the boy and the relationship is depicted with such disaffecting sourness: the more the viewer wishes to disagree with her the more the viewer sides with Kidman, even in the face of budding incredulousness.

What does Kidman do as Anna to help produce "real" moments with Sean? Two things in particular, both of which are directed from without and yet energized to a heightened degree in her working to be credible. As she converses with the boy, she drops the mask that adults wear in Western society when interacting with children, the mask that makes constant and unremitting reference to the fact of the child's "childishness" and difference. This mask is a way of using the voice, a choice of words, a mythologizing and generalizing tendency in discourse, a romanticization of minute experience, as well as a prurient circumspectness in regard to physical posture, alignment, and contact. Children apparently being in this society not simply people, one filters and restrains one's emotional and active participation with them. But Kidman begins not to perform this distancing, and becomes someone to whom Sean the boy is only Sean the person, the person who might be her husband, or herself.

Then, building on this, she gives the boy full ocular devotion, the devotion typically reserved for an object of adoration. One night, for example, he stands on the sidewalk outside the apartment building, reaches up to draw her face down, and kisses her on the mouth. As her face approaches his, Kidman's eyes never lose their intense focus, as though through an apotheosis of vision she is transforming Sean's material self and the material world into a spiritual truth, into something beyond what everyday commonsense behavior takes for granted. She is seeing in him what he seems to believe he really is. Part of the awkwardness and tension of this and other similar moments is exactly that, locked in our position as viewers, we have trouble going as far as she does; that we are tempted to side with her mother and discard this boy as a perverted imposter, Anna as lost. Yet the stakes for her could not be higher. Her marriage was all she had, and all she has. To deny the possibility that Sean has been reborn would be a denial of life, of possibility, of reality, of the world. And it is in her open gaze, fixated upon him, that her conviction becomes palpable. That gaze, of course, is the same gaze the viewer is using to watch the film. And so the gaze depicted onscreen reaches out to—forms a kind of blood relation to—the Principal Gaze that is the watcher's; like Anna believing in the Sean she is seeing, audience members can believe in Anna believing, whom they are seeing. Later on, when Kidman thinks about this—whatever it is that, in the face of life and death, thought may be—she lowers her eyes, turns them inward.

One can err by giving an actor too much credit or credit of the wrong kind. Kidman's great sensitivity and expressive capabilities are evident all through this film, yet one of her signal strengths is recognizing what is around her, the details of set decoration (antique furniture with tranquil bouquets in crystal vases), scenic design, costumes, lighting, and other people's performances, all of which, in an ensemble, form the vase in which the flowers of her own performance must bloom. She tones the level of her expression to match the color of the walls, just as the cinematographer tones the level of his lighting to accentuate the color of her eyes as she looks into the boy's. And there is a certain out-of-frame quality to her gaze and attention, as though what she is thinking of, looking at, concentrating upon, and desiring is someone who is not here, not present to the film, yet at the same time thoroughly represented by someone who is. She is looking not at young Sean, but at older Sean who is inside or around him—just in the way that any player of roles is outside or around a dramatic role he is playing.

In *Birth*, one of the reasons the matched performances of Kidman and Bright are so believable is that the script permits a sense of recentness and spontaneity, even surprise, in their connection. Another is that Bright, while he is now an international sensation for some audiences because of the *Twilight* saga films, had at the time made only a small number of screen appearances, mostly in Canadian made-for-TV fare, and had always been cast in a background role. He was relatively unknown when Kidman organized her performance around him, and her actions and responses constituted an identity for both of them.

Uniquely intriguing is the problem of family performance when the actors involved are all very well known, and, among other things, well known for not being connected to one another. When a number of stars, each identifiable in relation to a star persona and star context that has been

meticulously built for years through the studio system, appear to link up
onscreen as members of the same family, one can see a real challenge to
the art of screen performance. To simply play out one's star persona is to
alienate one's character from others. To utterly relinquish the star persona,
even if this were possible, would detract from the film's box office allure:
yet, too, it is not really possible. Further, when stars are busy playing familiality in the narrative framework of military relationships, the identical
uniforms and differences of rank can easily serve to cover over kinship,
so that the family bond is harder to establish in a way that audiences can
see. With a 1965 film, Otto Preminger produced just such a pairing of cinematic performances, establishing a father and son onscreen against significant odds.

In Harm's Way

Set in and around Hawaii after the Pearl Harbor attack of December
1941, *In Harm's Way* highlights a reprimanded naval officer, Rockwell Torrey (John Wayne), now brought back into action on a dangerous Pacific
mission. (The filming itself was dangerous for Wayne, who was not feeling
in the best of health.) He meets and falls in love with an American nurse,
Maggie Haynes (Patricia Neal). Shuffling from island to island in the
company of his impassioned and alcoholic friend and fellow officer Paul
Eddington (Kirk Douglas) and his efficient adjutant Egan Powell (Bur-
gess Meredith), Rock happens upon a handsome young ensign (Brandon
De Wilde), his son from an estranged (and socially superior) wife back
home. Jere, as the boy calls himself, has become doubly attached: first to
Annalee Dorne (Jill Haworth), another nurse and Maggie's friend and
roommate; and then to the manipulative and self-serving Neal Owynn
(Patrick O'Neal), a congressman in peacetime but now a highly placed assistant who has access to secret war plans and the ears of many very senior
military officers. Rock has neither patience nor respect for schemers like
Owynn, and while he is deeply touched to make the acquaintance of a son
he has never known he finds himself at the same time disappointed in Jere
for his blind, too ambitious commitment to Owynn and the man's un-
derhanded principles. When Eddington drunkenly rapes Jere's girl, leaving
her to kill herself, it falls to Rock to inform the boy, who is devastated. Jere
volunteers for a mission from which few are likely to return, and is indeed
killed in action. Eddington, for his part, steals a plane and flies off on a

suicidal recon, having time only to radio in the intelligence Rock needs for his battle mission before crashing to his death.

Saddled with a somewhat equivocal script by Wendell Mayes—the *New York Times* would find the film "a straight, cliché-crowded melodrama" but the carping Brendan Gill wrote in the *New Yorker* that he was absorbed only "because I am starved for movies that accentuate the positive"—Preminger enthusiastically transported his entire cast and crew to locations in and around Honolulu; arranged for Loyal Griggs (who had also shot De Wilde in *Shane* [1953]) to do the cinematography in dramatic black and white—a signal statement of serious intent for the mid-1960s; and drew from his actors performances of extraordinary depth and sensitivity, so that in its final (165-minute) cut the film is sharply paced, pithy, direct, and surprisingly moving, especially in the performances given by Neal, Wayne, De Wilde, and Douglas working with the rather thin material.

Clearly central to the narrative success of *In Harm's Way* is a viewer's ability to grasp Rockwell Torrey as a man who is tortured by the limitations and mistakes of his own past—less the misadventure that caused his reprimand just before the film begins than the distance he has maintained from the family, especially the son, he left behind. Onscreen, Wayne would be a powerful force, indomitable, compassionate, direct. A critical fulcrum for viewers, Preminger knew, would be the casting of Jere Torrey, and the exact performances he would be able to film from this actor and Wayne working in tandem in scenes written to emphasize their difference, their distance, and their hidden fears and love. Two such scenes would be pivotal, in each of which the father-son bond, erected between two performers who were not father and son, had to be fully and scrupulously believable, else the melodramatic center of the film would collapse. First, on a docked torpedo boat one evening as Rock meets the ensign on duty: a confrontation about his paternal absence, the boy's resentment, and Rock's eagerness for a relationship of some kind, souring when he learns of the boy's too eager "affiliation" to the slimy Owynn. This is Scene 140 in the final script:

> Torrey is waiting on the pier. Jere comes quietly out of the hatchway, moves along the deck until he can see Torrey from behind some deck gear. Jere knows this is his father. For a long moment he studies the older man before he steps into view himself.

Torrey tries hard to initiate a conversation: "Well, how do you like motor torpedo boat duty?" The boy is recalcitrant: "I don't like it, sir." But he has also learned the sort of political craft his father finds utterly alien:

Jere: I volunteered on advice, sir. This unit's assigned to Admiral Broderick's command. I was advised that once I was in Broderick's command a transfer could be arranged to the admiral's staff.

Torrey: Mind if I ask who gave you this advice?

Jere: Commander Neal Owynn, the admiral's public relations officer. I'll be his assistant. I expect you've heard of Neal Owynn.

Torrey: No.

Jere: He's quite a well-known congressman, sir. He resigned from office to join the service.

Torrey: Your mother's family could usually pull strings for about anything they wanted.

He makes his exit from this tête-à-tête abruptly, grumbling that he has to leave "Before I pick you up and throw you to the fish."

The second scene is 258:

Torrey: I have bad news for you. The nurse—Ensign Dorne—

Jere: Yes?

Torrey: She's dead. From an overdose of sleeping pills.

Jere (after a time): But why? Why?

Torrey: Whatever the reason she thought of you. She left this ring for you. *Jere takes the ring and turns away.* I'm sorry about the girl. Very sorry.

Jere: Thank you for coming all the way over here, sir.

Torrey: I know this isn't a good time for it but—well—I'd like to—somehow—we're father and son—it seems there ought to be— *He bogs down.*

Jere: I know what you mean, sir. I wouldn't know how to say it either, but I know what you mean. *He turns and they look directly at each other for a long moment.*

This scene works to frame Rock's difficulty informing Jere that Annalee has killed herself as a result of being raped by Eddington. These two PT boat scenes were made in Hollywood, between Wednesday, November 4, and Monday, November 9, 1964, with De Wilde appearing for makeup each day at 7:30 in the morning so that within an hour he could be ready on set at Paramount's Stage 15. A third scene, considerably lighter than either of these, shows the two men confronting one another uneasily outside Maggie and Annalee's apartment (shot under the shadow of Diamond Head at La Pietra estate on Poni Moi Road, Honolulu, July 17) on an evening when they have both come for dates; softer and slightly comic, it displays a pointed social awkwardness between the older and the younger male, both of whom are in the throes of romance at the same moment and in the same place.

Principally in the two conflict-ridden scenes of dyadic interaction between Wayne and De Wilde, the tension between Jere and his father had somehow to be made palpable on the screen. More fundamentally, De Wilde had to manage to be convincing as the abandoned son of John Wayne, Wayne to be similarly convincing as De Wilde's distanced father. If the two actors had become popular and known onscreen by way of (among other films) cowboy vehicles in the 1950s and early 1960s — *The Searchers* (1956), *The Horse Soldiers* (1959), *Rio Bravo* (1959), and *The Commancheros* (1961) for Wayne, *Shane, Night Passage* (1957), and *Hud* (1963) for De Wilde — they had never shared the screen, had not played out family relationship together to any audience. I should add a fact that might be axiomatic for some readers, although it is typically not openly in evidence in Hollywood productions that, like this one, involve family portrayal: off-camera, Wayne and De Wilde were neither friends nor acquaintances. Indeed, there is no evidence in the production files that the two had even met prior to filming their scenes. Wayne was formal and stiffish off-camera, and his only personal connection with De Wilde was by way of a gift mug offered when shooting was complete (Jesse De Wilde, personal communication). The "reality" of paternity, even mutual recognition, in this film, then, was wholly a fabrication of the actors' craft. They did not share a Hawaiian experience, either. Along with "perhaps the largest location troupe to ever be dispatched out of Hollywood" (Press Release, May 28, 1964), De Wilde and Wayne, accompanied by nearly 200 cast and technical craftspeople, made their way to Hawaii in late May and June of 1964, De Wilde in the company of his wife at the time, Susan Maw, being in fact one of the last in the caravan and departing on United Airlines Flight 197 at 6:45 P.M. on June 29 (Operations Desk Memo). Wayne traveled separately, with his own family, and earlier; with his wife and two children he resided in a house rented for $300 per week by Paramount, who also paid his grocery bills, covered his television rental, procured him a station wagon, and sprayed his house for bugs (Grosser to Caffey). Offscreen, Wayne was a resident of the Los Angeles area but De Wilde lived on the East Coast. Shooting back in Los Angeles, they also did not socialize, Wayne spending off-set time at his residence and De Wilde likely living, as he typically did when filming in Hollywood, at the Montecito on Franklin Avenue. As they labored together for *In Harm's Way* De Wilde was twenty-two, Wayne was fifty-five, this in the first years of the 1960s when generational discontinuities were palpable in American culture.

One may think of the performances that Wayne and De Wilde constructed together here, and indeed the greater body of film performances, as having three more or less discreet facets, which are both within and without any one actor's own province of control. I take these to be understood structurally, not necessarily as characteristic emanations of specific human intent, since photographic "presence" can be rigged through negative duping and filmic "performance" can be reconstructed or digitally composed. In all events, what is believable in a moment of performance remains in the jurisdiction and judgment of those who watch, a gallery whose epistemology and values must be taken to heart by those who act, fabricate acting, or only stand in.

First, the skeleton of a performance is written in advance, which is to say, bound and realized through some (published) articulation of verbal expression. Generally, the instrument of vocalization belongs to the actor, although there are notable cases where this is far from true: for example, although they frequently contain text meant to emanate from a character being performed, the title cards of silent cinema are typically penned by an illustrator working for the producer independently of the actor whose character's words are being shown; in dubbed foreign film, the voice we hear almost always does not emanate from the body we are watching speak; and with great frequency even in directly recorded cinematic speech the vocal track has been laid down by the visible performer but not at the moment in which his lips were moving (Oliver Stone's *Nixon* [1995] is a striking example). Movie musicals, in which performers will lip-sync to a pre-recording (in the 1940s and 1950s, this recording was called a "dream"), constitute only the most obvious case of temporal separation. In *Forms of Talk*, Erving Goffman is careful to note how the content of a spoken text (its "authoring") and the set of values or institutional requirements in the name of which that speech is made (the "principle") need not, and very often do not, correspond with the "animator," the being whose body or equipment is technically being used to produce the sound.[8] Regardless of whose body is actually used to manufacture utterance, in performance action and saying are scripted; and so, what is seen onscreen is there to be seen because it has been pre-ordered. In the case of *In Harm's Way*, Rock actually said to Jere the definitive phrase, "I'm your father": John Wayne was the animator (as Rock), and appeared to be the author as well, but the actual author was Wendell Mayes and Rockwell Torrey was the principal.

If speech is considered as an element that contributes to the realism of the Torrey-Jere conversations, it becomes evident how appreciably authentic characteristics of shared and mutually known family life have been embedded in the utterances—the father's comments about his wife and her family, for example—so that filmgoers are in a position to believe as they listen that no speaker but a family familiar could be saying such things. The situation of the meeting as military and its inherent (and more than military) hierarchy are contained in the kid's continual address to his father as "sir." The more probable a speech sounds onscreen the more "real," and the more audiences may need reminding of the obvious truth that the words they hear, spoken so engagingly and realistically, were not written or invented by the speaking figures themselves. "A fundamental for the director, which has only very rare exceptions," wrote Nicholas Ray, "is that every sentence, thought, or phrase that is spoken on screen must sound as though it is being spoken for the very first or very last time" (76). Here, neither Wayne nor De Wilde really originates his part of the discourse. Anyone's sense of the performance coming fully from them relies in part upon their faithful adherence to the script and the capacity of their memories—during the shoot itself—to retain dialogue correctly as well as upon their ability to speak a line, over and over again if production contingencies require, without losing freshness. This means both that the realism of the performance has been created in part by people who are not visible onscreen; and that in part it has been created exactly by those who are, yet by aspects of their being that we cannot see. Often, dialogue seems improvised even when it is not because viewers have invested themselves in the conceit of the actor's realistic performance, and because, without a script to turn to, they are in no position to see how much fidelity to written words an actor is showing.

Rock and Jere "are" father and son, then, because in speech they behave the way a father and son "would behave," it being relatively immaterial that all this "being" and "behaving" is being structured from without. I elide from this discussion the general fact that paternity is expensive to verify, thus, that anyone could be imagined by Jere as his father, especially a man who openly claims to be.

A second eminent feature of performances and their realism involves wrappings or surrounds of the performer's body, principally setting and clothing (although of course props and the work of other actors can work in this capacity). Wrapping and surrounds are outside the frame of the actor's direct control except that he may perform the sorts of manipulations for which the setting or costume has already been designed (the steering column of an aircraft will turn; the sails of a fake sailboat can be manipulated; a door will be designed to open and close, a bed to be stretched out upon, a table lamp wired to produce light, a jacket shaped to come off, a pair of gloves to be spoken about—as in *On the Waterfront* [1954]).

A performance can abruptly seem unreal if the performer suddenly loses the assured control of space and things, which we expect from competent persons in everyday interaction. For this reason, actors will rehearse with their props. One such loss of control, theoretically speaking, is a failure on a character's part to react to any climatological or scenic event that members of the same culture would normally consider astonishing or remarkable: in the background of a shot, an unknown person suddenly collapses; in the distance, a tornado brushes through a landscape. Because characters must be distinctively reactive, and appropriately so, to such eventualities—eventualities that through audience distraction would ruin the continuity of a sequence—crews go to considerable trouble during a shoot to isolate the goings-on that will be filmed, thus gaining total control over the environment and gaining the ability to filter out any such potential "happenings" that would call for (unscripted) reaction. Location shoots are accomplished with traffic cordoned off for several blocks around, and so on.[9] The unintended happening might very well not, in and of itself, collapse a scene, but a performer's casual and unreflective failure to attend to it, when the audience could see it perfectly well, would.

Important to note is that both scripted language and designed setting are largely beyond any actor's personal control, at least beyond the control of actors who have not come into the film as producer or director.[10] An interesting atypical example that worked quite differently is given by the parental argument scene in Nicholas Ray's *Rebel Without a Cause* (1955), where Jim (James Dean) comes home after a nightmare experience with a car accident on the bluffs to find his father (Jim Backus) waiting up, with the television on. To rehearse this, Ray brought Dean to his apartment bungalow at the Château Marmont, on Sunset Blvd., where their interaction was so fluid, their work so productive, that Dean wanted to shoot the actual scene in the same place (Douglas Rathgeb, *Rebel* DVD commentary). I can attest that Ray's bungalow at the Marmont had very tiny rooms, and although Ray's home may have been charming it did not permit the necessary space for camera placement and proper lighting. Accordingly, and mostly because of Dean's desire (and Ray's great permissiveness with his actors), the apartment was re-created point by point on a Warner Bros. soundstage, but larger. Usually, however, it is not the actor who decides where a scene will be shot, or how a script will reflect his character's response to the scene or to other actors. Since much that we see onscreen is characters behaving *in situ* and expressing themselves through articulate dialogue—using a place designed by someone else and reading out lines written by someone else—the realistic effect of screen performance is often largely due to performers' passivity, responsiveness, and obedience to formal demands.

In the Preminger scenes, the realism of De Wilde as an ensign is partly in what he says, but also partly in his familiarity with the space of the torpedo boat (a set in which he can have rehearsed and walked around considerably before the camera turned). He is believably an ensign, too, because his uniform perfectly—even a little too perfectly—fits his body. Actors' agents have their physical measurements on file and provide these to productions when casting is completed; producers can then provide their costumers with the right guidelines for designing. Central to cinematic costuming as a profession is a tacit understanding that producers will want costumes to fit the characters being given in performance, and, absent specific instructions to the contrary, clothing designers make it a practice to tailor garments exactly to the body measurements they have been given. An exceptional case in this regard was the performance by Sammy Davis Jr. of the role of Sportin' Life in Preminger's *Porgy and Bess* (1959), where because the producer needed the clothing to fit Davis's body with absolutely perfect tightness through and through, as though it were a skin, special measurement sessions were required and a fabric selected that would "give" during Davis's elaborate and accomplished choreographic movements. In *In Harm's Way*, a subtle but readable distinction is given onscreen between Torrey and Jere by virtue of the differential fit of their clothing: the older, more settled, and therefore more relaxed Torrey wears clothes that fit comfortably but not snugly over his large frame; the son's uniform fits tightly and crisply, showing off his youthful physique but at the same time calling attention to his rather brittle posture and attitude and the deference required of his rank.

The setting can act as a skin or shield to enhance and establish an actor's performance. (The following chapter considerably elaborates setting as a function of the "reality effect" in cinema.) Makeup can also function as a "garb" or covering of the performing body, and more than an assist it can be a distinct problem for the working actor. The discomfort of Max Factor's yellow pan-cake makeup designed for early soundstage Technicolor shooting is legendary, since all visible skin had to be covered with it in order that actors' bodies would not look blue onscreen in the bath of cold arc light to which they might be subjected (see Factor). For the Canadian Broadcasting Corporation, Michael Ironside discussed with me in 1983 his performance as the villainous Overdog in the science-fiction adventure *Spacehunter: Adventures in the Forbidden Zone*. The several hours each morning he had to endure being fitted into metallic prostheses and latex masking converted him so thoroughly into an alien other that, said he, he found it impossible to discover himself in the mirror; the experience was alienating and made the daily labor of performance a serious challenge.

The actor's embodied personality is a third aspect of his performance important to consider, even though our access to it is always at best indirect. By "embodied personality" I refer to an amalgam of body shape and size, ostensible range of attitudes and postures, characteristic vocal timbre, and typical speaking rhythm, all adding to a set of recognizable physical features that can be identified with a singular person and can be seen developing through a performing career. When Janet Staiger discusses a movie star as a "monopoly on a personality" (Bordwell, Staiger, and Thompson 104), it is necessary to understand this alleged personality as always, in perceivable fact, a complex of muscular tensions and exertions, locative tonalities and pauses; the personality is ultimately the expressive body. In the case of movie stars, who are marketed intensively on the basis of their embodiment (in early scholarship on Hollywood stardom, Hortense Powdermaker noted that tricks of the camera "give intimate details of the actor's physical being" [207]), we may detect a notable consistency from role to role, even a typification: John Wayne, Jerry Lewis, Robert Mitchum, Katharine Hepburn, Elizabeth Taylor, Jake Gyllenhaal, Meryl Streep, Tom Cruise, Anne Hathaway are all instantly recognizable as themselves regardless of the roles they play (unless, as for instance with Dustin Hoffman in *Dick Tracy* [1990], the makeup hides the actor's face). While a star persona to some extent mitigates against the realism of an actor's performance—it is the star herself, a human being working in the

Hollywood system, and not the character in whom one is being asked to believe and whom one is watching—it is also true that star performance is augmented by the attractiveness of the star and the relative rarity of his appearance. Wayne's Torrey in *In Harm's Way* seems larger than real because he always already calls up the familiar (gigantesque) Wayne, and also because every nuance of Wayne's action is magnified and intensified for the viewer through the mechanism of his stardom. Character players, such as De Wilde, are typically not known by their features alone, and very often make significant changes to their physical appearance from film to film, the better to become dissolved into, or hidden within, the role. Indeed, much of De Wilde's screen work was accomplished as he physically matured through childhood and adolescence, retaining some characteristics—the ocular twinkle—while others changed. If Torrey is very much like John Wayne, he is much like a man to whom the viewer has no access (exactly because he is so much seen): Wayne the quickly recognizable is simultaneously Wayne the unapproachable, thus Wayne the untouchable and unknowable. Wayne the star is immense upon the screen, and yet this Wayne-as-star has virtually no content, is almost evanescent. The John Wayne who underpins him is almost a complete mystery (although after this film was done, Wayne's offscreen life took on more form for his fans). Onscreen, and magnified over and over by his profound stardom, Wayne actually diminishes in presence, but Torrey expands.

In an important sense, the body of the cinematic performer *is* the camera. A long or a wide-angle lens can produce radical distortion of perspective and objective form, so that when photographed any actor's body can take on a whole new shape. For example, when Matt Damon is directed by Gus Van Sant and photographed by Jean-Yves Escoffier for *Good Will Hunting*, a 50 mm lens is used predominantly, mimicking the spatial perception of the normal human eye. Damon's body takes on certain proportional characteristics as a result. Five years later, directed by Doug Liman and shot by Oliver Wood for *The Bourne Identity*, he has gained a little weight, notably in the face, but is also often seen in extreme close-up or extreme wide-angle, with the effect that the body is at once made less rotund, more topographical; and exaggerated in form. Added to the power of the lens is the fact that most viewers of a movie have not met the performers in person, and are thus ignorant of their absolute size. The qualities, proportions, and dimensions of a performing body onscreen are thus largely constructions, not facts. Some actors are very short, but must appear taller than other cast members, and so they wear shoes that have lifts built in or stand on unseen platforms for two-shots: Christopher Plummer working with Julie Andrews in *The Sound of Music* (1965), or Claude Rains, or Al Pacino.[11] The camera cranked up on its podium could make Glenn Ford and Peter Graves appear onscreen shorter than they were in real life, too; Ford was more than six feet two inches tall, but manages never to tower over his co-stars, and Graves was a good six inches taller than that.

If their responsiveness to scene, articulateness, and physical appearance in *In Harm's Way* convincingly establish Torrey and Jere as navy men, differentially accomplished and at home in combat, what exactly is it that makes the discerning viewer believe in a "reality" where they are father and son? They say what father and son would say to one another, of course, because as characters they have been imagined this way by the writer Mayes, who can borrow as he needs from James Bassett's novel and from the experiences of fathers and sons that he has observed in offscreen life (he died childless in 1992). Yet there are plenty of very beautifully written interactional scenes in American cinema of the 1960s that posit familial relationship but are entirely unbelievable in performance. In *Bye Bye Birdie* (1963), Paul Lynde is supposed to be teenaged Ann-Margret's father. Lynde is thirty-seven but looks closer to fifty; she is twenty-two and looks thirty as the camera turns, but covers with a persistent display of curvature that is meant to take our eyes from her too canny face. Lynde, meanwhile, regardless of the fact that every word he utters adds up to paternity, seems so entirely and devotedly self-conscious, so overtly "performative," that anyone might reasonably find him hard to believe as being aware of anyone else on earth, least of all a wife (Mary LaRoche) with whom he purportedly produced his children. It could be argued that this film is a parody of the middle-class mid-American family, not a portrait. Portraiture is the intent in Stanley Kramer's *Guess Who's Coming to Dinner* (1967), however, where Katharine Houghton is meant to seem the daughter of Katharine Hepburn and Spencer Tracy. The casting doesn't work—bizarrely so, since offscreen Houghton was Hepburn's niece—largely because the young actress is entirely self-effacing in the presence of the two stars who flank her, not to mention that of Sidney Poitier as her love interest. While there is nothing in the performance bluntly to forbid reading familial relationship, nothing encourages it, either; but the setting is perfect and the dialogue could not be more astute or more on point.

Perhaps what strikes viewers so forcefully about John Wayne and Brandon De Wilde is some visible trace of a concentration and mindset that each of them brought to the filming, out of some devotion to the project, to the filmmaker, to their own careers, to each other in mutual respect, it is impossible to say what—a devotion that cannot always be said to be present in film acting. Beyond filling his own role, each of these actors convinced himself that the other was related to him by blood. De Wilde crossed some kind of boundary when the camera rolled, and believed entirely in Wayne as his father—a belief that the physical resemblance encouraged, permitted, perhaps even facilitated but did not demand. And Wayne saw in De Wilde some son with whom he could bond, and also, of course, given the requirements of the story, spectacularly fail to bond when on some very deep level he wished otherwise. These commitments of performance were not necessary for either actor outside of the acting work: Wayne had children of his own, and De Wilde had a good relationship with his father. There is a glow to the eyes and a steadiness of gaze revealed again and again in close-ups of the two actors as they gab it out. That the glow is produced by key lights does not detract from our coherent interpretation of it as warmth. Wayne was of course known for his steadiness of gaze, and so was De Wilde; but here is to be seen something unrelenting, the eyes of each actor apparently boring into those of the other.

Often in performance there is no particular key to the viewer's acceptance at all (beyond the viewer's intense desire to accept), except that actors carefully avoid actions that might cause discontinuation of belief in their characterological relationship. If Wayne and De Wilde are cautious not to do anything to disrupt the illusion of being father and son, an illusion created on their behalf and outside of themselves, the audience may be willing enough to go along as part of the narrative contract. Thus, part of the performance is a sense of moral commitment in the actor's professional posture. Typically in everyday life, the same moral constraints apply, although this fact hardly makes performance easier. The possible pitfalls, poisons, sabotages, and other ruinations of performance are legion. Here, for example, a minute aversion of the gaze toward the wrong part of the screen, for even a split second, could have thrown the magical bond down.[12]

In *Acting in the Cinema*, James Naremore is interested in the relative fragmentation and coherence of a rendition. He notes a particularly interesting feature of an actor's job in realist films, "to split the character visibly into different aspects" (75). None of us always identifiably produces the exact same manifestation, in every situation, on every day. Our attitudes toward different people, our moods, the ongoing events of life all pressure us to modify expressiveness and alignment. So, for instance, Wayne's tenderness in his confrontation with De Wilde after Haworth's character's death marks a notable shift from his stiffness and superiority when first he meets the boy on the torpedo boat. Yet Wayne and De Wilde must not travel in this tender moment too far from the positions they have staked out emotionally in other scenes. Part of the actors' work involves modulating between the fragments they provide to the camera (and not necessarily in chronological order) in such a way that reasonable coherence is established without the performance appearing to be rigid, stale, or tedious. Balance and consistency among the fragments of performance can be a nightmare to achieve, since films are typically not shot in sequence for the final editing; and since for many sensible reasons an actor might not have a clear view of what he did on a previous day before the camera (not all performers watch their rushes, or, if they do, make notes to themselves about what can be seen there). As to a stimulating sense of spontaneity in a scene, one recipe is to respond to one's scene partner on the spot, with a minimum of prearranged business. The character appears to be hearing and thinking through his screen "existence" as it is unfolding, much as persons do in real life. Until one actually tries one's hand at doing this, it can be difficult to believe how difficult it is to say a line of scripted dialogue as though one has never read or thought it before: to behave honestly on a breath, when in actual fact one is shamming, because one knows everything that will be said now, and indeed later, in a film before one opens the mouth.[13]

Broadly interesting is the fraught extremity of the bond De Wilde and Wayne manage to make us see in the face of their discreteness and even alienness to one another as actors. Something of this sort had been part of Howard Hawks's *Red River* (1948), between Wayne as Thomas Dunson the cattleman and Montgomery Clift as Matthew Garth, his adopted son. Here, Wayne reportedly came into the project with genuine antipathy toward his co-star, who had to prove himself by spending four weeks on location prior to shooting, learning how to ride and rope (McCarthy 413–18). The urbanity of Clift, his gentility, his thoroughly disarming physical beauty in place of challenging ruggedness as could be seen in every angle of Wayne's face all conspired to drive the two performers apart: but the story depended on precisely this distance. Had that negativity been part of Wayne's relationship with De Wilde seventeen years later, *In Harm's Way* could not have worked, since the final resolution of the Torrey-Jere relationship had to be pure and unrestrained, yet also unspoken, paternal love.

However screen performance is theorized, there always remains an inexplicable residue, something of the human action that, insinuated into awareness, strikes with a certain force. Watching these two actors at work is to be fully convinced of the "reality" of their presence with one another in character. Indeed, while the rest of the film, its effects, its bizarre concatenation of personalities and events plotted onto the screen, may easily fade from memory, this father-son bond floats securely in the center of the diegetic array, pulsing and lambent and true. It is also a truth, of course, that the feelingful complexity of fatherhood and filiality do not necessarily portend complexities of appearance: much of seeming to be related in a familial way lies in merely saying one is, merely looking upon other people as though one has looked upon them all one's life. The element of personality, then, may play into performance less than scene and script do, though in the case of the Wayne–De Wilde case it does seem evident that some real commitment of self has been achieved on both sides of the scene, achieved exactly in the moments while the camera was turning.

In some instances an actor can wend his way through a performance taking advantage of the inherent "authenticity" of the script, in a process I would call "script-playing." While people are sometimes thought to be deceitful, scripts are not, it being a fundamental convention underlying all theatrical endeavors that the words coming out of the performers' mouths are to be understood at face value as they are uttered (sarcasms, jokes, and ironies being expected to be coded as such for the audience by fillips of the actor's intonation, gesture, and so on). If, as with Jeff Daniels and Jesse Eisenberg in *The Squid and the Whale* (2005), the script continually makes reference to one being the father of the other and the second being the son of the first, the actors need do little more than reiterate their words in order to set up for the viewer some understanding of the alignment between them. A close inspection of the scenes between these two players in comparison with the De Wilde–Wayne scenes in *In Harm's Way*, however, will show how the more recent film takes advantage of script acting to establish the paternity while the earlier one takes advantage of personality. It is not merely that less reference to the relationship is made in the Preminger film; but that Wayne and De Wilde, through posture, hesitation, aversion and focus of gaze, speed of talk, and minute facial gestures convey a screen "reality" that goes beyond what the very capable Daniels and Eisenberg are asked to do (playing characters, it must be admitted, who care less about affiliation, care less, actually, about everything). If the two scripts were read out as radio plays, with no vision to fill in the scene, *In Harm's Way* would fail utterly, while *The Squid and the Whale* would lose little of its presumable "authenticity." With Daniels and Eisenberg, the "reality" is in the words; with Wayne and De Wilde, it is in the faces, the body distance, the physiques so powerfully visible during the pauses.

While the Preminger film would have a gala premiere and its central performances would receive considerable attention inside and outside of Hollywood, both Wayne and De Wilde had to remain, at least temporarily, silent. The former proceeded directly to a medical examination when his scenes were complete, there to learn that he had a tumor the size of a golf ball on one of his lungs; surgery was immediate. As to the younger actor, he had developed a polyp on his vocal cord, and entered Lenox Hill Hospital on March 31, 1965, for an overnight stay in order that it be removed; he was prescribed nine days of speechlessness, during which period *In Harm's Way* premiered at the DeMille Theater (Press Release, March 29, 1965).

"Reality" Aids: Casting and Technical Arrangements

The Wayne and De Wilde performances in *In Harm's Way*, accomplished and technically brilliant though they are, hardly represent pinnacles in screen acting or especially important moments in the history of the acting craft. In a way, they only exemplify what all screen acting normally and typically is when it sets out to model the social world that viewers do, or can, know. The two scenes I have discussed, far from overwhelming, typify what screen acting can produce when it is conscious, refined, well worked, and devoted. Two other facets of the performance need to be mentioned when film acting is up for discussion (which it is, of course, only when one is not in the process of being captivated by it). First, in the case of star performance, a great deal of what is experienced in watching a film may be arranged in advance, or at least prepared, through publicity. Audiences see what they do because they have been led to expect to see it. The dignity and staunchness of John Wayne, for example—characteristics that tend to accompany his performances and augment them—are part of the poster persona of this actor that viewers come into the theater already knowing and adopting. As to the angularities of his presentation in this film: family tension, sexual appeal, interpersonal conflict, historical trauma—all these can be signaled and illustrated in poster designs (about the power of which see Haralovich) so that viewers do not need a detailed inspection of actual scenic performances in order to elicit representative clues that cumulate to establish them. As a fairly slick example of this phenomenon: when Brad Pitt and Angelina Jolie appeared together in *Mr. and Mrs. Smith* (2005), they were already widely known to their public, through weekly headlines at the grocery counter, as lovers who teetered on the edge of separation or fidelity. To perform realistically two lovers on the edge of separation or fidelity, they knew, required a labor much of which had already been done for them by the press. The Wayne of *In Harm's Way* was always already a stalwart, militarily oriented, patriotic, dignified, and straight-from-the-hip type of screen male because of his work in such classics as *Stagecoach* (1939), *Fort Apache* (1948), *Red River, Rio Grande* (1950), *The Quiet Man* (1952), *Island in the Sky* (1953), *The Searchers, Rio Bravo, Hatari!* (1962), and *Donovan's Reef* (1963), among many other films. And in a smaller, but no less acclaimed, group of pictures including *The Member of the Wedding* (1952), *Shane, Night Passage, Blue Denim* (1959), *All Fall Down* (1962), and *Hud*, Brandon De Wilde had established himself in the public imagination as the eager and loyal young male looking—or at least desiring to look— to a father figure or other masculine idol with adulation and wonder. (Of his actual father, Fritz De Wilde, Brandon "confided" to a columnist, "He's always given me good advice about girls. He probably got around himself when he was young" [Ardmore 2]. "Kids," he continued, "like to sit around and yak about how *old-fashioned* their parents are and how little they understand; but if you get them into a good sober discussion, they'll usually end up admitting that their parents' attitudes are sound enough" [5].) In *Shane*, indeed, he had established a presence (with both Van Heflin and Alan Ladd) that became iconic. Part of the performance for *In Harm's Way* was thus inbred in the casting process itself.

Technical arrangements contribute to screen performance in ways that critics have heralded insufficiently. The faces of actors will be made up so that their skin tones match in front of the lens: for two men who are father and son, this relationship between visible tonalities will be a central, but unobtrusive, signal to viewers. And the lighting provided by the cinematographer and his crew is critical for lifting the body of the actor out of

the surround and giving it a rounded presence on film. Fill lighting, in particular, and bounce lighting from behind help shape the bodies. But from
an actor's point of view, what is principally important about the precision
of key lighting is that it restricts mobility and narrows the territory of the
performance. The expressiveness required of both Wayne and De Wilde
in both of their key dramatic scenes here must be contained and shaped,
in order that the torpedo boat on which they are playing can remain relatively underlit and thus a secondary aspect of the scene.

In classical acting for camera, the overall shape of a moment in performance is ultimately given not by the actor's force but by the film editor's
choices and dexterity. The rhythm of a silence before or after an utterance, for example, and the relationship of any utterance to one made by a
second performer, will be structured in the editing regardless of the way
actors contrive to behave on set. Bette Davis was an actor who understood this implicitly. In this account by her longtime editor Rudi Fehr of a
chance meeting between the two of them at the St. James Club on Sunset
Blvd. (now the Sunset Tower Hotel), where she was to receive an award,
we get direct evidence:

> I wanted to look this place over, I was so impressed by it. I wanted to go out
> in the lobby. There was a lady standing out there. "You can't go out there. *Life*
> magazine is doing a layout with old stars with new stars, and they are doing
> Bette Davis." I said, "Bette Davis is here?" So I waited when they made a
> break and I walked out and I walked up to her. I said, "I just felt compelled
> to shake your hand, Miss Davis. I'm Rudi Fehr."
>
> "Rudi! You're *it*!" That's exactly what she said to me.
>
> I said, "May I return the compliment? I think *you're* it, Miss Davis. You
> look wonderful." She did. She had a beautiful gown on and her makeup was
> perfect. Six weeks later she died. (Bell 139)

There are no matching reports that either Wayne or De Wilde played a
similar game of tag with James S. Fowler or George Tomasini, who cut
their scenes for Preminger, but these actors would have known how an
editor could shape their breaths, prolong or curtail their pauses, sculpt
their forceful mutual gazes.

I choose these two performances from the legion that could present
themselves for discussion because here, mutually constituting family relationship—in the face of sufficient star visibility that if it were any less
poignant audiences could have seen through the construction and found

the acting "self-referential"—Wayne and De Wilde signify together one of the limiting cases in acting achievement, where what is built for the audience's entertainment is a set of entirely fictitious but also entirely credible signs of closeness, bonding, and knowledge. In all such cases of "realistic" screen performance, one is looking at work undertaken by actors, technicians, publicists, writers, and, indeed, viewers themselves. *In Harm's Way* is significant, too, because it came to be at the end of the Hollywood studio system, wherein a large body of professionals of various kinds—screenwriters, publicists, directors, cinematographers, designers, makeup artists, costumers, and actors—collaborated on a routine basis, and with a wild productivity, to make characters come "real" on the screen. By the 1970s, much of this system had been broken up, and by the 1980s and 1990s many of these professionals were no longer working on the scene.

Screen Performance Renovated

Indeed, most of the technicians and artisans who populated the studio system and labored to manufacture its "reality effects" are now gone. Only a relatively small number of performers remain active in filmmaking today, people who were also working intensively during the heyday of studio filming: Lauren Bacall, Angela Lansbury, Mickey Rooney, Dean Stockwell, Martin Landau, Eva Marie Saint, and Max Von Sydow come immediately to mind. Alive but not filming very much or at all are Olivia De Havilland, Debbie Reynolds, Joan Fontaine, and Joanne Woodward. In screen work of the 1970s, 1980s, and 1990s one can see performances by other luminaries from the 1940s and 1950s no longer with us, including: Jack Palance, Laurence Olivier, Alec Guinness, Jack Lemmon, Jack Warden, Barbara Stanwyck, Bette Davis, Katharine Hepburn, Elizabeth Taylor, and Ernest Borgnine. Such actors as Michael Caine, Gene Hackman, Clint Eastwood, Warren Beatty, and Dustin Hoffman got their start later, but tasted the end of the studio system. They work today (some of them rarely) with memories of what screen acting was "back then." To examine the most popular films of the early twenty-first century, however, is to find that they are cast almost brimful with performers of an entirely different generation, whose work exhibits a new quality, being extensively bounded by the requirements of blockbuster cinema. As the *New Yorker's* Tad Friend reports, "'All the furor surrounding Elizabeth Taylor's death was an elegy for the kind of movie star we used to have,' Terry Press, a leading film-marketing consultant, says. 'People were mourning the loss of larger-than-life personas'" (48). These young actors, having learned to perform athletically more than dramatically, tend not to vocalize particularly well (Peter O'Toole complained of this gently during an April 2012 on-air interview with Robert Osborne), often, indeed, slurring their language. They are typically "treated"—with computer and makeup effects—to have surface appeal, while the roles they are called upon to play demonstrate little depth of personality. Often their glamour stems from their being young and inexperienced. Their film work is studded with effects jolts—if possible, one every few seconds—and so they must be athletic and pliable in the hands of special-effects wizards. Their principal function is to deliver narrative bits, not to convey a sense of the palpable actuality of an emotion, a look, or a statement. In blockbusters, scenes are written to seem blockbuster-worthy, which means they are exaggerated, more and more representing bizarre and imaginary worlds or visions as viewed through some transformative matrix of ideology or high-tech magic. While Stephen Prince quotes Cedric Gibbons, long-time head of the Art Department at MGM, as saying a challenge for the art department "is to make something look real which is not" (in Prince 180–81), he is pointing to a view that, in view of blockbuster cinema, incorporates a relatively old-fashioned conceit. Now art departments and designers work to dramatize, emphasize, and exploit what is already palpably not real and what is intended to stun only by virtue of its explicit technical complexity and cost: the film has become an advertisement for its own techniques.

In this context the actor is transposed into a model, if not to show off fashion then to cast off the flitting impression of an attitude, a connection, an intent. Plot (typically very complicated plot) dominates character, rather than character dominating plot; and neither plot nor character work to fill in a picture of the world: instead, plot and character occupy beats in a rhythmic flow. Lest the scene, usually visually elaborate, appear like a mere diorama of prehistoric nature at the museum, it must be populated; and characters are used to provide that effect.[14] Jonathan Mostow's *Surrogates* (2009) is a beautiful example of a film that briefly held out the promise of a "real" situation, as is Luc Besson's *Leon: The Professional* (1994)—in both cases, the agony of a person who could not find the self within the flux of modern life—but in the end, as the market now demands, and as both Mostow and Besson repeatedly led us to expect in their earlier work, action sweeps in and takes over, special effects dwarf personalities, and the "realism" is stymied by simulants for the viewer's uninterrupted adrenalin rush.

Beyond having come to mean a form of posing with clothes or props, screen acting is often today a case of modeling as a skeletal and muscular reduction for computer-generated animations, a process discussed with consummate brilliance by Prince, who notes of malleable audiences that "much character animation takes advantage of the human perceptual system's fine-tuned propensity to scan objects and environments for signs of intention and to read these signs often on the basis of scant and incomplete evidence" (107). The kinematic algorithms that animators use nowadays are integrated in such a way that when one part of a "body" moves, associated parts will move in accord (111) and in general screen performance can be thought of as a "composited element" of film (114 ff.). On "Larry King Live," November 5, 2010, the chameleonic Jeff Bridges raved—or wept, it was impossible to tell—about new "cameraless" filming and "performance capture," in which for *Tron: Legacy* (2010) the wired actor's body is mapped out electronically in a green room called "the volume" and then laid over with makeup, clothing, movement, and expression in post-production.

Given that as the actor's stock-in-trade, posturing has replaced feeling and gestural experience, there is nothing illogical about the use of very exploitable young talent onscreen. Life has not yet etched lines on their faces that the makeup artists need to brush away (or that compositors might have trouble etching instead). And being young laborers, young actors have good strategic reasons for not complaining, for enthusiastically missing the fact that they are being manipulated for profit. In the classical Hollywood cinema, very young actors did not typically have starring roles—Mickey Rooney and Judy Garland were exceptions, not the rule— and in general were rarely used (except to play the parts of children, as, for example, with Barbara Bel Geddes in *I Remember Mama* [1948]). De Wilde, who was just out of adolescence when *In Harm's Way* was filmed, was another exception at the time, indeed an exception that worked, since Jere was intended to be callow and smooth, a boy without experience who wanted to think himself more mature than he was.

For many actors the opportunities for emotional expression are limited to extreme close-ups (see, for example, David Bordwell on "intensified continuity," where attention is given to the extraordinary increase in

the number of shots per film since the 1960s, and to the preponderance
in contemporary film of dialogue shot in close-up). In this context, it can
become newsworthy when a performance is based on the relatively old-
fashioned technique of expressive movement, as with Heath Ledger's
performance in *The Dark Knight* (2008). Some of the considerable (and
much deserved) praise lavished upon it may have been inspired by viewers'
sheer delight at the atavistic pleasure of seeing him leap and crawl on the
screen—in short, actually use space, both cinematic and geographic, with
some evident physical control: a relatively classical acting form—although
even this notably complex performance is structured in the editing fundamentally for producing action jolts, not connections and catharses. Action
film has no time for the mess of catharsis.

Perhaps, indeed, given the spectacle of the technologically inflected
screen (movies with effects that announce themselves as such, both onscreen and in surrounding publicity), attachment to action has itself been
altered. "Realism" is now the movie experience itself, however false or
contrived, and the telling moment has been lost in a maelstrom of sensibilities. If the movie as a package is already "real," the viewer need not
look for "reality" inside it. Given the plethora of reducing devices through
which screen images are now downloaded and watched, watched in miniature, the very idea of establishing a place or condition is bypassed by the
rhythm of editing, the splash of color and light, and the seductive promise
of pornographic visions and acts. Place on the palm screen, as in Google
maps, is purely relative, a matter of signpost definition and point-to-point
calibration. It lacks the absolute sense of magnitude and extension that
the 1950s widescreen, for example, worked to emulate. What doesn't fit the
system, now as always, seems wrong, outdated, antique, perverse. And the
new "realism" of screen acting is that it must seem rigged.

Perhaps the cinematic "reality" of classical works is utterly eclipsed, the
depiction of experience replaced by the depiction of appearance, the surface of surfaces, or what Wilhelm Worringer called imitation of the real.
In watching film, audiences do not any longer feel obliged to root themselves in the "earth" of social relations and experiences, settling instead
for the thrill of pace and flicker. Thus, blockbuster and download cinema
bring with them a whole new sense of order. "The farm," the poet Donald
Hall reminds us of those sunny days of the 1930s (when cinema was blossoming), "had an order to it. . . . Everything done was part of a motion we
didn't control but chose to implement . . . the farm was a form: not a set

of rules on a wall, but like the symmetry of winter and summer, or the balance of day and night over the year, June against December" (qtd. in Nye 289). Now that farms are disappearing for real, so are the films that farmed our sensibilities. Cities and modes of transportation are expanding without apparent limit. Electricity that brings warmth to winter and coolness to summer, that makes day and night interchangeable, has now also become the very subject of what we see, since the performances are very generally electric: the actors are electrons in motion *through* the resistance of the script.

To look comparatively at the work of two young icons of the screen, the Andrew Garfield of *The Amazing Spider-Man* (2012) and the Brandon De Wilde of *In Harm's Way*, is thus to see—beyond the bodies strapped into their costumes and intentionalities strapped into their scripts—acting work of two different kinds, accomplished, in the earlier case, as the studio system was shifting toward independent production and, in the latter, as blockbuster cinema had begun to pervasively shape filmic form. Both young actors had done considerable work before; both had technique to burn. And both, in the contexts of their films, seem "real." One cannot say of a contemporary performance like Garfield's that it is "realer" onscreen than what De Wilde did, although it plays to a contemporary conceit as to what screen "reality" is in being electric, more the sort of phenomenon that is received and appreciated at a glance. In his work here, and in *The Social Network* (2011), *Lions for Lambs* (2007), and *The Imaginarium of Doctor Parnassus* (2009), Garfield onscreen is a commodity to be quickly seized and consumed; he doesn't build a perduring character, but inhabits a preestablished form with brio and athletic grace. Whatever his body does, De Wilde's presence onscreen moves more slowly, changes less mercurially, haunts by simulating an objective reality that teases the viewer's tactility and thought. As for audiences in 1964 and now, they watched then and watch in our own time with a stunned sense of engagement in what seems to be a progressive movement of performance, a thoroughly up-to-date and galvanizing thrust that seemed then, and continues to seem, "real" because absolutely up to date.

As for up-to-dateness and the "real," Peter Gay reports a stunning conversation from 1881:

> During his American lecture tour, Oscar Wilde went to visit Walt Whitman, one outsider interviewing another. They talked about poetry. When his host wondered whether he and his friends would renounce Tennyson

and other leading versifiers of the previous generation, Wilde thought that they might. True, he said, Tennyson was "of priceless value." But he acknowledged that, regrettably, this national icon had withdrawn from his age. "He lives in a dream of the unreal. We on the other hand, move in the very heart of today." (49)

In an emergency anybody can use a brush.

—Roy Brewer (IATSE), at the time of the CSU strike, 1945

4

A Fairy Tale

Two Worlds: The Doubling Experience of Cinema

Where is it that one can claim to be, while watching the action of a film? In which of two incomparable, undocumented, unresolvable realities? In the world of the theatrical auditorium, with its dimmed lights, its plush seating, its sweeping screen, its modest projection booth, its hidden projector, its paid projectionist, its garlanded box office, all attached to—or at least occupying the same social dimension as—those Mole-Richardson fresnels and barn doors, coated lenses and obedient cranes, dressing trailers and laundered costumes waiting to be fitted and word-processed performers' contracts waiting to be countersigned by the producer: that world the viewer recognizes as functional on entering it, and then quickly works to dissolve?[1] Or else in another domain altogether, the imaginary space of the story, which can never manage to appear or feel like the place the watcher sits in—even with the case of *Singin' in the Rain* (1952) or *Play It Again, Sam* (1972) or *The Purple Rose of Cairo* (1985) or *The Dreamers* (2003), where what is depicted is actually a movie theater with an audience similar to the audience watching—but instead insists on suggesting a fabular zone to which he progressed only through a portal crossed in that now-vanished place, thus a portal forgotten?

Each person watching a film "gives himself over," as Erving Goffman suggested of the filmgoer's counterpart in the theater. "He is raised (or lowered) to the cultural level of the [writer]'s characters and themes, appreciating allusions for which he doesn't quite have the background, marital adjustments for which he doesn't quite have the stomach, varieties in style of life for which he is not quite ready, and repartee which gives to speaking a role he could not quite accept for it were he to find such finery in the real world" (*Frame Analysis* 130). Each person watching a film surrenders in the watching a self and a world.

The issue is frames of reference, involving the distinction between characters and actors; between acts and performances; between places and sets. To give a case:

When, after it premiered September 8, 1954, people were watching Vincente Minnelli's *Brigadoon*, was it Tommy Albright in his spanky forest-green Viyella shirt who was holding their attention or Gene Kelly (wearing the same shirt at the same time)? And during the moments of their absorption, were they situated in the lost forests of the Scottish Highlands or in Culver City on an MGM soundstage (or in a theater seat in one of the Loew's theaters owned by the company that still, at this time, controlled not only productions but also exhibition spaces and also paid Kelly's fee)? Where did those watchers think they were and who was the apple of their eye? Certainly the body in which any filmgoer finds herself occupies a space that pulls upon it, pressures it, conforms and reforms it. Is that space the motion picture theater, dark yet radiant—perhaps a place where one would choose, above all other places on earth, to be—or the sun-dappled little village of Brigadoon with its vale, its hills, its little bridge, that is only here one day every hundred years, wherever "here" is? If the body exists in history, consider also Marc Augé's comment that "there is no room . . . for history unless it has been transformed into an element of spectacle" (83). In this case the studio "had to construct indoors one of Hollywood's biggest, fanciest outdoor sets," said *Life* magazine: "Rolling moors, sturdy enough to support a troupe of Highland fling dancers, were planted with heather (California sage sprayed with lavender paint). Low-lying Scottish mists were made with dry ice, more buoyant fogs with vaporized oil. Clumps of huge plastic trees were rigged with live foliage, and a 75-foot stream was tuned up to gurgle musically through the glens" ("Highland" 94). Even knowing all this (before or after a screening), is it a dry ice effect that viewers see, or is it mists; heather or sprayed California sage?

As to frames of reference, the American abstract expressionist Irene Rice Pereira (1902–1971) mused, "One of the dilemmas of the twentieth-century man is finding a position in relation to frames of reference in space and time; otherwise he will be driven from pole to pole, only to be lost or overwhelmed by the infinitudes of anxiety as the picture of the

universe opens up to the human mind, displaying more and more gran-
deur" (*Nature* 4). It is not, of course, only in space and time that frames
of reference are necessary as guides. We need to know, and are puzzled as
we search to discover, where to place ourselves socially, politically, ideo-
logically, and phenomenologically. For more than two centuries now, the
Kantian distinction between the noumenal and the phenomenal has an-
chored Western thought as it struggles to negotiate between the eventual
and the apparent, between (reliable) reality and (vulnerable) perception.
The Kantian problem is always worth rehearsing again: an observer sees a
world, but not the world that is there. Or: incapable of perceiving the true
reality, observers construct and substitute an elaborate illusion that they
nominate as reality instead, this illusion sometimes containing particular
constructions pointed to openly as "illusions" but as often as not constituting what is taken as "untransformed," or "authentic," or "actual" presence.
All of it, even what is thought actual and imminent, is just an illusion.

About the noumenal and the phenomenal worlds there has been a
long-lived argument as to which dominates the other or which ought be
considered with more gravity, a debate that has riddled aestheticians and
political philosophers alike. Should I rely on my senses, knowing that it is
only by means of them that the world is accessible; or should I discount
that dependency, concentrating instead upon what the intellect can deduce
through rational principles (that flow from some a priori axiomatic position taken, "reasonably," to be fundamental)? To put this perhaps too simply, yet simply enough to provoke: should the looker take seriously what
he sees (knowing that it is only appearance)? "Your spellbound thought,"
writes Nabokov, "mistakes every new layer of the dream for the door of
reality. . . . Is this reality, *the* final reality, or just a new deceptive dream?"
(*King* 20–21).

This is a vital question, because the thrill and mystery of cinema are
available, fully, only to those who do take seriously what they see. It is possible to know the world of production that underlies an image without
reifying it as the principal object of real consciousness, without thinking
to ourselves, "There is singing and dancing, but it is *only* the contracted
work of singers and dancers." Much conventional cinemagoing is based on
this way of knowing and seeing, in which fantasies, pictures, illuminations,
and unaccountable sights, for all their manifest power, are treated as mere
décor upon a substantial material armature. It is equally possible to disattend production, giving over one's belief so fully to a fictional world that
one is unable to see it as the product of seriously laboring and perduringly

committed skill. Seen this way, movies just appear, and moviegoers just watch them. What cinema challenges is the achievement of a double vision, however: to see what is on the screen at once as both phenomenon and noumenon, enchantment and creation, poetic reverie and technical achievement. Every lyrical vision is the result of hard work; and in Hollywood, the outcome of hard work is lyrical vision.

In the Gloamin': Shooting a Complex Scene

In *Brigadoon*, there is a majestic scene in which Gene Kelly and Cyd Charisse, as Tommy and Fiona, stroll up a deliciously heathered little hill—high enough to lift them above the normal world, yet not so high as to necessitate a strenuous climb—and sing the Lerner and Loewe tune called (hardly a surprise) "Heather on the Hill." The camera floats above them, and they lean forward as they rise up, vast tracts of purple blossom sweeping past their feet. They turn, they spin. They touch hands, look into one another's eyes—everything by the book. He swings her around, and the vast extensive valleys of the Highlands speed past, with green and purple hills mounting upon themselves it would seem without limit. The passion of their song—

> The mist of May is in the gloamin'
> And all the clouds are holdin' still.
> So take my hand and let's go roamin'
> Through the heather ... on the ... hill. . . . . .

—mounts as they are suddenly frozen in a pose, and then mounts again as the notes of the song climb higher and higher with sailing, yearning violins playing in accompaniment from some invisible cloud. The dappled light, the majestic promontories in the distance, the earthiness of this private little hillock, the rich yet modest heather: all of it adds to the melody and movement to produce a sense of transformation, elevation, and extremely intense purity: say, if you are not too jaded, the sublime.

At the same time as one experiences this phenomenon one is also caught up with a relatively noumenal reality: the actual studio production, as recorded on film, of what will be taken as diegetic reality. Every moment on film is both a dramatic reality and a record of its own making. (For a limiting exhibition inside a diegesis of so-called noumenal reality

ger's *The Day of the Locust* [1975], where other characters climb a different
hill, with much more frightening results.) Here in *Brigadoon* is the accomplishment of the cinematographer Joseph Ruttenberg and his gaffing crew
as, on Stage 27 at MGM, they worked to photograph Kelly and Charisse,
themselves laboring under Minnelli's direction Monday through Friday,
January 5, 6, 7, 8, 9, and Monday, January 12, 1954, often with the assistance
of Kelly's choreographic assistant Carol Haney and "dance-ins" (dancing
stand-ins) Jeanne Coyne and Jimmy Thompson, all this in the presence of
art director Preston Ames and his crew and a grip crew that could move
the camera, switch it from its normal dolly to the (high) Chapman boom,
realign pieces of set, and so on. Here are some tidbits, selected from the
daily production reports from this short period: January 5 from 9:00 until
10:32 A.M., "director & art director dressing set with flowers—spraying
same with paint—building stile with stones next to fence at bottom of
hill." January 6, from 12:55 until 2:43 P.M., lighting and lining up a dolly
shot that would cover the first cut of the dance routine, rehearsing with
the cast from 2:43 until 2:50, rehearsing with stand-ins from 2:50 until
3:00 with the director "riding boom to check setup and colors" (a notably Minnellian gesture: he loved his boom) and the cast busy changing
into wardrobe, then shooting four takes from 3:00 until 3:06, with the first
two of these completed and unsatisfactory, the third unfinished, and the
fourth printed. Kelly himself riding the boom January 7 from 12:07 until
12:20, then from 12:20 until 12:35, a decision being taken "to change setup
slightly," re-dress the foreground set, re-lay the camera track, all in an effort "to get longer shot of scene. Discuss best angle for camera." A lunch
break is called at 12:35 for an hour (but half an hour for the crew), and at
1:35 a continuance of lighting and lining up the camera. From 2:20 to 2:30,
a rehearsal with the cast, Minnelli on the boom to check the setup. From
2:30 to 2:50, continued lighting on the dance-ins, while the cast changes
wardrobe. From 2:50 to 3:05, a continuation of rehearsal, "to check setup
and wind effect." From 3:05 to 3:47, thirteen takes made, with unfinished
dance action in 1, 2, 3, 4, 5, 7, 8, 9, 10, and 11, takes 6 and 12 put on hold,
and take 13 printed. (Here as before, Minnelli is pleased to have one print-
able take of a shot, and works until he gets it.) On January 8, Gene Kelly
worked out some "slight changes" for the fourth cut of the dance routine
from 9:15 to 9:45, and stagehands lined up the foreground brush for the
camera; then at 9:45 for fifteen minutes the crew lit the stand-ins while
Kelly and Charisse dressed and Minnelli stuck leaf branches onto the

foreground tree on the set. On January 9, the cast worked past the normal deadline of around 6:00 P.M. At 7:10, they were waiting for Gene Kelly, who was experimenting with his makeup, "recovering up his beard—decided had to put on new 'makeup'"; the director needed a rehearsal before shooting, this from 7:35 until 8:00. At 8:00 they spent five minutes shooting one take of dialogue and action to end the musical number, but there was no print, and the company was dismissed at 8:05 "due to going on meal penalty at 8:10 P.M." Work picked up January 12, with Kelly called for 8:15, to be on set at 9:00 (and Charisse called for about an hour earlier, the standard procedure for her during these shooting days); from 9:00 until 9:40 the crew awaited Kelly, who got into makeup at 8:50 and wasn't onstage and ready until 9:40. From 9:40 until 9:48 they waited again, while Kelly rehearsed off-set to the playback. 9:48–10:00, rehearsal, with director riding boom to check setup. 10:00–10:18 final makeup and hair check, with director and cast discussing the scene. Then twelve takes made between 10:18 and 11:15, 1, 3, 5, 8, 9, 10, and 11 unfit because of action or synch; takes 2 and 4 completed but no good because of bad synch; takes 6 and 7 on hold; and take 12 printed. This gives only a fragmented picture of the style and type of work undertaken on Stage 27 for this number, which often involved moving the camera onto or off the Chapman boom, repositioning and redressing parts of the set, rehearsing every single dance move for camera and lighting, and so on. All of this, and the more than a hundred daily production report entries I have not reported here for this sequence only, constitute what lies *underneath* the phenomenal reality of the "Heather on the Hill" number in the film.

The production on set of this sequence, as partially detailed above, is exemplary of virtually all studio filmmaking in the period of the 1940s and 1950s, when Hollywood was populated by an army of extraordinary talents bound together by contract and commitment (see, for other discussions, Powdermaker; then Bordwell, Staiger, and Thompson). One can note some general features of the activity: obsessive meticulousness about the use of time, with detailed record-keeping of work activity minute by minute and annotation of workers' prompt or late arrival and any distractions from scheduled activity (Kelly needing to redo his makeup); adherence to a ritual of rehearsal before exposing film, and the repetitive technical task of lighting and lining up a shot ("L&L," as it is notated in the actual reports at MGM) rather than just arbitrarily selecting a camera angle and proceeding; and moving through the working day on the basic assumption that all members of the working crew and cast are not only expert in their activity but familiar with the script, therefore needing minimal face-to-face consultation about what they are to do. Some discussions exist, but they are brief and to the point. The script, in short, constitutes a veritable blueprint of what will be done in front of the lens.

By complete contrast, however, for some of what is to be seen there never was a blueprint, and exist no records, the film itself being a kind of file of the spontaneous decisions made by workers (typically performers) before the lens. Further, as a standard operating procedure, focus checks, lighting arrangement, and camera moves are all established with the help of stand-ins or dance-ins, not with the principal players, whose energies must be concentrated on the action during a take. In the case of this production number, Charisse's dance-in and Kelly's both made about a hundred and fifty dollars a week, for a one-week engagement with a one-week guarantee.

From the daily production reports on the "Heather on the Hill" song and dance number, even in their grossly adumbrated form as given above, it is easy enough to deduce some interesting features of the working methods of a principal player in this activity. Vincente Minnelli had an obsessive desire to see in advance what a framed shot would look like: to visualize the entire dramatic space, to conceive the action developing in that space, and to picture for himself the precise framings that the camera would obtain. (Look at Hermes Pan's direction of Fred Astaire's "No Strings" number at the beginning of Top Hat [1935] to see a looser use of cinematic space.) Hence his passion for riding the Chapman boom, and the very oft-repeated notations of him checking the setups for lighting, for color, and for composition. Color, in principal, attracted this artist, and he was always sensitive to ways in which it could be accentuated. More than rehearsing for the composition, he would trouble himself to arrange it from far above, and in peace, while his actors were dressing. And he was not above stepping down onto the stage and adjusting a branch, a flower, or a prop to suit the needs of the composition. In terms of an issue central and vital to producers—even to Arthur Freed, with whom Minnelli was on the best of terms and who went out of his way to support the artists who were working for him—an issue around which the entire process of filmmaking rotated, namely, financial expenditures and savings, Minnelli can be seen to work with notable efficiency. He does not, for example, make insurance takes—that is, after finding a take that is completely acceptable and ordering it printed, going for a second or third acceptable take, so as to have a choice in the cutting room later. The takes that are out of synch or unacceptable for one reason or another are stopped mid-way or else completed but not printed. He seems never in this sequence to have made more than about fourteen takes of a shot—and this only rarely since most shots were accomplished with six takes or fewer—and never to have printed more than one take. While it costs to run film through a camera, it costs much more to send that raw stock to the laboratory.

There is also a sense in which Minnelli exudes calmness, patience, and matter-of-fact workmanship. Consider that on the first day of work the cast and crew were present from 9:00 A.M. until 5:20 P.M. for rehearsals only. On the second day, January 6, six takes were made in the morning (with Kelly insisting on singing to disk), four takes on one setup, then two on a second; in the afternoon four takes on one setup, four takes on a second, then five takes on a third, none of which were printed because "Miss Charisse looking very tired—so decided to dismiss and start shoot-ing with Take 6—on same setup tomorrow morning." This is four com-pleted shots in total, with the crew on set from at least 8:15 A.M. until 6:10 P.M., and the principals from 9:00. During each take of each shot, Kelly and Charisse are expending themselves with profound energy and disci-pline—"going all out"—sometimes for only seconds at a time, and with a focus on grace and elegance of movement (in poses however taxing) all the while smiling and mouthing the words to the pre-recorded song track (five minutes and fifty-six seconds long, and made by Kelly with Charisse's voice dubber Carol Richards on January 1 and March 25, 1954 [Memoran-dum on recording dates]).

Contrasting with this laborious and technically astute work is the finished sequence, the "phenomenon" as it were: gloss, ambience, gliding movement, supreme emotion, harmony, agility, balance, color, depth, rich-ness, and brilliance, all of which appear natural, as though Tommy and Fiona merely throw themselves forward into song.

Is phenomenal perception to be regarded as nothing but a delirium, a withdrawal from the reality of existence into a pleasure dome of ab-stractions and deceptions designed to lead people away from the truth? An exceedingly critical view can be taken of this kind of withdrawal. For example, adopting the theoretical framework of the Frankfurt School of cultural and political philosophy, Russell Berman argues, perhaps with far more stress than makes sense, that the force that "transforms the world into a visual object" is nothing less than fascism, the producer of a "spectacular landscape of industry and war" ("Written" 99). In riposte, Thomas Elsaesser proposes that a view such as Berman's would take every cinematic image, every illusion, as fascist, and this is surely going too far ("Berlin"). Beyond the question of how, and to what degree, the viewer can usefully and safely rely upon the world presented to the senses lies the deeper question: how to rely upon anything else?

Case Studies of Fabulous Perception

As well as referencing the places of experience—a hill, a swath of flowers, a mountain range—images may invoke a world that does not exist outside of them. In that case, the sight exists as it is seen, and only then, so that its manifestation and the viewer's inspection are wedded. Take, for example, a screen close-up, a kiss forty feet high and fifty feet wide. Mouths, noses, eyelashes, cheeks . . . This does not represent an actual gigantism, a collision of beings the size of a bank who linger just behind the screen (as in my very first viewings of film I thought it did). Nor can it be summed up as a mere articulation of cinematic grammar in which, for emphasis, a face or two understood to be normal yet magnified by a technology for diegetic reasons take over the screen. While it does point out particular details relevant to an ongoing narrative (as well as featuring the star performer successfully), the facial close-up, while it lasts, offers a face that is simply and absolutely enormous, looked up to in a kind of all-absorbing infantile appropriation. The face is glowing, is radiant, exists without a body, offers the pronunciation of dark ocular tunnels, and so on. Does it not, too, recall other faces? Italo Calvino in *Invisible Cities*: "I thought: 'You reach a moment in life when . . . the mind refuses to accept more faces, more expressions: on every new face you encounter, it prints the old forms, for each one it finds the most suitable mask'" (95). In close-ups and in all screen imagery, the picture constitutes not only a map but also a territory. I am interested here in pictures principally as territories, yet as territories carefully fabricated for the screen.

A strange and wonderful example of the harmonious juxtaposition of practical and phenomenal realities is provided by the interior designs executed between the 1940s and the 1960s by Tony Duquette, a (somewhat idiosyncratic) creative spirit (and, among other things, the costume designer of *Kismet* [1955]) who had a penchant for covering surfaces with such treasures as green malachite, sea shells, and faux leopard skin. His studio was on Robertson Boulevard in Beverly Hills, and he did a lot of celebrity homes and film sets, as well as corporate commissions. In all his designs, the eye is stunned by shapes, colors, and textures that seem un-earthly and, thus, otherworldly, yet also grounded in a kind of productive array, where the technique of Duquette's assemblage is made bluntly ac-cessible. The Beverly Hills living room of Mr. and Mrs. James Coburn, for example, had seashells covering the ceiling beams so that as one moved beneath them, around long coral sofas laid out with orange, avocado, and gold silk cushions, the beams could sparkle and flicker through the day-light that flooded in past high blue brocade curtains lined with coral velvet (Goodman and Wilkinson 166). For the penthouse of the Hilton Lagoon apartments in Honolulu, he covered walls with crushed abalone. At his own estate, Sortilegium—"twenty-one structures, each one based on a dif-ferent theme," and cobbled from "architectural fragments, Georgian shop fronts from Dublin, Chinese roofs, columns, doors, windows, bathtubs, pavilions, mobile homes, backs of trucks, old windows, and much more" (257)—one could gaze, at least before it was all burned away in the Green Meadows fire of October 1993, at a tree sculpture made out of green gar-den rakes attached to denuded red-painted branches (246) or at a Chinese garden gate decked out with bleached elk antlers and aloe; or repose in the master bedroom under a leopard-skin canopy or walk among malachite-green pagodas. Burt Lancaster, Merle Oberon, Ann Blyth enjoyed his lamps, used his candlesticks, wore his jewelry and thus experienced the mixed pleasures of Duquette design. Hired by Arthur Freed to work on the "This Heart of Mine" sequence in *Ziegfeld Follies* (1946), Duquette sur-rounded Lucille Bremer and Fred Astaire with a revolving ballroom that featured "an elaborate ruby-and-white interior with dipped plaster drap-eries with antler and tree branch tiebacks as well as fanciful 'Duquettery' figural candelabras. The outdoor garden was decorated with white painted trees sprinkled with mirrors and Duquette figurines standing twenty-eight feet tall" (102). To experience these designs is at one and the same time to understand the materials that have been manipulated—through paint, through glue, through repositioning, through artful and unexpected combinations—and to be transfixed by environments that so thoroughly exceed or flout convention they become transfigurations of space.

Two further case studies will illustrate the problem of establishing the value of phenomenal perception, that issue of central importance in the experience and assessment of cinema, given that seeing a spectacle always involves the negation of a production, seeing production the negation of spectacle, yet any viewer may shift concentration to see both. First is the wax reconstruction of a scene from Émile Zola's *Germinal* (1885) that was opened at Paris's Musée Grévin in January of 1886, as described and discussed by Vanessa Schwartz in her book *Spectacular Realities* (122–23). On the Boulevard Montmartre near the Rue Jouffroy, this rather intoxicating museum, still very much thriving, and a haven of such meticulously produced and dramatically staged waxworks that they often seem alive, doted from its first days on simulacra that were fashioned with an exceptional attention to detail and then posed in settings arranged to discombobulate the viewer's sense of spatial reality. In the case of *Germinal*, instead of copying the props from the Zola play, which was set in a coal mine, authorities of the museum directed that materials and samples should be taken from an actual mine at Anzin, the place that was reputedly the real source used by Zola when he wrote. Since the "realism" of the spectacle for the crowd depended heavily on their preeminent familiarity not with coal mines but with the Zola play that the wax model reflected, writes Schwartz; and since the reviewers hadn't been to Anzin and therefore couldn't recognize its aspects, the presentation was somewhat disorienting. About *L'Illustration*'s summative comment that "Everything is the most exact nature," Schwartz is moved to wonder: "What was 'real' in this tableau? Its recreation of the theatrical adaptation, of Zola's novel, or of a mine? What was the claim to reality of this novelistic/theatrical scene when juxtaposed with other scenes at the Musée Grévin, such as a tableau of the Chamber of Deputies? Perhaps for the visitors who might never see the president of the republic or a coal mine, the diorama's simulations were satisfyingly real." This wax tableau seemed to constitute a picture of what audiences already knew how to see and love, the Zola play, which was related to, but not in fact the same as, the mine replication it actually was.

Also noteworthy is that merit was attributed to the Musée Grévin presentation based on its phenomenal value: no one thought they really *were* in Zola's "mine"; they thought they were in a place that was *"like"* it. In short, they were experiencing an effect. When I visited this museum in 2010, I was able to meet someone very much *like* George Clooney at a cocktail party and to sit behind "Charles Aznavour" in a tiny theater as he gazed at the stage. A poignant case of the opposite effect can be found in audience reactions to various scenes in Michael Mann's *Public Enemies* (2009), which recounts the final days of John Dillinger. At the Congress Hotel in Tucson, Dillinger (Johnny Depp) is quite believably arrested—believably in large part because of the character's recognizable perturbation and irritation at the event. In fact the building labeled as the "Congress Hotel" is not, and does not look like, Tucson's Congress Hotel, where I had breakfast one day. If with the Musée Grévin viewers thought they were seeing a simulation of a simulation when they were seeing a simulation of reality, here viewers are convinced they are seeing a picture of a reality when they are seeing a picture of a simulation.

My second case suggests that the fascinating example of the Musée Grévin is not necessarily a model for every audience interpretation of "reality." In the gale scene of Michael Powell and Emeric Pressburger's *I Know Where I'm Going* (1945), Wendy Hiller, Roger Livesey, and Murdo Morrison are in a long boat with its motor out, circling a huge whirlpool in a blasting storm off the Isle of Mull. Alternating for the viewer here are (a) long shots of the craft and the whirlpool—made with a miniature and figurines, and (b) close shots of the live performers, water splashing up into their faces, simulated with rear-screen projection. Both types of shot supply reality effects—that is, the shots can all be edited together to give a seamless representation of three people trapped desperately in a stormy whirlpool. But given these two sorts of reality, viewers may accord one with more gravity than the other. Confronted with both a real, if miniature, whirlpool and a rear-projected picture, and sliding back and forth willingly and comfortably between the two, yet viewers can tend to value the "real" image, however misproportioned, over the construction, this in the face of the fact that real whirlpools this size are things that very few viewers have experienced while cinematic artifice, on the other hand, is more familiar. The reaction to push away the rear-projection shots as fake, but to buy into the reality of the miniature shots, suggests viewers who do *not* opt for what they know how to look for, indeed, who reject it.

Regarding so-called theatrical "realities"—by which I mean moments onscreen when the audience is clearly subjected to the sort of construction that can only happen in the movies: these are, in every way, purely cinematic moments, and guaranteed to please especially audiences who are in love with cinema. Those who think of cinema as a window for looking upon a real world that happens to be out there cannot fully appreciate what it is to sit and stare at something that has been made up entirely to be stared at. It would be painful to wish for a real "real" presence near that whirlpool, Corryvreckan. Such a "direct" exposure to a terrifying natural phenomenon like this would present all kinds of problems, not least our magically remaining dry at such proximity to threatening wetness—comforting safety would also disable the fiction. (And of course, how could filmmakers manage to get the shots?) Although audiences may like to think they prefer hard realism (and, in the case of viewers today, boast

about the virulence of the realism they can tolerate watching), perhaps the
most efficient screen image for producing audience pleasure is one that,
while hinting at the noumenal world, actually presents a clear-cut phenomenon designed to be seen as such.

Brigadoon's World: The Travails of Artificiality

In that light, turn again, and patiently, to *Brigadoon.*

Far and away in the "high hills" of "Scotland," deep in a lush, green,
deer-filled "forest" and tucked beside a gushing "stream," where the horizon
is mauve with heather and the air is crystal clear, and with tiny thatched
cottages and friendly folk always wise, nestles the tiny village of Brigadoon. (Doon = Celtic, "dark"; Brig = bridge; Brigadoon = "Bridge over
Darkness.") One travels long and hard, as it were, to find this place, and
must use not only the eyes but the eyes of the soul, because Brigadoon is
a village with strange powers to vanish in the mists, which it does do, in
"fact," for all but one day in every hundred years. Hither and with a passion for hunting Tommy Albright (Gene Kelly) comes from the outside
world (Manhattan!), accompanied by his chum Jeff Douglas (Van Johnson). Discovering this remarkable village he falls in love with the comely
lass Fiona Campbell (Cyd Charisse), a long-time resident: indeed her way
of "living" is atypical in the extreme, since in many ways she is a ghost.
Fiona seems younger than springtime, but Tommy soon discovers (in a
reprise of the English novelist James Hilton's 1933 novel *Lost Horizon*—
which in 1937, having become an international hit, was filmed by Frank
Capra) that she is hundreds of years old. She is as old, actually, as some of
these hills! Love, however, is love. When finally the cynical Jeff attempts to
draw Tommy back with him to the urban pressures of New York, Brigadoon's call proves to be stronger. He does agree to depart, but finding the
city an intolerable jungle soon takes off again to be with the girl he loves.
When he finds her,[2] one can take leave of the village, and of the two of
them along with it, and the whole illusion vanishes into the shroud of time
(exactly what happens with every motion picture, when it ceases unspool-
ing in the projection booth and leaves us straining to remember its lyric in
the far less exciting everyday world).

In the formula of the fiction, the enchantment of Brigadoon, the charm
which saved it from destruction, will hold only so long as no citizen makes
bold to cross the bridge. Should anyone leave, the village itself and all its

inhabitants would be lost forever. This story is adapted from a German work of fiction by Friedrich Gerstäcker (1816–1872), centering on the charmed village of Germelshausen and a voyager, Arnold, who, chancing upon the place in the one day of the century when it appears, falls in love with Gertrud, who lives there. At the end, he abandons both her and the village to time—

> Arnold turned away, and slowly proceeded on his way. Only when he had reached the top of the slope which commanded a view over the whole of the valley did he pause once again and look back.
> "Farewell, Gertrud!" he murmured softly, and as he walked over the hill, tears were streaming from his eyes.

—but in Vincente Minnelli's version of this tale, the hero is heading back over the bridge and into the village when the story closes. This is a central change, since it urges the privileging of the fictive over the pedestrian, the phenomenal over the everyday world. Gerstäcker was a pragmatist, Minnelli was a dreamer. They took separate paths at the fork, and we must ask ourselves which way we would choose to go.

A hint, if we need it, is that the film constantly links the magically appearing and disappearing village, its spontaneous but evanescent population, and the colorful, musical intimations that strike the visitor immediately on arrival there, with the world of cinema. If cinema is merely a purveyor of cheap and unredeeming falsehoods, one need have no special consideration for it. If, by contrast, the enchantment it provides is valuable in itself, socially and personally valuable, because it charges audiences with affection for sensory experience, that is a higher matter indeed. Cinema can be seen as an art, but it is not necessary to elevate it this way in order to consider the regard aesthetically important. Both the cinematic process and the ghostly Brigadoon appeal to what is deepest and least known in experience.

Brigadoon was pure Broadway. Set in Scotland instead of Germany (in the immediate aftermath of World War II), it opened at the Ziegfeld Theater, 141 West 54th Street, on March 13, 1947, and played 581 performances in a production organized by Cheryl Crawford, conceived and written by Alan Jay Lerner, with music by Frederick Loewe. During the run the screen rights were purchased by Arthur Freed, whose unit at MGM had been responsible by that time for many of the most sparkling musical productions in the history of film. It was some while before the property could be turned into a working film project, in no small part because by the early 1950s the Hollywood studio was no longer the fabulously profitable dream machine it had long been. While it is true that the Freed musicals, expensive and complicated to produce, had been a source of significant profit to MGM during the 1940s, not to say a repository of exceptionally talented performances and a showcase for a persistently engaging camp sensibility (as Matthew Tinkcom suggests [see "Working"]), by the time *Brigadoon* was being conceived Nicholas Schenck and other controlling forces in New York were getting impatient with Louis B. Mayer's old-fashioned, rather regal style of filmmaking. It was costing a fortune and obstructing the adjustments in production that were evident at Warner Bros., Fox, and other big studios where it had openly been recognized that television was a force to contend with (see Schatz, *Genius* 367–70).

By July 1948, Mayer had been ousted. His replacement, Dore Schary, a man dedicated to making what he would call "good" pictures and pressured to cut costs, was enacting hard decisions through the first years of the 1950s that would have no little effect on what Freed and his associates could produce. Schary did not want to curb the talents of Freed's crew — Roger Edens, Keogh Gleason, Johnny Green, and the other talents (like Betty Comden and Adolph Green) whose collaborations had made *Easter Parade* and *An American in Paris* (1951), not to mention *Singin' in the Rain* (1952) and *The Band Wagon* (1953), such huge successes. At the same time, however, he could not afford to let the studio gamble on expensive propositions that weren't absolutely guaranteed to bring in a profit.

Already committed to the production, but living in the early 1950s in Paris, Gene Kelly had given thought to Moira Shearer (the star of *The Red Shoes* [1948] and *The Tales of Hoffmann* [1951]) as his female lead,[3] and rumors also circulated about Kathryn Grayson. But thinking of dollars, Schary announced that Cyd Charisse, already contracted to the studio, would be fine in the part. As Green, the film's musical director, recollected, this meant that the original Broadway vehicle, composed by Lerner and Loewe as an operetta "in effect, for two simple vocal figures — a soprano and a baritone," would now be centered upon "a fellow called Gene Kelly … one of the closest friends of my life, and utterly and completely brilliant … who sings with a kind of appealing, husky, Irish high baritone to low tenor" and, of all possibilities, Cyd Charisse "who is (putting it correctly) monotone—not tone deaf. . . . Cyd Charisse cannot carry a tune, okay? She can hear it. If she couldn't hear it she couldn't be a great ballet dancer, which she is and was. This is primarily a vocal role! So we've got two dancers in a vocal operetta" (Burk 100–101).

Beyond this tonal irregularity came a more central problem: what might the film look like? Kelly's original desire had been to shoot entirely on location:

> We thought when we bought *Brigadoon* that we were going to make one of the great revolutionary breakthroughs in screen history, because Cinemascope had come in and widened the screen and, and the costume pictures had proven this was a great vehicle for costume and Western films. So we said, "Now, we'll do a movie musical." This, this is Kelly and Minnelli talking, you know. (Slight laugh.) We were, this was our hope, that we would do *Brigadoon* as an outdoors picture the way John Ford would do a picture as a Western. We would do it as a Minnelli and Kelly musical, but do it outdoors. So we originally planned to do it in Scotland. (Davis, *Kelly* 49)

He envisioned the dancers moving through real hillsides covered with heather and recollected that "we wanted all the clans to gather out-of-doors and meet them with the camera eye and see the, the four clans approaching from the North, the South, the East, and the West, with the bagpipes skirling and the drums banging away, and it would have been thrilling" (50).

In February and March of 1952 plans were indeed reported congruent with such a *plein-air* approach. "Alan J. Lerner and Frederick Loewe are switching about completely on 'Brigadoon' by going to Europe, instead of coming to Hollywood for this picture," William Schallert wrote in the *Los Angeles Times* in early February. "They will meet producer Arthur Freed in Scotland, where the film will be shot this summer" ("'Brigadoon' Format"). Two weeks later, *Daily Variety* announced Minnelli as the director, and said the film "will be rehearsed in Paris, and shot in Scotland and England" ("Minnelli Assigned"). A month later, Lerner still had plans to "go to Scotland when Arthur Freed's production plans for 'Brigadoon' jell" ("'Brigadoon' to Get Overhaul"). He and Kelly took the overnight train from London to Edinburgh in April 1953, staying at the Caledonian Hotel (Patricia Ward Kelly, personal correspondence, February 25, 2009). Forsyth Hardy recollected:

When we met in Edinburgh [Freed] told me he wanted to find a village in the Highlands which could look unchanged with its inhabitants just awakened after the passage of a hundred years.

I took him first to Culross on the Firth of Forth, explaining that it was not a Highland village but was certainly very little changed since the seventeenth century. The domestic dwellings with their crow-stepped gables, lintel stones carved with initials, and sun-dials on the corners of the houses were right. We travelled northwards, noting the little houses in Cathedral Street, Dunkeld. Comrie, set against the Grampian foothills on the Highland fault, I thought might give him what he wanted, especially as it had an old humpbacked bridge, necessary for the storyline. Braemar, next on the exploratory journey, had the sought-for Highland ambience. Then a long leap west to Inverary, its shoreline buildings well preserved and enjoying a highly picturesque location on the head of Loch Fyne, which I thought would have an appeal for him. He insisted on seeing Brig-o'-Doon, although I assured him it had nothing to do with the Highlands.

Then Arthur Freed went back to Hollywood and declared: "I went to Scotland but I could find nothing that looked like Scotland." (Hardy 1)

For his part Kelly found that there was constant gray weather around Edinburgh, and with the slower film stocks they were using those days it would have been extremely difficult to get proper color. But "we got a promise from the studio to, we could shoot it up in the mountains back of Carmel in California. We had found some places with, that looked *just* like Scotland up in there" (Davis, *Kelly* 49). Schary, however, insisted to Freed that

> television was beating motion pictures to the ground. And we had to budget this thing so low that it had to be all shot on one stage at MGM, which we did. . . . It's true that we lost a lot of our enthusiasm for making the picture, but we, we were professionals, and we, we faced it with, and did the best we could. . . . The first thing that happens is you feel a sense of betrayal. You feel, "Oh, those fellows who promised us the great outdoors now are confining us to a pen." And then you realize that, no, that, that they are just as helpless as we are. (Davis, *Kelly* 49)

CinemaScope was not a good frame for dancers even if it was a good outdoor frame (Patricia Ward Kelly, personal correspondence, February 25,

2009). Thus was introduced to the project a certain "interior" style that pointedly marks the finished product: Minnelli's penchant for intensively designed narrative spaces and his immersion in the history of art, as well as his frequent use of a "self-conscious" or "involved" camera; the trademark MGM devotion to luscious and exorbitant setting and décor, not to mention high quality performance; and a realism contingent upon scenic artists' ability to conjure, inside the soundstages of Hollywood, a touching sense of place.

A further decision was made by executives at MGM (not, as some have suggested, by Freed, Minnelli, or Kelly themselves) that the film would be shot in Anscocolor, for processing at MGM's Metrocolor lab, tests for this process being executed at the studio as of the end of March 1953 (Gillespie-Eiseman Communication).[4] Still in 1954, the Technicolor three-strip process could have been used instead (the Eastman recording stock it involved would be discontinued by Kodak a year later [see Pomerance "Some Limits"]). And Kodak's Eastmancolor negative could have been used as well. Although the General Aniline & Film Corporation was advertising its Ansco process as bearing "Truer color," it remained true that "Ansco Color negatives lacked the resolution and sharpness of Kodak color negatives," as Richard Haines notes (59). Another result of using a color negative process rather than Technicolor's dye printing was a release print that soon began to fade, and that for many years, when viewed either in direct projection or through the agency of a commercially sold tape, gave yellowed and faded images. By the late 1960s and 1970s, the mists of the "Highlands" were smoky and acrid looking, the hills sere and tawny as one might expect to find in Arizona, all of these fading effects owing to the quality of the prints that were originally struck, that is, to the wearing of the color stock to which the negative had been contact-printed, not to the original Ansco Color negative itself. The camera negative recorded Minnelli's production with stunning fidelity; and anyone who treats herself to a viewing of the DVD, which was made by direct transfer from that negative (Richard Haines, personal correspondence), will see nothing less than a fabulous world of variegated greens and blues and purples, with hillsides awash in lavender heather and crags falling away into the darkest emeralds and jades, not to mention a silvery lake winking at a population dressed and dancing in every conceivable tartan. This is the "COLOUR beauty of the Highlands!!" as the British pressbook touted. The nocturnal "Chase" sequence alone—in which to the tattoo of rumbling underbeats the villagers scour the woods for Harry Beaton, who has announced he will leave Brigadoon—is one of the preeminent examples of saturated color cinematography in the history of the medium, with the forests of Brigadoon gleaming in the darkness around the rushing river, a fleeing stag, and tartan-clad Harry being tracked by the heroic Kelly in his forest green viyella shirt covering a flaming crimson T-shirt.[5] Yet at the same time it is a pure form of dance in CinemaScope, through which format "everything has changed. . . . The dance becomes a chase, the chase becomes a dance" (Burdeau 206; 207; my translation).

Perhaps it is not surprising that *Brigadoon* has raised the hackles of many critics for pandering to myths and received notions about Scotland. One viewer estimated it "the zenith of Scottish kitsch" (Martin 140). The film is seen as a mere hollow construction serving contemporary cultural and commercial ends rather than reflecting sophisticated truths about the real Scotland or Scots heritage (see for example the particularly vituperative Colin McArthur; or even well-meaning David Martin-Jones, who cannot refrain from pointing to this and other films' use of "tired mythical images" [102]). The film, wrote Anita Schmaltz recently, is set "in a concocted Technicolor plaid-clad Garden of Eden with a 'puppet show' residue . . . the residents of *Brigadoon* look like the love children of Mother Goose and a Scotsman's caricature . . . song-belting, taffy-stretching, kilt-wearing, unnervingly happy folk." Colin McArthur takes a distanced view of the film as having been influenced throughout by the commercializing and misrepresentational tendencies of Kailyard and Tartanry. And reviewing when the film was released, Bosley Crowther pronounced, "It does look artificial." *Time* archly called it a "Scotch-potch," with "the village green set in by hand, the sheep marcelled like chorus girls, the cottages authentic from the dew on the thatch to the sweat on the hob, and even the cricket on the hearth selected for what sounds like a Scottish burr" ("New Pictures").

John Brown notes the angry attacks that have been mounted on *Brigadoon* by people within Scotland itself:

There is a profound distaste for what might be called the infrastructure of [the film]: for the way the Scots are insistently portrayed as quaint and old-fashioned, comically innocent or comically cunning, and for the way the country is characterized as no more than a natural paradise of romanticized mountain, loch and glen. This is made worse by the consistent thematic use of "Scotland" as being superior to the real modern world, sophisticated and industrialized, by which the natural paradise is blessedly untouched—how fortunate these peasants are, to be close to the land and the sea and the eternal verities, to be free of materialism, class conflict and other neuroses. (41)

All this with passionate ire, even though any film fiction at all could be subjected to precisely the same complaints by any who might choose to see themselves represented in it.

The Scots had been irritated with Freed and Kelly even on their early visit to scout for locations. When the two men gave an interview in Glasgow, Freed got angry because the journalists were dressing them down for presuming to know all about Scotland after spending only two days there (Patricia Ward Kelly, personal correspondence, February 25, 2009), it apparently never having occurred to the Scots that what Kelly and Freed did "know all about" was making cinematic musicals, for which it was necessary to create a space more mythical than historical. Kelly, at any rate, later suspected that Freed's motive for the Scotch trip was to put himself in a position to go back and report to Minnelli that Scotland was too expensive for a location (Kelly correspondence).

While critical sniping has proliferated about this film, very little has been written in depth about the actual effect of watching it, an effect that depends largely on the viewer accepting the filmmakers' constructions as a phenomenal, not a noumenal Scotland, a Scotland not *as it is* (or can be claimed to be, by any advocate) but one designed entirely and only to be apprehended. The "claim to represent or exemplify" that is attached so frequently to Hollywood films is a feature of the paradigm through which watchers read them, not a feature of the films themselves. To persist in taking the movie screen as a window on the world—indeed, a magical window, since it can show a world gone by or a world to come—is to fall prey not only to the pressures of an unending critique, which would point out every one of the myriad ways in which the productions turn away from historical "reality," but also to the deflations of sincere disappointment, the images turning out with truly disturbing frequency *not* to be visions of the world at all. In experiencing this film, the fact that *Brigadoon* isn't really Scotland isn't really alarming. Indeed, it's essential to the delight of the fiction. If real Scotland doesn't come and go every hundred years; and if the people who live there don't manage to live forever, still we can wish it could be so.

Like Tommy Albright, I will return to Brigadoon, after a short divagation that bears intrinsically upon my regard for it. The issue, indeed, is the viewer's mode of regard.

Interlude: Subjunctive Sights

Jonathan Crary writes that between 1810 and 1840 models of subjective vision emerged. The rendering of vision became "faulty, unreliable, and, it was sometimes argued, arbitrary" (12). Nevertheless, in that vulnerable subjectivity it was not necessary to suspect what one saw while one was seeing it. Lookers take looking seriously, even if there are good reasons for not doing so. Perhaps after ages of looking to understand and navigate, humans have learned to conclude that considering sight indeterminate is unproductive.

Of all images, those in cinema press their directness and "realism" with exceptional force. Three aspects of the cinematic image tend toward lending a quality of "reality," "directness," or "presence" in the face of "unreliable" vision. First, blemish and purity. Just like what can be seen with the unaided eye (seen, at any rate, by persons with normal vision: Nabokov describes how for poor myopic Franz in *King, Queen, Knave*, who has just replaced his shattered glasses, "the haze dissolved. The unruly colors of the universe were confined once more to their official compartments and cells" [45]), the film image normally appears relatively free of grain. At least for extended spates of time, it is clear of dust, embedded celluloid skivings,[6] or other optical imperfections. Thus the viewer's possible direct perception of an artificial layer standing intermediate between him and the depicted world—say, the chemical grain in the photographic emulsion—is diminished, finally for all intents and purposes extinguished, by advancements in film chemistry, processing techniques, and projection. Screen images come to be viewed as immediate and direct presentations of something tangible (even when the images represent altered subjectivities, such as alcoholic perception in Billy Wilder's *The Lost Weekend* [1945], drug-induced euphoria in Ken Russell's *Altered States* [1980], or alien eyesight in John McTiernan's *Predator* [1987]). In films that show subjective perceptual warping—nightmares, hallucinations, shocks, panics, and the like (for instance, Matt Reeves's *Cloverfield* [2008])—the perceptual exaggeration of the image is usually dissolved into the diegesis: the viewer considers himself to have direct and undisturbed access to a *character's* transmuted vision, due to factors or circumstances adduced in the plot, and does not read the transmutation as applying to himself by way of the projection that is before him. The presumption in viewing is that all images *as images* are as perfect as they can be, thus, that image workers have offered an ideal rather than an arbitrarily constructed vision that suits the needs of producers, technicians, and performers (not to say the exigencies of the moment). Of course, what they have offered is precisely an arbitrary construction, a negotiation meant to be satisfying to viewers but manageable on the producer's wallet. To purvey the ideal on a day-to-day basis would put them out of business.

It bears upon cinema spectatorship that most people who go to the movies do not know much about the structure, composition, or history of imagery, and recognize onscreen more or less what they are told to recognize by the advance publicity. When they have been prepared for a "sweeping panoramic vision," or for something that "isn't human yet," or for "amazing 3D," or for "the entertainment experience of a lifetime," that is what they see. With *Avatar* (2009), for example, customers were led to believe they would see authentic 3D, and many believe they did, although of course the screen remained flatter than the three-dimensional world in which it existed: what they saw was planes of focus with heightened contrast. With *Hugo* (2011), Martin Scorsese's publicists promised "an extraordinary adventure"—a prize easier to deliver (Scorsese goes much further). If publicists and critics rave that a film presents a "stunning vision," viewers are stunned, this through such a thoroughgoing pedagogy that it is difficult for many to be stunned unless they have been told they would be. Having no trouble believing as they watch it that the screen image fundamentally replicates in clarity their unaided vision, film viewers see what looks to them like a picture of the world, one only occasionally distorted or warped by blatant effects (such as the facial makeup, thick as Van Gogh's impasto, in Roland Emmerich's *Anonymous* and Clint Eastwood's *J. Edgar* [both 2011]). Yet the crispness of sight unhampered by blurs, color shifts, unintended glare, and so on is not a natural condition but has been cultured to some extent by motion picture experience. (If movies do not exactly look like real life, real life is often thought to look like movies.) While the materiality of the cinematic medium is not generally taken to occlude the viewer's perception, this is largely because most viewers are incompetent to judge the occlusion.[7]

Innocence of constructive techniques thus helps to make for cinematic "real"ness. Secondly, consider size. At least in conventional theatrical projection, the image is notably large in relation to the perceiver's own body, occupying almost all of his visual field. The projected screen image thus fills in more of the visual field than such material as is represented there would occupy in everyday life in its real size. The image thus becomes a monument. Given the power engendered by absolute image size, the bounding frame of the exhibition space is easier to disattend than to incorporate. Easier still is to reduce the status of that frame to that of a denigrated slave merely serving to augment attention to the image. The image then becomes not only paramount but overwhelming, as William James suggests: "Other objects whisper doubt or disbelief; but the object of passion makes us deaf to all but itself, and we affirm it unhesitatingly. Such objects are the delusions of insanity, which the insane person can at odd moments steady himself against, but which again return to sweep him off his feet. Such are the revelations of mysticism" (309).

Beyond innocence of technique and the absolute size of film images is a third factor, light. In theaters, the screened image is discreetly luminous. "Sensible vividness or pungency," writes James, "is . . . the vital factor" (301). Because of the general darkness of the auditorium, the brilliance of the screen is special in and of itself.[8] With the advent of home and computerized viewing, where films can be watched on ever smaller screens and in environments that obtrude more and more into the field of vision, the "reality" of filmic imagery is vulnerable to recession and diminution (see Pomerance "Wings"): the more social and political experience is apprehended by way of images, and such small images, the more its reality and significance seems to diminish as well. With or without special effects, any film will come to look increasingly constructed (or at least irrelevant) in comparison with the relatively lively surround, and so it is that blocking out the surround becomes a relevant feature of film screening. It may be impossible for any viewer inculcated at an early age with the stunning experience of seeing images on a large screen in a darkened space—a space, further, filled with strangers who have come away from their privacies in order to share these delights (see Arlen)—to produce an intense gaze at a hand-held screen. But whatever rapture one can experience with hand-held or computerized cinema is entirely an achieved one—exactly as it always had been, but now in the face of a technology that tends to play against such achievement rather than with the flow of a technology that was designed to facilitate and enhance it (see Gomery; Belton *Widescreen*). More popular in the age of the hand screen is a flitting, fractured, casual, and motile attention that intercalates instants of film viewing with other business in a kind of experiential multiplexing.

Film offers a world "out there," subject to continual and active study and fascination, as Crary indicates through his discussion of entoptical phenomena—"particles, specks, and other tiny aggregations suspended in the fluid medium of the vitreous humor of the eye, often called *mouches volantes*"—that for him evidence William James's selective attention, which "excludes from consciousness sensations that are non-referential, that are irrelevant to knowledge about the world" (215–16). Speaking of descriptive rather than narrative literary moments in his beautiful essay, "The Reality Effect," Roland Barthes shows a similar fascination for the "irrelevant" and the "non-referential." Our tendency is to call urgency, engagingness, and reference presented together in unity, "reality."

If cinema has a tendency to seem real, however, one can know that it is not. A useful way of resolving this paradox is through a *subjunctive mode of attention*. Rather than proclaiming, "This *is*," one can say, "If this were, it would appear in this way." Not, "There is a world that is being represented directly" but "If the world were such as we are now asked to believe, this is how it would look." I mean something different here than Stanley Cavell invokes when of Hitchcock's *Vertigo* he writes, "We are made to share the hero's quasi-hallucinatory, quasi-necrophilic quest *in the realm of the subjunctive* for the woman he imagines dead" ("What Becomes" 180, my emphasis). His subjunctive, in this case, is a narrative subset, a paradigm of belief unfolding from within the narrative (and possibly, of course, inspiring echoes in the viewership). I mean to suggest a tentative mode of perception that is more frequent among audiences than among film characters; a reliance upon maps that are hypothetical, not actual and functional in geographic territories. Scottie Ferguson is trying to find among the living someone "he imagines dead," but in watching the "reality effect" in cinema we are trying to find in conditional depictions an unconditional truth.

What subjunctive attention makes possible is an experiential linkage between two "realisms," that of a social drama—*Grand Hotel* (1932), *The Mortal Storm* (1940), *The Heiress* (1949), *The Man in the Gray Flannel Suit* (1956), *Cool Hand Luke* (1967), *Annie Hall* (1977), *Ordinary People* (1980), *Good Will Hunting* (1997), *The Notebook* (2004), *The Squid and the Whale* (2005), *The Reader* (2008)—and that of a fantasy, like *The Last Airbender* (2010) or *Pinocchio* (1940). In both sorts of cases, the "if" can be invoked. For a somewhat extreme case, take Michael Bay's *Transformers* (2006), a film about giant mechanical robotic entities encountering one another in battle here on Earth, with the benevolent interference of a nerdy California teenager: viewers aren't asked to believe that transformers exist, but simply to watch as though *if they did they would look and behave as they can here be seen looking and behaving*. In respect of their believability, the transformers are hardly different than Claudette Colbert and Clark Gable in *It Happened One Night* (1934): not that this man and woman really did meet on a bus one night in this way but that, *if a man should have met a woman one night on a bus,* this is how *one may reasonably believe* they could have behaved together. He might string up a blanket in the bedroom they are forced to share, in order that she could dress herself in "privacy." As there is nothing exclusive about subjunctive attention, it opens the way for multiple renderings. Orson Welles (1953), Paul Scofield (1971), James Earl Jones (1974), Patrick Magee (1976), Michael Hordern (1982), Laurence Olivier (1983), Ian Holm (1998), Brian Blessed (1999), Michel Piccoli (2007), and Ian McKellen (2008) were each, equally and believably for a moment, King Lear, which is to say; if a king existed in England at such and such a time, with three daughters, and who carved up his domain, and who went mad in a storm, *this* is what he might have looked and sounded like, this Welles, this Olivier, this McKellen . . .

Our way of perceiving subjunctively offers the chance to open the imagination with certain technical constraints. "This place" apparently appearing is always "that place," one that might conceivably appear. Viewing is a continually unfolding assent to possibility and plausibility, not actuality. Given the possibility of existence, a viewer can be led to agree to the features of a design when nothing in the presentation works to contradict the proposition of presence, immediacy, and form. Further, regardless of the structure of the world presented on film, the very fact that it is presented and the nature of its presentation are accepted as paramount and taken for granted by viewers, who find delight, one must suppose, simply in this presentability. Most of the time I do not stop in the middle of a film and say, "Wait! This looks only like the sort of place one sees in films, as though it has been filmed by a movie camera!" When I am watching film there is no such thing as film—not, at least, film of the sort I am watching. (People in films often watch a film-within-the-film, which is altogether a different sort of film.)[9]

To actually believe as one watches a film that there exists now, here, in front of us, a world subtending the appearance we apprehend, may be to go beyond cinema; but audiences do that, too. The pungency, the directness, the swollen pith of the presentation are all engulfing. Always the subjunctivity of the cinematic tale contends with its perceptual quality, with the fact that it can be made to appear more or less "real." Every enunciation, "Imagine that because you have permitted it, a tale like this is being told to you . . ." struggles against, "Look! Here! This exists!" If we sense ourselves to be at a distance, knowing that the movie isn't constituting or depicting the reality of a life, still, of all art forms cinema is the one that riddles that proposition most excitingly and disturbingly. Humphrey Bogart telling Ingrid Bergman on the tarmac at Casablanca that if she doesn't get on the plane she'll regret it, "Maybe not today, maybe not tomorrow, but soon, and for the rest of your life," all this in riddling black and white and as the camera rests upon Bogie's face with his moist eyes and then cuts to hers with her moist eyes and with that stunning hat sweeping across her brow like a horizon of the future: they are so real, yet, as we fully know, Rick and Ilsa are phantoms; this is not the actual Humphrey Bogart or the actual Ingrid Bergman, not the man whose marriage was driving him to the bottle or the woman whose illicit love would later condemn her in Hollywood; and seeing this I am not at an airport, not in Casablanca, not—while watching this screen—in the middle of that war. Bogie and Bergman seem like people would seem to be if the world they lived in was just such a place as this Casablanca seems to be, a world in which one's gaze, like a restless bird, could swoop into a man's face . . . or in which giants trod the earth. And yet: look! . . .

Setting and Ambiguous Engagement

The setting of *Brigadoon* works as a vivacious and active participant in the goings-on, not only backing and grounding the action of characters in a narratively believable if completely subjunctive zone but also looming forward into the audience's attention as an active form itself. The film immediately escorts the viewer to a strange and transcendent locale, which may be called, for better or worse, the Highlands of Scotland, or else the "Highlands of Scotland," since it is persistently evident, from the meticulous placement with a decorator's taste of every tree and every clump of heather, that all of what is given to be seen is an evocation of a spacious outdoors scene that has been carefully recreated in the closed space of a studio. Yet so sweeping and perfectly executed is the vision that it never ceases to persuade the viewer of its freshness and natural allure. It is always, in other words, both set and place, both the work of a scenic designer and an apparently actual spot. In describing it through these antinomies, I immediately raise one important way in which this locale is "strange," "uncanny," or "*unheimlich*," namely that as one observes it the reading of "reality" is torn between two points of commitment. First, refined techniques have been used to render artificial scenery credible as actuality. Secondly,

in the looking itself the gaze fixes not on pictures of mountains but on
mountains themselves. The forwardness of the setting urges (substantial)
consideration, while its meticulous execution blurs the line between artistry and nature.

Blue mountains these are, rising beside a long silvery lake that trails
away in the misty distance, while the camera, tracking back and leftward,
reveals leafless trees and a hillock of wild ground covered with heather.
Dissolve to a rightward tracking shot, where some steep and substantial mossy crags, lush and green, dropping down into a misty crevice,
background our protagonists who seem lost in a confusing tangle of
undergrowth: Jeff, dressed in a gray tweed suit, staring around with consternation, and Tommy, who has stepped forward and is looking upward,
his tan jacket, brown fedora, and knapsack tilted back casually and a rifle
loose in his hand. Dissolve to a copse of trees, still on the hillside, with a
flock of cooing pigeons fluttering around, and the camera pans right to
a hump-backed stone bridge arched over a gurgling stream full of twinkly appeal. As the camera cranes upward, sunlight that has apparently
emerged from behind a cloud begins to gild this stream and the stones of
the little bridge, then discovers a pair of tawny longhorns. One of these
leaps to his feet, looks at the camera without interest, turns away. In yet
another shot of darkened branches the warm gilding sun sweeps across
the field of sight, and the camera cranes up to show flowers and a cloud
of green and pink mist. When the mist clears, cozy little structures of the
village of Brigadoon can be seen, the quirky inhabitants met one by one as
they rise to the sunny morning.

This panorama segues into an energetic market scene with the people
of Brigadoon walking toward, then reveling inside, MacConnachy Square:
singing and dancing citizens, in contrasting tartans, leading a pony cart
along a rough scrub path to bring a heifer for sale, bearing baskets of wool or
leafy vegetables, carrying piglets in their arms—"Whenever we see the little girl with the pigs during the MacConnachy Square number it would be
nice to have some pig squeals," wrote Arthur Freed's assistant Lela Simone
(Simone to Steinere)—or hauling braces of wild fowl; young and old citizens, bearded and smooth, hefting bundles of sticks, kegs of whiskey, with
a herd of black-faced sheep chased by a collie; all set against a woodland
and with what seems a never-ending view of those rolling heather-covered
hills. The village square itself sits in front of a turquoise lake and vast sun-
drenched hillsides. By the time the opening song, "Come Ye to the Fair,"
is in full (and, in typical Broadway style, rhythmic) swing, there are some

forty joyous cast members in action in the clearing between the cottages with their thatched roofs. Dyeing wool and weaving, pulling taffy, dairying, and gossiping, the joyously singing dancers seem bound up in limitless commitment to the workaday pleasures of their pastoral community, but the viewer's attention, hardly uninterested in their pulsing chant and gymnastic fervor, cannot quite attach itself to the scale of local happenings—the buying and selling, the talking, the casual introduction of the boy and girl who are to be married today (or of the boy's rival for the girl's affections), the shifting of animals, the expressions of satisfaction and curiosity that each performer deftly flashes upon her face—because of a passionate interest in the fabulous place where these goings-on are going on.

Later, in that ballet *pas de deux*, "Heather on the Hill," the contrast between foreground action and background intensification is heightened still more. As Tommy woos Fiona in the hills near Brigadoon, the expansive and emotional dancing—iconized by her flaring dress as she turns and by his upward climb through the blossoms with arms outstretched—is arranged against long loden promontories. Tommy races after Fiona and an enormous swath of lush magenta heather recedes behind his footsteps. Behind them, as they hold hands, the light green of a rolling hillside is covered with what seems an endless rash of heather. The camera pans and they are suddenly dancing in total absorption with one another while, at the same time, it is impossible to move one's eyes from the yawning surface of that lake extended like a silver finger between steep furrowed mountains and receding as far as can be seen. Loch Ness is this kind of lake, and Loch Lochy, Loch Loyne, Loch Garry, Loch Arkaig . . .

In this sequence, Kelly's choreography is designed in a number of ways to work with the particular technical features of the décor, as rendered through the anamorphic lens (that was required for the CinemaScope process).[10] He and Charisse are almost always moving across the (very wide) screen, with the extension of an arm or the bend of the torso indicating the direction in which they intend to head. The dance is given a sense of expansiveness, matching the sweeping background. But because the painted backing is hung circularly in the studio, it is also possible for the dancers to change direction or for the camera to move around them, all the while keeping the "Highlands" present and focused in the background. Cinematographer Joseph Ruttenberg recollected,

We had one scene . . . built on a stage 360 feet long and 150 feet wide. And Minnelli wanted to make it all in one, the scene all in one shot. And with a

boom, we had to go from one end of the stage to the other end, and then
turn the camera around, continue our shooting, and shoot back towards the
other direction, all in one shot. And you've got many problems—lighting,
boom, movements, and many others. This took one week to prepare, but I
was very proud of that shot. (Davis, *Ruttenberg* 84)

While it is always advantageous in screen choreography to minimize edits,
screen dancing almost always seems a little contrived, placed inside a manufactured set. This effect is mitigated by only the most superlative dancers,
whose style and technique take the eye away from scenic detail. In this
routine, because the dance moves are so elegantly harmonized with a moving camera in a set that can withstand all this motion without breaking
apart into its constituent components, the sense of movement in place is
never interrupted.

Further, even more than Charisse's opulent orange skirt and Kelly's rich
dark green shirt tend to alternately blend with and then suddenly separate
from the colors of George Gibson's backing, Kelly has arranged it so that
Charisse frequently leans back or bends over with a leg out, in a classical
ballet pose that seems inadvertently to mimic the lines of the hills that
Gibson has painted. The dancers appear to be "at home in" the landscape,
then, because as graphic figures they are actually merging and remerging
with it from one moment to the next.

A full appreciation of *Brigadoon* calls for some attention to this scenic
backing and the man who created it.

The Gibson Technique

As a young Glaswegian during the 1920s, George Gibson (1904–2001)
was a student at the Edinburgh College of Art and studied further with
the scenic designer William E. Glover. He worked in Wolverhampton and
elsewhere as a theatrical scenic painter in an era when the technique of the
painted stage backing was as yet in its infancy. By the early 1930s he had
moved himself to Hollywood, where, having begun work at Twentieth
Century-Fox, he met forerunners of the California scene painting movement, including Phil Dike and Millard Sheets. By 1934 he was at MGM,
and four years later, under the mentorship of Cedric Gibbons—"He gathered around himself competent people and gave them almost complete
autonomy" (A. Arnold Gillespie, qtd. in Heisner 63)—he became head of

the scenic design department there, specializing in backdrops "so realistic that the audience didn't realize the setting was on a soundstage, which was the goal of the studio" (Blake 2). It was not long before the demanding and erudite Gibbons estimated Gibson "an extremely valuable man and one that cannot easily be replaced" (Gibbons to Spencer). Gibson was responsible for the scenic backings for a huge number of films at MGM, notably among them the cornfield vista of *The Wizard of Oz* (1939) and the marvelous green-skied alien environment in *Forbidden Planet* (1956) (see Heisner 93, 105).

The idea of the scenic backing—that Gibson was instrumental in developing—involved a two-dimensional extension of the built set, a form of constructed geotopical environment. Because even the smallest backings depict considerably more space than can be framed by the lens, the painting itself suggests not so much an artifice as a world, yawning without frame beyond the confining aesthetic limits of the picture. Backings were painted on canvas sized with a cornstarch-and-water mixture, then strapped or screwed to long beams that were strung from the rafters of the soundstage. Often finished backings are appreciably immense, curving around the corners of the stage and thus contributing to the "limitless" aspect of the cinematic vision. The paint employed, report Scarfone and Stillman,

> was a type of watercolor made of ground, dry pigment mixed with a glue binding to create a sort of poster paint. (The powdered color was requisitioned by the pound from paint companies.) Gelatin glue in dry chips of about 1/8-inch thick and no more than two inches square were put into a double boiler. The pigment was added to the mix until the color ran a certain thread consistency, formed a bead, and dropped down into a paint bucket. This was the only way to tell if the amount of glue was sufficient or needed tempering. The general recipe for backing paint was a teacup of glue to a gallon of water. The paint itself was 60-to-70 percent dry color to 40 percent water, mixed in 5-gallon crocks. [After the 1930s] huge quantities of paint were mixed in the 100-gallon drums on [MGM] Lot 3, which had a paint shop to accommodate its own huge backing around the water tank used for miniatures at sea. (129–30)

A well-executed backing has no point of focus (since that would distract from any shot composed upon it and would thus severely limit compositional possibilities), and is lit homogeneously and intensively with a bank of sky-pans—neutral or cold fixtures embedded in dish-shaped reflectors that spread the light evenly across a surface. (MGM had a policy of using very high-key lighting, so as to make films that could play to audiences even in theaters with poor projection [Heisner 58].) Any lighting "effects" intended for the "environment" of the shot—sunset, for example—are either painted into the backing in the first place or created additionally on set through the use of additional lights possibly equipped with filters.

The lay viewer of motion pictures, who is often predisposed to give the scenic backing a mere glance and to take it as a "natural" or "automatic" part of the presentation, might be astonished to discover the depth and complexity of the problem it raised for scenic designers and workers through limitations to their materials. In an extensive memorandum in March of 1954, Gibson made it clear to his supervisor Cedric Gibbons, and to executives at MGM, why the paints they had been using until then were far from suitable for backdrop work. Gibson needed, said he, to procure a type of paint which would:

1. Be easy to mix, match and work as easily as watercolor.
2. Be as easy to spray, spatter and blend as casein or rubber type paint.
3. Be impervious to spoilage and its ensuing waste.
4. Remove the need for matching and rematching colors periodically on work which covered an extended period of time.
5. Eliminate double mixing of two mediums and the taping and masking of areas which would be subject to painting in two mediums.
6. Have complete flexibility, softness, coverage and adherence, thereby adding to the life of the backing, which would be less subject to cracking and mutilation of surfaces due to handling.
7. Dry with the same or similar characteristics of watercolor.
8. Make it possible to mix and work on stages where heat or hot water is not easily available and which is necessary where water-color is employed.
9. Have as little effect on the purity of the colors when mixed. (while glue is an excellent binder it does have some dulling effect on color although not nearly so much as casein or rubber binder.) (Gibson with Hill)

Gibson was being sensitive to the fact that backings were not sufficiently resistant to rough handling or to the wear and tear that resulted from frequent reuse; that a good all-purpose paint "handling just as easily as a *brushed color* or as a *sprayed color*" was still, by the early 1950s, unavailable; that presently, as paints cooled off, their glue sizing was jelling or hardening; and that spoilage of the glue being used as a binder had a bad effect on color (Gibson with Hill). As a master of scenic painting at MGM, then, Gibson was not only executing designs on canvas but also continuously evaluating the materials and painting process toward finding economical improvements. Some paints that were fine for brushing didn't work in the atomizing spray guns for covering vast sky areas, and vice versa. Much of the paint degraded, or dried to a different color, or stiffened. The actual labor involved in producing the backings was therefore intensive, complicated, and constantly aggravating in one way or another.[11]

Scenic art, Gibson reflected in an interview with Donald Knox (who used part of the material in his book *The Magic Factory*, about Minnelli's *An American in Paris*), is "one of the very oldest art professions in the amusement industry . . . because it began in the early renaissance. . . . Even Michelangelo, you could say, was a scenic artist" (Knox 951). Gibson cites such artists of the seventeenth and eighteenth centuries as Maria Oriana Galli Bibiena (1656–1749) and Giovanni Batista Piranesi (1720–1778). At MGM, under the guidance of Gibbons and with the full support of studio production manager Joseph J. Cohn, Gibson brought scenic painting to the point where it "overcame all expectations" (952). He reports that Gibbons told him scenic art "would become a thing in itself. It deserved as much feature as the set deserved. The only thing we couldn't do is to put a bird in there flying around or an animal or another man or something like this. We couldn't put life into it, although we did put life to a degree" (952).[12] ("We had to make it believable that the set went on there, and it was done," said Gibson. "It was done to the point where it's been a common happening for birds to try to roost on a barn that was painted on a backing" [953].)

The Gibson team included Ben Carre, "an old-time art director and a man who had worked in pictures from 1908 or something like that" (Knox 970), John Coakley, Harry Tepker, Wayne Hill, and Clark Provins, "all in there, interested, enthusiastic" (970). These painters had to work with consultants Henri Jaffa and Al Eiseman to determine the relationship between what colors looked like on the canvas and how they would appear when transformed through the photographic process, always knowing that the laboratory could and would make color corrections to please the director. Further, decisions might always be made on set to increase the key lighting on the star, a move that would shift the relative intensity of illumination on the backing and possibly alter its finished look in the film (950).

Previous to and in the early stages of *Oz*, painters made backings on the soundstage itself. "We painted them right in place," Gibson said (947). "We had a scaffold devised . . . these backings were about 40 feet high . . . scaffold was on five levels . . . we had to have one of these power machines, high lifts, to move the scaffold" (Fordin). There had been a "paint frame," a stable and accessible giant easel setup, on Stage 6 for some time in the early sound years, and it had been used intensively in the filming of Robert Z. Leonard's *The Great Ziegfeld* (1936). After that picture, however, the apparatus was dismantled. Working afterward with scaffolding made it difficult to maintain control of what a number of artists, spread vertically and horizontally away from one another, were doing as they worked simultaneously at various points of the grid outline that was their guide (see Scarfone and Stillman 126). Toward the end of the *Oz* production, Gibson complained to his boss, "Look, this is absolutely ridiculous to try to work under this condition. We have to have a building" (Knox 1001).

Working closely with the architect Martin McArthur and Norwegian designer John Bossert, and completely supported by Gibbons in the undertaking, Gibson designed and oversaw the building of a new MGM paint frame, housed in the Scenic Art Department adjacent Stage 14, and opened on Christmas 1939 (see Scarfone and Stillman 127, 129). The cost of construction was around $85,000 (Knox 1003).[13] This is a two-story building about one hundred and thirty feet long, fifty feet wide, and about ninety-five feet high. "At each end of this big oblong building would be windows. The whole wall would be a window so that we had daylight" (Knox 989). Strung from the rafters is a mixture of incandescent and fluorescent light, so that any lighting condition can be simulated (the color of different lights affects the way the eye registers and interprets the color of paint or filmed material, with daylight being relatively blue, incandescent light being relatively yellow, and fluorescent light being cyan-green).[14] The painters' atelier is on the second floor of this building, reachable by a slow-moving cast-iron elevator big enough to hold three very thin people not quite comfortably. On the ground floor underneath, backings up to a hundred feet long are stored in rolls, with the cloth (sprayed with sodium pentachlorophenol fungicide [Horning communication]) screwed between two pieces of wood and rolled eight or nine inches in diameter (955). Through long slits in the floor of the atelier, unpainted canvas from below is hauled upward by electric motors in front of the painters' eyes as they stand working at floor level. The sky is painted first and then, as the canvas is slowly raised, the horizon and the territory beneath. The studio's length accommodates three canvas frames each forty feet tall and a hundred feet long, one forty feet high and sixty feet long, and one forty by forty, but Gibson noted that the MGM group had painted backings as high as sixty-four feet high by extending the frames (955). Virtually all the painters who were young trainees at the time of *Brigadoon* graduated later to television, where some are still working, and the MGM paint frame is still in use at Sony Entertainment with artists making drops as big as ever.[15]

All aspects of the paint frame building were designed with studio efficiencies in mind. For one example, the canvases when fully raised hung within eighteen inches of the floor. When a backing was completed, the grip department had no trouble just lifting the canvas off its frame and down onto the floor, for easy transportation to the relevant soundstage (Knox 974–75). Hanging the canvas on its frame and removing it when it was finished were always matters for the grip department, as was delivering and mounting the backing so it would be ready for principal photography. The canvas material that would become the backing was muslin sheeting bought in three-yard widths. "They had these tremendous sewing machines downstairs," said Gibson,

and they would sew these things together in nothing flat. The sewing machines were in the grip department in what they called the sewing room. In the making of motion pictures there is a need for a great deal of sewing in the way of gobos, tarps and backings and all kinds of things, so they would fabricate the backing in the sewing room to whatever the dimensions would be and, naturally, nothing over 100 feet because that was all we could put on a frame at any one time and length, and then they would bring them up, and we would have the battens on the frame, and they would be tacked to the battens and a sandwich batten put on top. They would be tightened up a little bit, very lightly, and tacked up down the sides of the frame, and then we would prepare them with a size . . . usually a cornstarch size much like the paste that you sprinkle your shirt with when you iron it . . . sort of a lightly viscous starch which in turn filled the fabric and laid down the knap and prepared a nice surface from which we could work. We could draw easily, and we could paint easily on it. (971–72)

Working with Minnelli was challenging for Gibson because the filmmaker didn't say a lot. Gibson recollected, in fact, that it helped to be a "mind-reader" to know what the filmmaker wanted. While it is always problematic to speak of origins, the vision in the backing may have germinated from Minnelli's studies. Asked by Charles Bitsch and Jean Domarchi in 1957 if it wasn't true that on *Brigadoon* he had been influenced by Dutch painting for his interiors and English Romantic painters for the exteriors, he said, "Exactly. A good part of my use of color in *Brigadoon* comes from English painters I was able to study who represented Scottish landscapes: in all of these pictures one keeps finding exactly these colors bordering on yellow, a certain treatment of the sky, an atmosphere" (10; my translation). The foremost of the English Romantics—Gainsborough, Constable, Turner—painted almost exclusively in England (and some painters voyaged to northern Wales), but for historical views of the Highlands Minnelli could very well have interested himself in the work of the fifth son of the landscape artist Edward Williams (1782–1855), Sidney Richard Williams (1821–1886), who, to distinguish himself from his five brothers— each an accomplished landscapist as their father had been—went by the name of Sidney Richard Percy.[16] His *Highland Landscape*, represented in Jan Sterling's catalog of the work of the Williams Family, shows the dappled waters of a typical mountain lake and just the sort of tumultuous twists of verdure and tufts of cloud over the high hills that show up in Gibson's backing.

Minnelli's taciturnity was understandable. A director is often bombarded with suggestions while he is trying to work out his own method for a film. In this case, the filmmaker had been sent fulsome letters, over a period of several weeks, by Iain F. Anderson, assistant secretary for administration of the Scottish Tourist Board, who saw it as his task, unbidden, to furnish copious notes about the details of Scottish life: "Thinking of outdoor scenes, and keeping in mind that you have such geological formations not dissimilar in California I thought these [photographs] might be of interest" (June 10, 1952); "This is the bridge over the River Doon just outside Ayr, within 200 yards of Burns's cottage. It is quite in keeping on a smaller scale i.e. not so wide in arch, as would be the stone bridge to the 'Brigadoon' of the film" (July 16, 1952). In March of 1952, further, J. B. Atkinson, a photographer with the Scottish Tourist Board, had written to inquire,

Do you want strictly Lowland features or would you like pictures of Highlands as well including pipers and mountains and thatched cottages? I want to help you, but there is within its 200 odd mile length such variety of ancient cultural remnants, that I ought to know which type of Scottish terrain you wish to use most! What I have in mind for you is: Tartan—dancing and piping—mountains and thatched cottages—pine trees and rushing rivers—spinning wheels and tweed and so on.

Gibson knew how to handle the situation.

I was a Scot, and I knew Scotland, so I did a bunch of set backing sketches which carried a feeling of Scotland. Well, despite all of the attitudes that had been discussed à la Arthur Rackham, the English illustrator of fairy tales ... they had discussed a lot of ways to do this but the thing that became the most acceptable to Minnelli was a Scotsman's sketches ... from there we just went from one thing to another. . . .

[Preston Ames] had this big mound, the heather on the hill set. Meanwhile, he's doing the village, and he's doing all these other things. I'm trying to catch up with sketches for backings, not sets ... he was doing sets. He was taking my backing, and he was having the illustrator use the backing, of course, using the set for the feeling of the thing. . . . We had about 7 or 8 hundred feet of backing, and it ran all the way up to 40 or 45 feet high, I think, but that was the way Minnelli worked. (Knox 978)[17]

Discussing the film in 1972 with Hugh Fordin, Gibson recalled that

the big problem we had was the heather. You see, heather is small, the texture of heather is small, and of course they couldn't get enough stuff that would look like heather, so we wound up painting sumac purple to represent purple heather, because when it was back against the backing it resembled heather. Sumac is way out of character for heather, but painting it you had texture and the quality of color for heather. It felt like heather. You can't shoot the normal thing and expect it to work.

Gibson's work makes *Brigadoon* an oneiric vision in which, as Jean Douchet wrote, discussing Minnelli, "living means conquering the world to shape it in the image of one's dream by means of a décor" (Bellour 407). Writing of dreams, Raymond Bellour is convinced of their personality and idiosyncrasy, convinced that they are forms of privacy, and so he concludes that Douchet's appraisal can only mean "taking from others, through theft or destruction, the very nature of their own dreams" (407), quite as though in the cinema, as perhaps in other forms of art, a gravitational force exists that could draw us toward Minnelli's dream and away from our own. Yet, given the publicity of the film image, given the fact

that many strangers at once sit to be involved with it, there might seem
to be truth in imagining that no director's dream is his own exclusively,
and that the dream vision Minnelli plays out upon the screen is already in
some way the viewer's, because it is built of a shared language or iconogra-
phy that reduces experience and expectation to common shapes and signs.
"Even the loveliest young woman is a terrible devouring force, not by her
soul, but by her dreams," Gilles Deleuze had written. "Beware of the other
person's dream, because if you're caught in the other person's dream, you're
screwed" (in Bellour 407).

Yes, but.

The loveliest young girl's dreams and mine are not as different as our
two narcissisms might wish, but are shaped of the same kind of life, which
is life in the world as it is today. I am caught up in her dream no less than
I am already caught up in my own. Or perhaps it should be said that regardless of the shape and content of one's dream—of the dream one's
conceit appropriates to oneself—its décor is not so very personal. To reflect again on the ostensibly idiosyncratic designs of Tony Duquette: they
seem outlandish, alien, overwhelming until on a second look they reveal
the mundane objects of everyday life. Another person's dream—Minnelli's dream—may reside and turn in some inner inaccessible world, yet
its décor is manifest and interpersonal. The embodiment of that décor in
the Gibson backing, that both advanced toward the viewer's imagination
and retreated from it, gave both perspective and weight to the built sets:
the huts and open public space, MacConnachy Square, the charming little
stream, its hump-backed stone bridge, its surrounding forest all built by
the Gibbons crew.[18]

The Gibson backdrops were so powerful that even technical personnel
working on the soundstage, not to say visitors who dropped in, were as-
tounded. "So real," said cinematographer Joseph Ruttenberg.

One woman from Scotland was standing there when we had visitors, she
said, "My it looks exactly like this place in Scotland." And another thing,
when we had the big doors open . . . the birds would fly in toward the set,
where it was lit, and go for the skylight. And they'd (claps hands) hit it like
that and they'd get killed. . . . They'd come so swift and they'd go right for the
backing, thinking it was the sky. (Davis, *Ruttenberg* 84–85)

It was not only for aesthetic and phenomenological reasons that the decision was made to use a painted backdrop rather than, say, a photographic

projection of the actual Highlands of Scotland. Rear projection was in frequent use in 1950s Hollywood. A second unit crew could have been sent to Scotland with instructions to seize background shots of exactly the sort of place that Gibson's drops apparently "looked exactly like." But beyond the fact that rear projection was far from suitable with the CinemaScope process, because Scope exaggerated large grain (Gillespie to Gibbons), it was impossibly difficult as an aesthetic choice for another reason. A passable rear projection composite can be made only if the process plates are projected perpendicularly to the screen, any and all desired angles having been included within them, in reverse, when originally they were shot. Once plates have been made, they cannot be modified. Thus, inexorable constraints would have been placed upon Kelly's choreography, with all the angles planned and rigidly fixed in Scotland before live action was shot in Hollywood. Imagine the stress that would have fallen upon the dancers themselves should any single step have been off-angle to even the slightest degree. As a choreographer and dancer, Kelly was obsessive about precision and accuracy. Rear projection is just not ideal for dance numbers, in which live movement is complex in its relation to the background.

Only a painted backing, and such a backing as George Gibson was able to create, could have aided in fostering for viewers the idea that they were being given unmediated exposure to Scotland itself. That, or at least unmediated exposure to the fantasy of having unmediated exposure.

Finale: A Patriotic View

As conceived by Minnelli, Kelly, and Freed, *Brigadoon* continually and openly reflects the marriage of creative imagination and technical process, a central perplexity and wonder of studio filmmaking. James Walters observes, "*Brigadoon* seems to assert the 'story' traits of its world with particular transparency" (169). It is not a flaw of the film, as so many critics scathingly thought at the time, that viewers are partly conscious of the artificial nature of the setting: "George Gibson's diorama looks like the world's biggest *nature morte* . . . distant lochs glint like silver cardboard, unseen clouds cast static shadows on a flat sea of heather," wrote one carper (Harvey 130, qtd. in Walters 171); "The several ensemble dances . . . seem as calculated as Rockette parades," wrote Bosley Crowther in the *New York Times*; and the *Morning Telegram* grunted that the film was "considerably less than what might have been expected. It is overdone, overlong and overpowering" (Mishkin). To the contrary, Minnelli has carried the delirious artifice of a setting to extremes never before achieved on film. The technical quality of the backdrop painting (and the lighting that illuminates it) is prodigious, and the shots that open a view of it are temporally extended far beyond expectation. Viewers of *Brigadoon* thus have a deliriously mixed sensation of reality and illusion. They are the beneficiaries of the filmmaker's attempt to—in the words of Roger Caillois—"momentarily destroy the stability of perception and inflict a kind of voluptuous panic upon an otherwise lucid mind" (Caillois 23).

Dore Schary wrote to Arthur Freed, "I have just run the set test on *Brigadoon*, which I think is magnificent. . . . I urge you not to make changes that will in any way destroy the simple and illusory quality, which I think is something very special" (Schary to Freed).[19] A Birmingham, Alabama, viewer raved, "It was to me breathtaking to go into the theatre, and forget where you were, and what was going on in this disturbed world" (Stovall to Freed). Viewers seem at once to detect a world of direct presence, the transcendent and ethereal village of the story, and a practical space in which talented effort has been extended to structure a décor and a perspective, effort that includes the choice of palette, the size of the brushstrokes, the choice of vista, the movement of the camera in the choreography, and so on.

> The stage 27 door opened to reveal only the gray expanse of a 50-foot-high cyclorama. We set out, at a fairly rapid stride to walk around it and see what it was like from the front. When we finally emerged at the open end, we were in the kirkyard of old Brigadoon—and a delightful sight it was. At the right was a hill—steep, and topped with a wood. Straight ahead, all in ruins, an old chapel stood. At the left were more highlands. (MacCann)

The *place* that is Brigadoon is always—yet also never—merely the commercial space of MGM's studio and its backing, all utilized to promote a particular observational style and achievement.

Every Hollywood movie operates in this way, placing creative technique and budgetary planning at the service of illusion and tying illusion to money and technical capacity. But no film before *Brigadoon* so sumptuously and openly placed this equation in view (and few films after it have done so), or so provoked the viewer's desire to escape from the grounding of a practical knowledge into the freedom of desire. No film has asked its audience so complexly to consider the riddle of cinema: that in watching one ongoingly is where one is not, that we are not where we are.

Interestingly, the film itself addresses this profound phenomenal/noumenal conundrum. "The whole thing is too unreal to be remembered—emotionally, that is. You might think about it, but you won't feel anything," read a speech from Jeff in the Broadway play script as typed for the MGM Script Department on November 6, 1951. Seven months later comes a considerably spiced up and sharpened tête-à-tête between the two chums (immediately following the chase, in which Harry Beaton—"a hunted thing" [Jones synopsis 9]—has been slain trying to escape from, and thus obliterate, Brigadoon): "I don't know if this town is a miracle, a bad dream, or a training camp for lunatics. All I know is that whatever it is it's got nothing to do with me and nothing to do with you. Anything that happens here to either of us just doesn't count. It can't. It's too unreal. Every bit of it. Probably by tomorrow morning you'll forget all about it. I know I will" (June 23, 1952). Still more bounce and anger filtered into the scene by October 20, when it was locked:

Jeff: After a while, Jeff thought he saw a bird perched low in a tree, and shot at it. Something fell to the ground. He ran over, and what do you think it was? It was Hothead Harry. Yessir, the boy dervish himself, lying there looking all dead. (Tommy is stunned.) Now, to kill somebody somewhere else in the world would have been an awful thing. But you see, Harry was a citizen of the little town that wasn't there, and he probably never lived in the first place. And the chances are there weren't even any woods. In fact, the whole day probably never even happened. Because, you see, this is a fairy tale.

Tommy (almost whispering): Jeff . . . Good Lord . . . You poor guy . . . You must feel horrible.

Jeff (turning on him suddenly and violently): What do you mean, "I must feel"? What am I supposed to feel in a voodoo joint like this? This is dream stuff, boy. All made up out of broomsticks and wishing wells. It's either that or a boot camp for lunatics. I don't know what goes on around here. All I know is that whatever it is, it's got nothing to do with me and nothing to do with you. Anything that happens to either of us just doesn't count. How can it when you don't understand it? And you think you're going to give up your friends, your family, your whole life . . . for this! It's not even worth arguing about. Now go say goodbye to the "little people" and thank them for the picnic.

is *confused.* "You know," he adds, "if you believed as much as you think you do, you wouldn't be."

The provocation in *Brigadoon,* then, is not only that it poses a dramatic space so elegantly composed on the cusp between the fantastic and the everyday; not that it optically challenges the sense of the real and even the meaning of reality; but that beyond doing these things it openly asserts that it is doing this, openly and very bluntly asserts the problem of experiential "reality" as central to engagement and purpose. Had it been produced as an outdoor spectacle, I cannot imagine how *Brigadoon* could have made this point seem anything but trite and forced. In Minnelli's rather overwhelming construction, however, the issue of reality—and principally optical reality—is stated or implied at every moment and built up powerfully so as to culminate in this speech of Jeff's. Jeff the *nebisch* observer, Jeff the bungler, Jeff the goofy sidekick, whose action with his rifle turns the story—even in an act of perfect ambiguity involving a mistaken apprehension of reality: he thought he was shooting at a bird—and whose assessment of himself and his circumstances so chillingly summarizes a pungent, troubling human theme.

It was a "mythical place" that Kelly and Freed had in mind when they conceived this film, not something that would be actual (Patricia Ward Kelly, personal correspondence). Yet the actuality is continually hinted at, as must always be true in myth. Because in watching *Brigadoon,* and most intensively in its set pieces like "Heather on the Hill" or "MacConnachy Square" or "The Chase," two worlds appear at once, an illusion and the mechanism that supports and mobilizes it, the film goes beyond simply grasping that things and perceptions of things are not the same to a point where phenomenal reality *presents itself as such.* The phenomenon is no longer hiding underneath, beside, in an implied cloud around the hard truth it represents, but is now something to be digested and considered in its own right, with its own bizarre flavor.

If for a supreme experience of *Brigadoon* one must alternate rapidly between Scotland and "Scotland," watching it one may discover a real self in this suspended time "when no man was his own." Discussing patriotism, George Orwell wrote that it is "devotion to something that is changing but is felt to be mystically the same" ("My Country" 247). A kind of patriotism is called for in watching *Brigadoon* with love. Losing, abandoning loyalty to the cinema *per se,* that hollow chamber with its whirring mechanism and hot light; and at the same time letting fly loyalty to the shabby, flimsy imagination, one gains the truth that reality is both of these together and neither of these alone. A patriotism not for Scotland, nor for "Scotland," but for both.

And patriotism, adds Orwell, "might seem an impossibility, if one did not know it to be an everyday phenomenon."

Notes

Prelude: Corn

1. See for example, Georges Seurat's 1884 drawing of a monkey (as a study for *La Grande Jatte*) and his 1883 conté crayon drawing of a colt, which illustrate the *ébauche* and the *étude*, respectively (Courthion 62; 58).

1. Vivid Rivals

1. This is a cheat, of course: in "reality," the little boy is not having his focus pulled, but we can solicitously imagine that he is, and thus protect ourselves from having to fully engage with what is fictionally engaging his young and unprepared consciousness.
2. Even this depends for our sense of its authenticity on the conviction that it is really Hitler we are watching, and not one of the many actors who have pretended subsequently to be him (see Pomerance "Villain" for a partial listing).
3. The "far-below" shot is neatly deconstructed in Mike Nichols's *Postcards from the Edge* (1990) where we see the horizontal mechanics of such a "vertical" perspective as actors work on a diegetic soundstage.
4. Other specialists work in other films to produce *realistic*, as opposed to "real," effects, making things look as presumably they would look if they existed in our world while avowedly they do not: Jack Pierce making up Lon Chaney Jr. in 1941 or Rick Baker and some thirty-odd others doing Benicio Del Toro in 2010 as a "wolfman," for example; the age of blockbuster spectaculars has been rife with "aliens," "monsters" and hideously wounded humans, "mutants," or "zombie/undead."
5. A moment like that in *The Purple Rose of Cairo* (1985), in which a character walks *out of* the movie screen and into the audience, being the exception that proves the rule.
6. Cinematic history is replete with cases of films about filmmaking (*8 ½* [1963]; *Alex in Wonderland* [1970]; *The Stunt Man* [1980]) and, as Jane Feuer has artfully pointed out, musicals about doing musicals (*Footlight Parade* [1933]; *Singin' in the Rain* [1952]; *Three for the Show* [1955]), but a film in production

at this writing raises the bar by migrating into "real" territory. This is the Ivan Reitman production of Sacha Gervasi's film *Hitchcock*, based on Steven Rebello's discursion *Alfred Hitchcock and the Making of Psycho* (1999), in which Scarlett Johansson will play Janet Leigh, and Helen Mirren and Anthony Hopkins the happily married Hitchcocks. One may expect that the degree to which any of the actors will have been cast, or will be made up, to resemble real persons no longer alive (Hopkins has already been photographed in a typically puffy profile shot) will reflect the "knowness" of the character. To miscast Hitchcock would be a problem for the general viewer. To miscast Barney Balaban, Bernard Herrmann, or Joe Stefano would be a "reality" breaker for only film scholars; but perhaps film scholars have become the core of a new audience. Perhaps, too, the general population has become indistinguishable, as far as Hollywood producers are concerned, from scholars of film.

7. Ferren was even struck himself by the finished work. "I liked *Vertigo*, both as a picture and my sequence," he wrote to associate producer Herbert Coleman. "I saw it twice. The first time I was put out by some technical roughtnesses [*sic*] the second time I thought that I had a real kick and was fine in and for the story. Incidentally Bob Burkes [*sic*] photographed the thing (I mean the entire picture) beautifully" (Ferren to Coleman).

8. On the not dissimilar rhetoric of the biblical spectacular, see Sobchack "Surge."

9. In January 2009, I screened *The Mummy* for a delighted audience of adults and students at Toronto's Royal Ontario Museum. Afterward, there were numerous comments and questions, not a single one of which reflected any doubt on the viewers' part that they had been seeing not "Egypt" but Egypt.

10. "Pure" because unformed by arbitrary human action (and thus "natural"). While Zombie and surgical adventures could show bodies erupting with mechanical parts (as in *The Terminator* [1984] and its sequels), the constructions they use tend to be hyper-organic, and what "leaks" is usually biological matter, that which is beyond our aegis to create (that is, that which is created only through the "magic" of human sexual reproduction). Most cyberadventures, such as David Cronenberg's *Videodrome* (1983) or Jon Favreau's *Iron Man* (2008), offer a body/machine hybrid expressly built as such, rather than what is actually more common in real life, the organic body into which some nonorganic stent or plate or additive has been set.

11. For an interesting observation of a painter's observation on such matters, see Sebald, *Rings* 13ff.

12. I recall, in fact, that one of my own very earliest stage performances was as a corpse underneath a blanket, in a kind of open-air theater where audiences would move from tableau to tableau. The principal difficulty I faced

was determining when I should hold my breath and when it was all right to breathe normally, since from beneath the blanket I could not see whether observers were present or not. The extra who played the dead Comanche whose eyes are shot out by John Wayne in *The Searchers* (1956) had almost the same problem, and his dubious timing was caught on film.

13. In *Wings of Desire* (1987), Wim Wenders had suggested the same idea of beings who could invisibly watch earthly goings-on, these a pair of angels who circulated over and around Berlin taking meticulous note of the daily experiences and undertakings of a number of discrete individuals (see Pomerance "Laddy").

14. The "attractions" of cinema that dazzled the eye and wit of the viewer through their self-conscious exhibitionism were related, in a way, to excesses and focusing of illumination, hyper-realities that became evident as constructions due to their very intensity of production. Schivelbusch cites Diderot's eighteenth-century distaste for "splendour," the "colourful, peacock-like display of the aristocracy," which the *philosophe* found "not beautiful." Splendor could "dazzle the eye, but it cannot touch the heart" (qtd. in Schivelbusch 201–02). In cinema a real moment can be fractured by overdecoration and overlighting, which are ostentatious and self-indicating. The point of cinematic "realism" was not mere intensity of illumination onscreen but a relationship between film and its audience in which substantial, healthy, normative quantities of light flooded the image while an audience subtly attended in a pool of relative darkness.

15. All of this drawing only the skimpiest sketch of the kind of catastrophic horror that was produced, writes W. G. Sebald, on July 27, 1943, with the bombing of Hamburg, in which "the fire, now rising two thousand meters into the sky, snatched oxygen to itself so violently that the air currents reached hurricane force, resonating like mighty organs with all their stops pulled out at once" (27).

16. Motivated, I feel certain, by his childhood wonder at the elaborate train crash sequence in Cecil B. DeMille's *The Greatest Show on Earth* (1952).

17. Notwithstanding what Ridley Scott suggests in his narratively tortuous 2012 "prequel," *Prometheus*, where we learn that there is indeed something disturbingly human about the genetic history of the alien.

18. Jean-Philippe Tessé: "A structure of vocabulary topples—the one that reared the Lumières, Bazin, Rossellini. A lexical field that treated the ontology of the cinematographic image as Bazin conceived it: the window on the world, the imprint of reality, revelation, impression, persistence of vision, etc. These words—it's no accident—easily circulate through the ontological discourse in the glossary of techniques (to develop a film is to reveal it). Henceforth these words have no use. Filming no longer consists of recording a mysterious chemical trace on film (*pellicula* means little skin) that in projection a beam of

light reveals on a screen but, in the digital age, stocking a quantity of information. . . ." (translation mine).

2. The Two of Us

1. Since its first use in 1937 for *Wings of the Morning*, and consistently through such startlingly beautiful renditions as Jack Cardiff's photography for *The Red Shoes* (1948) and onward, British Technicolor presents a slightly crisper and more metallic color palette than Hollywood Technicolor does, possibly because of the mineral deposits in the Thames water source, which was used in the washing.

2. I am grateful to Christopher Lacroix for reminding me that in *Harry Potter and the Half-Blood Prince* (2005) J. K. Rowling invents the magical technique of "apparating," whereby through intensive concentration of mind a suitably trained person can move instantly through time and space to any place of her choosing. Harry, for instance, "felt as though he had just been forced through a very tight rubber tube. It was a few seconds before he realized that Privet Drive had vanished. He and Dumbledore were now standing in what appeared to be a deserted village square. . . ." (60). A catastrophic possibility evidenced here, but not in the films I am discussing, Rowling calls "splinching," which is the "separation of random body parts" and occurs "when the mind is insufficiently determined" (361). Apparating is made visible onscreen in *Harry Potter and the Deathly Hallows* (2010).

3. A film that had a rather inauspicious opening release at $22 million but that has earned more than ten times that amount worldwide as of this writing (boxofficemojo.com).

4. Noël Burch gives an extensive discussion of "spatiotemporal articulations between shots" in his *Theory of Film Practice* (30ff.). And John Carey has masterfully studied the way artistic techniques for effecting temporal and spatial transitions are negotiated between filmmakers and audiences, and how this process evolved over time ("Temporal and Spatial Transitions").

5. Scott Higgins notes a number of constraints imposed on cinematography by the Technicolor three-strip process in its early days (in the 1930s) and even later. The three recording stocks, he notes, had "a collective speed equivalent to around sixteen ASA," but considerable light was lost due to filtration inside the camera. "Altogether the filters accounted for a loss of light equivalent to at least two f-stops. These and other variables reduced the effective speed of the Technicolor system to around four ASA" (81), which would have meant that a tremendous amount of light was needed on the set.

6. Numerous other Hitchcockian masterpieces of rear projection are to be found in *Notorious* (1946).

7. On November 7, 2011, Dr. Conrad Murray, Jackson's physician, was found

guilty of involuntary manslaughter regarding this death, which through the judicial process had now found both resolution and ultimate definition.

8. The Jackson riddle was repeated with the death of Whitney Houston on February 11, 2012, just as it had been prefaced powerfully by the "immortality" of Elvis Presley, at once a corpse and a king.

9. From Patrick Hamilton's novel *Hangover Square; or, The Man with Two Minds; A Story of Darkest Earl's Court in the Year 1939* (London: Constable, 1941).

10. Adapted by Margaret Kennedy from *Uloupeny Zivot*, a novel by Karel Benes (that had been filmed in England in 1939 by Paul Czinner, with Elizabeth Bergner).

11. The transferred wedding ring theme will be picked up with Barbara Stanwyck (doubling) in Mitchell Leisen's *No Man of Her Own* (1950) and then twice reprised, with Nathalie Baye in Robin Davis's *J'ai épousé un ombre* (1982) and Ricki Lake in Richard Benjamin's *Mrs. Winterbourne* (1996); all of these are based in Cornell Woolrich's *I Married a Dead Man* (1948; signed William Irish).

12. A split-screen machine designed in 1938 at Warner Bros. involved a Mitchell lens mount and camera assembly, a 30×42-inch projector assembly, a 2×3-foot five-speed transmission with forward and reverse capability, and a considerable number of ancillary assemblies for accommodating the Technicolor camera (Patent).

13. Lightman credits Polito for the cinematography.

14. For *A Stolen Life*, both Ernest Haller and Sol Polito are the cinematographers of record. Polito was the principal camera artist, but he was overtaken with appendicitis around noon on Friday, May 25, 1945, and replaced within about an hour by Haller, who is recorded as the cinematographer in the daily production reports for June 25 and 26, 1945, when this bedroom scene was shot on Stage 15 at Warner Bros. (Warner Bros. Archive, *Stolen Life* file). Although an Inter-Office Communication from Unit Manager Al Alleborn to General Studio Manager T. C. Wright indicated that Polito would be replaced by Robert Burks, it was in fact Haller who took his place, and remained behind the lens for the rest of the shoot. Haller worked with his predecessor's crew until end-of-day, Saturday, June 2, and his own crew came on set Monday, June 4.

15. I am extremely grateful to Barry Salt for taking the trouble to help me decode this shot.

16. Originated in 1930 (Read and Meyer 65; 157).

17. David Cronenberg very generously took time to discuss optical printing film stock with me.

18. The flame is used here to cover—indeed, efface—a transition between shots. But it can be used, too, as an explicit dramatic device. In Ann Coates's

celebrated match-to-sunrise edit for David Lean's *Lawrence of Arabia* (1962), a metaphorical comparison between a tiny and an enormous flame carried the narrative forward in space and time. Onstage, the device is used to move from Act I to Act II of Arthur Miller's *After the Fall*, a lighter spark and flame at the end of the first apparently gliding directly into the spark at the beginning of the second, and thus eliding the Intermission.

3. Being There

1. With even more wonder, Stanley Cavell takes up this same performance for examination in *Notes Out of School* (152–72).

2. Sinatra, in fact, had been clear with Frankenheimer when they discussed the possibility of making this film: "I'm an entertainer, I am not an actor. So I'm always best on the first take. If a director isn't a really great director, they don't realize that, and they keep choosing my worst take—because the camera angle's better or something" (Pomerance, "He Loved" 39).

3. The considerably more spectacular case of Johnny Depp, whose presence has been transformed for viewers around the world by his work in the *Pirates of the Caribbean* franchise, I consider in depth in *Johnny Depp Starts Here*.

4. *40 Days* was shot in British Columbia and released in March 2002. Spike Lee's *25th Hour*, filmed in New York City, came out just less than nine months later, including a scene in which Phillip Seymour Hoffman, a high school teacher who has just been seduced by one of his pupils (Anna Paquin) at a nightclub, emerges from the cabinet of lust in a dream state and seems to glide across a balcony toward the camera. Here, again, a moving platform is used to achieve the jiggle-free motion of the actor's body, but in the name of suspended consciousness, not extended perception. As Thomas Dorey has kindly pointed out to me, Lee has used the character dolly in a number of films, including *Malcolm X* (1992) and *Crooklyn* (1994), sometimes self-reflexively playing with the technique by putting his actor on a crane (for a supercut of a number of these instances see http://vimeo.com/40689260). We can find the same character glide, achieved in the same way, as Guy (Nino Castelnuovo) brings Geneviève (Catherine Deneuve) to his aunt's apartment in Jacques Demy's *The Umbrellas of Cherbourg* (1964).

5. In his television broadcast of July 8, 2010, Charlie Rose interjected into an interview with the playwright David Mamet an extended clip from the Broadway production of *Race*, in which James Spader was shown in medium close-up making a long speech. The footage came from a videotaped recording of a performance, not from a carefully produced filming; and we were able to see, again and again, the actor glancing into the audience as he spoke, often in mid-phrase, as though to check for responses from his listeners. His eye movements were very swift, and would have been virtually invisible from seats

in the theater itself, but were here magnified because of the lens being used for the filming. When Spader and other actors perform for and with camera in motion picture production, any such eye movements are eliminated in the editing if they are not in fact withheld in the performance.

6. The artist Lucas Samaras has permitted visitors to replicate this effect with his completely mirrored "Room No. 1" (1964) at the Albright-Knox Gallery, Buffalo; and for a brief moment in Christopher Nolan's *Inception* (2010) mirrors are aligned to let a character do the same.

7. As in Antonioni's *The Mystery of Oberwald* (1981); see Pomerance, *Michelangelo* 131–56.

8. I recall still with laughter, for example, a speech one of my professors made to the class during its first meeting in September of 1967, the gist of it being that the class was unacceptably overenrolled, and that it would not be nearly as simplistic as most of us undergraduate morons thought. We should all think twice about coming back. This talk was given not by a living professor, however, but by a tape recorder brought into the room by a graduate assistant and turned on at the moment when we'd all fallen into speechless silence. At the second class the professor did appear, jovial and jokey, and also happy to see that only half as many people were there. "It always works," were the first words that came from between his living lips.

9. Bob Rubin, an assistant director on Michelangelo Antonioni's *Zabriskie Point* (1970), recounted to me the absolute "nightmare" he experienced marshaling road traffic along Wilshire Boulevard in Los Angeles as Rod Taylor and his business companion drove to the offices of Sunny Dunes. In such social settings as busy city streets, the production has control—by way of the assistant director—of every single moving person or object for blocks around the camera, and coordination of movement can be stunningly difficult to achieve.

10. An exception, at least during the 1940s and 1950s, was the clothing worn by principal male performers in non-costume pictures; suits and sport coats were typically supplied by the performer himself (whereas the leading actress's garments were designed, often by a name artist such as Edith Head, and purchasable at a sublime discount after production). Thus, the elegant "control" of the look and tailoring of his garb onscreen was a wholly personal matter for Cary Grant, who wore his own suits. In *North by Northwest* (1959), by contrast, the clothing of the supporting player James Mason was purchased by him, but at the production's expense, from a London tailor.

11. Shooting a scene with Claude Rains and Ingrid Bergman for *Notorious* (1946), Hitchcock had a ramp built so that as Rains moved forward from the doorway in the rear of the shot his body would seem to grow.

12. And not long previously, in John Frankenheimer's *All Fall Down* (1962), De Wilde had with the same believability re-created himself as Karl Malden and Angela Lansbury's son, this requiring an entirely different kind of

performance, more vocal and physical in a different way (see Pomerance "Ashes").

13. Naremore also brings to our attention Goffman's concept of "disclosive compensation," whereby we are allowed to see in a character what other characters cannot see (but the actors playing them can).

14. When special effects extravaganzas do not; see, for an entertaining example, Shawn Levy's *Night at the Museum* (2006) and *Night at the Museum: Battle of the Smithsonian* (2009), in which the dioramas are populated with figurines that come alive.

4. A Fairy Tale

1. See on lighting issues Schivelbusch *Night*; and Pomerance "Light"; and on the design of the movie theater and its appurtenances, Ackermann 47–51; Moore; and Gomery 40–56. (I am grateful to Paul Moore for some of these suggestions.)

2. Finds her, it bears stressing, just precisely as she was; so that time appears not to have passed at all and the village of Brigadoon to have become immortal. A good friend, recently turned seventy and returning to the English village of his youth, found a certain scrumpy house, the Golding Hop in Meopam, Kent, positively and completely unchanged after fifty years, "just like Brigadoon."

3. In order to convince various MGM executives that a filmed ballet would work in *An American in Paris*, he had in fact screened *The Red Shoes* for them "fifteen to twenty times" (McLean 166).

4. MGM had noticed that Twentieth Century-Fox was making "so-called 'glass shots" rather than doubly exposed in-camera matte shots, because of "Eastman color film deterioration" and noted, "On the other hand, the film which we will use, Ansco Mazda, does not deteriorate" (Newcombe to Gibbons). In-camera matte shots produced a combinable matte image by using one of the color layers, so deterioration would block the success of this. In general, while Eastmancolor 5247 stock was in use by the early 1950s, there were numerous problems with the color it achieved (see, in general, Haines). Barry Salt notes that until 1955, Ansco negative and positive stocks were the regular materials in use at MGM's Metrocolor lab (241).

5. Kelly could be watched in two different kinds of print that were available for exhibition, a 2.55:1 CinemaScope version, in which the expansiveness of the hills and the dancing space would have been alarmingly effective; or a 1.75:1 Metroscope print for theaters without the necessary widescreen facilities; both versions were recorded "in PERSPECTA STEREOPHONIC SOUND and managers whose theatres are equipped for this system" were "urged to give prominence in all advertising, showmanship and editorials to PERSPECTA STEREOPHONIC SOUND as an added attraction" (*Brigadoon* British

"without doubt . . . the single most important sound development of the 1950s," gave the music a "'spread-out-sound' even though it actually was monaural" (*Wide Screen Movies* 244–45); MGM used the process from 1953 through 1960.

6. *Skivings*: film that is run through mechanical processors is often marred when very thin slivers are stripped off in the machine and then, floating in the processing liquids, become embedded on the surface as the film is dried. These make for slight visual imperfections.

7. Similarly, most gallery visitors who look at canvases don't know much about painting, a fact that underpins much of Tom Wolfe's iconoclastic analysis of the modern art world in *The Painted Word*, culminating in his observation that without a theory people cannot see a picture.

8. In *Disenchanted Night*, Wolfgang Schivelbusch shows how as the stage became luminous, "the more distinct" seemed whatever appeared on it (206).

9. Even when, in other circumstances, it is not: Jerry Langford (Jerry Lewis) pausing as he enters his apartment in *The King of Comedy* (1983) to watch on his TV a scene from Samuel Fuller's *Pickup on South Street* (1953), a film, not a film-in-a-film, when it is screened in theaters.

10. CinemaScope was patented by Twentieth Century-Fox on the basis of a late 1920s invention by Henri Chrétien, in his Anamorphoscope process. It required a pair of anamorphic "hypergonar" lenses. One, on the camera, would compact a scene laterally; the second, on the projector in the theater, would expand that contraction outward. The end product was a projection in the 2.55: 1 ratio (sometimes abbreviated to 2.35: 1); it premiered with Fox's *The Robe* (1953), photographed by Leon Shamroy.

11. It was not uncommon around the time of *Brigadoon* for MGM—the leading scenic art department in Hollywood under Gibson's direction—to loan out backings to other studios, or to prepare them on custom order: for example, the Grand Canyon background for Walt Disney Productions' Disneyland theme park (opened 1955 [see Marling]) was executed by Gibson and his team (Gibson to Smith). The craftsmen at MGM would do a backing on the assumption, written into a contract memo, that strips of canvas would be delivered to them already sewn up into pieces of the requisite size for their workplace. MGM would handle any requisite touching up of backings at another studio after erection, including any normal seam work and any touching up required after transportation; but changes or alterations would be at the renting studio's expense (Horning to Spencer). In general, however, MGM made backings principally for itself.

12. It would be a gross error to assume that Gibson's personnel in scenic art or any of the specialists who worked in miniature photography, process photography, or full-sized special effects photography at MGM were getting rich

at their work. Special effects head A. Arnold Gillespie complained to studio production manager J. J. Cohn just as production on *Brigadoon* was getting underway about personnel cutbacks in his department and predicted that any further cutbacks would "effect the efficiency of our operation"; in this context he mentions two employees, long at MGM, one of whom had had no increase in salary for seven years and a second who had been working without increase for fourteen: "The cost of living index has pretty well by-passed the department" (Gillespie to Cohn).

13. Two years before the structure was completed, the cost had been estimated at slightly over $60,000, and the matter described by Cedric Gibbons as one "of which I cannot stress the importance too greatly"; in the final construction some items, such as plaster on the inside walls, were cut for efficiencies (Gibbons to Mannix; Knox, *Gibson Interview* 1003).

14. That is, until the invention of the variable fluorescent Kinoflo system by Frieder Hochheim in 1987: Kinoflo made it possible to effectively color fluorescent light on set.

15. A very different approach to painting large backings for the stage, the "continental" method, is described in great detail by Polunin, who to paint the designs of Picasso, Braque, and others for the Ballet Russe de Monte Carlo stretched canvas on the floor and walked upon it to work with long brushes, often in a building at 50 Floral Street, London. The "continental" method would not have worked in front of film cameras, with studio lighting and other wearing characteristics of studio work; nor in cases like *Brigadoon* where the requirement was for a backing that could not have been painted in one single piece.

16. Percy painted numerous impressive Scottish landscapes, any of which might have been sufficient inspiration for George Gibson's work on *Brigadoon*, including *Kilchurn Castle, Loch Awe* and *Autumn in the Highlands* (both 1855), *Highland Landscape with Cattle* (1863), *Loch Katrine* (1865), *Loch Lomond* (1867), *Looking into Glen Lockey, across Loch Tay* (1870), *Glencoe* (1873), *A Highland Stream* (1874), *Loch Ewe* (1877), *Sheep in a Highland Landscape* (undated), and *Glen Dochart, Perthshire* (1885).

17. In the spring of 1954, MGM was in the process of testing a new rear-projection system that would allow for the lateral or vertical juxtaposition of two "plates," so as to achieve a background image congruent with the framing needs of the Cinemascope process. On March 18, 1954, as a test of this system, "an all-over painting for the production 'Brigadoon' was photographed . . . in two halves with a 15% overlap" and the multi-projection was viewed and evaluated on March 24 by A. Arnold Gillespie, Douglas Shearer, Carrol Shepphird, George Brown, and others (Shearer and Gillespie affidavit).

18. Oliver Smith, who had been held "in abeyance," was finally not used (Hoyt to Freed). The forest and village combination was erected for $6,900, with an

additional $2,700 for the bridge/stream portion and another $800 for installation of circulating water. All this is shown by way of an elaborate choreography of technicians and machinery: more than $2,200 for greensmen to tend the forest, and, to give some idea of the complexity of the many boom and camera moves involved, eleven shots of the woods, bridge, and stream costing the labor of ten grips and three crane operators (Picture Estimate).

19. It was perhaps with an ear for its abrasive erosion of the "illusory quality" of the film that Schary complained to Freed and Minnelli about "the use of the dialect," which was originally being recorded to sound authentic. "I think much of it will be incomprehensible to an American audience, and while it can be argued that dubbing will take care of some of it it would be absurd for us to continue playing the entire picture with so much burr to it" (Schary to Freed and Minnelli).

Works Cited and Consulted

Archive Abbreviations

AFI   Louis B. Mayer Library, American Film Institute, Los Angeles

BFI   Library of the British Film Institute, London

HER Margaret Herrick Library, Academy of Motion Picture Arts and Sciences, Beverly Hills

USC Cinema-Television Collection, Doheny Library, University of Southern California, Los Angeles

WB   Warner Bros. Archive, University of Southern California, Los Angeles

Archival Sources

Alleborn, Al. Inter-Office Communication to T. C. Wright, May 28, 1945, regarding May 26 shooting, with comment about Robert Burks. WB.

Anderson, Iain F. Letter to Janet Ramsay Kay [Secretary to Vincente Minnelli], June 10, 1952, with advice on Scotland. Vincente Minnelli Collection, HER.

———. Letter to Janet Ramsay Kay, July 16, 1952, with further advice on Scotland. Vincente Minnelli Collection, HER.

Ardmore, Jane. "Brandon de Wilde tells . . . WHAT A BOY FEELS ABOUT LOVE AND SEX." Typed manuscript, HER.

Atkinson, J. B. Letter to Vincente Minnelli, March 27, 1952. Vincente Minnelli Collection, HER.

Bell, Douglas. *Oral History with Rudi Fehr.* 1998. HER.

"'Brigadoon' to Get Overhaul for Films." *Los Angeles Times* (March 23, 1952), USC.

Brigadoon British Pressbook. BFI.

Brigadoon Daily Production Reports for January 5, 6, 7, 8, 9, and 12, 1954. Arthur Freed Collection, USC.

Brigadoon Picture Estimate, December 1, 1953. Arthur Freed Collection, USC.

Burk, Ann. *Oral History with John Green.* 1975. HER.

Davis, Ronald L. *Oral History with Gene Kelly.* 1974. HER.

———. *Oral History with Joseph Ruttenberg.* 1978. HER.

Ferren, John. Letter to Herbert Coleman, July 25, 1958, regarding *Vertigo*. *Vertigo* file 995, Alfred Hitchcock Collection, HER.

Field of Dreams locations file. HER.

Fordin, Hugh. *Interview with George Gibson*. Audiotape, USC.

Freed, Arthur. "Lineup of Time" for *Brigadoon*, Arthur Freed Collection, USC.

Gibbons, Cedric. Inter-Office Communication to W[illiam] W. Spencer, April 25, 1951, regarding George Gibson. MGM Art Department Records, HER.

———. Memorandum letter to E[dward] J. Mannix, November 17, 1937, regarding rear projection process requirements. MGM Art Department Records, HER.

Gibson, George, with F. Wayne Hill. Scenic Art Department notes referring to experimental investigation of a new type paint mixture, March 19, 1954. MGM Art Department Records, HER.

———. Inter-Office Communication to W. P. Smith, c. April 8, 1957, regarding Grand Canyon backing after a visit to Disneyland. MGM Art Department Records, HER.

Gillespie, A. Arnold. Inter-Office Communication to All Departments Concerned, March 7, 1952, regarding triple-head projector. MGM Art Department Records, HER.

———. Inter-Office Communication to J. J. Cohn, March 30, 1953, regarding cutbacks in department personnel, MGM Art Department Records, HER.

———. Inter-Office Communication to Cedric Gibbons, April 7, 1953, regarding CinemaScope and rear projection. HER.

Gillespie, A. Arnold, and E. Eiseman. Inter-Office Communication to Gibbons, Strohm, Cohn, Nickolaus, Arnold, Chamberlain, Ceccarini, and Hoff, March 28, 1953, regarding Color Process tests for Ansco film. HER.

Grosser, A. A. Memorandum to Frank Caffey, June 9, 1964, regarding expenses for John Wayne in Hawaii. *In Harm's Way* file, HER.

Hall, Barbara. *Oral History with Peggy Robertson*. 2002. HER.

Horning, William A. Inter-Office Communication to W[illiam] W. Spencer, May 19, 1958, regarding backing rentals. MGM Art Department Records, HER.

———. Unaddressed Inter-Office Communication, August 26, 1957, regarding fungicide for painted backings. MGM Art Department Records, HER.

Horton, Howard. Inter-Office Communication to Herbert Coleman, W. C. Strohm, M. Pye, Robert Boyle, and K. Gledhill, August 19, 1958, regarding the *North by Northwest* cornfield sequence. HER.

Hoyt, Howard. Wire to Arthur Freed regarding Oliver Smith, July 30, 1953. Arthur Freed Collection, USC.

In Harm's Way Daily Production Reports. *In Harm's Way* file, HER.

Jones, W. Kendall. Synopsis of *Brigadoon*, May 27, 1954. *Brigadoon* folders, MGM Collection, USC.

Kalmus, Natalie M. "Motion Pictures in Colors." n.d. HER.

———. "The Importance of the Correct Use of Color in Every Day Life." n.d. HER.

Knox, Donald. *Interview with George Gibson.* Donald Knox Transcripts, Vol. 8. 237
    AFI.

Lerner, Alan Jay. *Brigadoon* play script, as copied for the MGM Script Depart-
    ment, November 6, 1951. Arthur Freed Collection, USC.

———. *Brigadoon* script, May 9, 1952 with rewrites from June 23, 1952. Arthur
    Freed Collection, USC.

———. *Brigadoon* script, Arthur Freed copy, October 14, 1953. Arthur Freed Col-
    lection, USC.

———. *Brigadoon* script, with October 20, 1953 changes. Roger Edens Collection,
    USC.

Memorandum on recording dates and personnel for *Brigadoon*, Rogers Edens
    Collection, USC.

"Minnelli Assigned 'Brigadoon' in MGM Directorial Shift." *Daily Variety* (Febru-
    ary 22, 1952), USC.

Newcombe, Warren. Inter-Office Communication to Cedric Gibbons, April 7,
    1953, regarding Cinemascope, Ansco film, and "Newcombe" shots. MGM Art
    Department Records, HER.

Paramount Press Release for *In Harm's Way.* May 28, 1964. HER.

Paramount Press Release for *In Harm's Way.* March 29, 1965. HER.

Schallert, William. "'Brigadoon' Format to Be Developed Abroad." *Los Angeles
    Times* (February 9, 1952). USC.

Schary, Dore. Inter-Office Communication to Arthur Freed, November 10, 1953,
    regarding set test on *Brigadoon.* Arthur Freed Collection, USC.

———. Inter-Office Communiation to Arthur Freed and Vincente Minnelli, De-
    cember 16, 1953, regarding Scottish dialect. Arthur Freed Collection, USC.

Shanks, Bill. Inter-Office Communication to Ruby Rosenberg, Plaza Hotel, New
    York, August 14, 1958. *North by Northwest* File, Alfred Hitchcock Collection,
    HER.

Shearer, Douglas, and A. Arnold Gillespie. Affidavit, regarding test of an over-
    lapping multi-image rear projection system. MGM Art Department Records,
    HER.

Simone, Lela. Inter-Office Communication to Mike Steinere, April 12, 1954, re-
    garding sound effects for *Brigadoon.* Roger Edens Collection, USC.

Stefano, Joseph. Letter to Janet Leigh regarding her performance in *Psycho*, March
    30, 1960. Janet Leigh Papers, HER.

A Stolen Life British Pressbook. BFI.

"A Stolen Life." *Los Angeles Herald Express* (June 16, 1945). *A Stolen Life* file, WB.

Stovall, Mrs. E. F. Fan letter to Arthur Freed, n.d. Arthur Freed Collection, USC.

Strickling, Howard. First Report of First Preview of *Brigadoon*, Encino Theatre,
    June 4, 1954. Arthur Freed Collection, USC.

Turner, George. *Oral History with Robert F. Boyle.* Interviewed by George Turner.
    1998. HER.

Unsigned memo, Paramount Operations Department, June 29, 1964, regarding "revised location movement #16" incorporating Brandon De Wilde's travel for *In Harm's Way*. HER.

Warner Bros. Patent for Split Screen Machine, Warner Bros. Archive of Historical Papers (Patent Department). WB.

Published Sources

Ackermann, Marsha E. *Cool Comfort: America's Romance with Air-Conditioning*. Washington, D.C.: Smithsonian Institution Press, 2002.

Acocella, Joan. "Walking on the Moon." *New Yorker* (July 27, 2009), 76–77.

Affron, Charles, and Mirella Jona Affron. *Sets in Motion: Art Direction and Film Narrative*. New Brunswick, N.J.: Rutgers University Press, 1995.

Almendros, Nestor. *The Man with a Camera*. New York: Farrar, Straus, & Giroux, 1984.

Ansell-Pearson, Keith, and Duncan Large. *The Nietzsche Reader*. New York: Wiley-Blackwell, 2006.

Arendt, Hannah. *The Human Condition*. Chicago: University of Chicago Press, 1958.

Arlen, Michael J. "Eros in the Emerald City: The Low Spark of High-Rise Towns." *Rolling Stone* (October 6, 1977), 43–44.

Arnheim, Rudolf. *Art and Visual Perception: A Psychology of the Creative Eye*. Berkeley: University of California Press, 1954.

———. *The Sense of Order: A Study in the Psychology of Decorative Art*. Ithaca, N.Y.: Cornell University Press, 1979.

Assayas, Olivier. "La Publicité, point aveugle du cinéma français." *Cahiers du cinéma* 351 (September 1983), 17–26.

Augé, Marc. *Non-Places: An Introduction to Supermodernity*. London: Verso, 1995.

Aumont, Jacques. "The Variable Eye, or the Mobilization of the Gaze." Trans. Charles O'Brien and Sally Shafto. In *The Image in Dispute: Art and Cinema in the Age of Photography*, ed. Dudley Andrew. Austin: University of Texas Press, 1997. 231–58.

Baker, Nicholson. "The History of Punctuation." In *The Size of Thoughts: Essays and Other Lumber*. New York: Random House, 1996. 70–88.

Barthes, Roland. *Camera Lucida: Reflections on Photography*. Trans. Richard Howard. New York: Hill and Wang, 1981.

———. "The Reality Effect (1968)." In *The Rustle of Language*, Trans. Richard Howard. Berkeley: University of California Press, 1989. 141–48.

Basten, Fred E. *Glorious Technicolor: The Movies' Magic Rainbow*. South Brunswick, N.J., and New York: A. S. Barnes and Company, 1980.

Bateson, Gregory. *Steps to an Ecology of Mind*. New York: Ballantine Books, 1972.

Baudrillard, Jean. *The Evil Demon of Images*. Sydney: Power Institute of Fine Arts, 1987.

Baudry, Jean-Louis. "Ideological Effects of the Basic Cinematographic Apparatus." Trans. Alan Williams. *Film Quarterly* 28: 2 (Winter 1974–75), 39–47.

Bazin, André. "The Ontology of the Photographic Image." In *What Is Cinema?* Vol. 1, Selected and trans. Hugh Gray. Berkeley: University of California Press, 1967. 9–22.

Bellour, Raymond. "Panic." In *Vincente Minnelli: The Art of Entertainment*, ed. Joe McElhaney. Detroit: Wayne State University Press, 2009. 405–13.

Belton, John. "Technology and Aesthetics of Film Sound." In *Film Sound: Theory and Practice*, ed. Elisabeth Weis and John Belton. New York: Columbia University Press, 1985. 63–72.

———. *Widescreen Cinema*. Cambridge, Mass.: Harvard University Press, 1992.

Benjamin, Walter. *Charles Baudelaire: A Lyric Poet in the Era of High Capitalism*. Trans. Harry Zohn. London: Verso, 1997.

———. "The Work of Art in the Age of Its Reproducibility (second version)." *Walter Benjamin: Selected Writings*, Vol. 3 1935–1938, Trans. Edmund Jephcott, Howard Eiland, and others. Ed. Howard Eiland and Michael W. Jennings. Cambridge, Mass.: Harvard University Press, 2002. 101–33.

Bergala, Alain. "Le Vrai, le faux, le factice." *Cahiers du cinéma* 351 (September 1983), 5–9.

Berman, Marshall. *All That Is Solid Melts into Air: The Experience of Modernity*. New York: Penguin, 1988.

Berman, Russell A. "Written across Their Faces: Leni Riefenstahl, Ernst Jünger, and Fascist Modernism." In *Modern Culture and Critical Theory: Art, Politics, and the Legacy of the Frankfurt School*. Madison: University of Wisconsin Press, 1988.

Beyer, Walter. "Traveling Matte Photography and the Blue-Screen System." *American Cinematographer* 45: 1 (January 1964), 34–45.

Bitsch, Charles, and Jean Domarchi. "Interview with Vincente Minnelli." *Cahiers du cinéma* 74 (August-September 1957), 4–14.

Black, Joel. *The Reality Effect: Film Culture and the Graphic Imperative*. New York: Routledge, 2001.

Blake, Janet. "George Gibson (1904–2001), Scene Painter." Online at www.tfaoi.com/aa/5aa/5aa332.htm. Accessed February 11, 2008.

Bode, Lisa. "No Longer Themselves? Framing Digitally Enabled Posthumous 'Performance.'" *Cinema Journal* 49: 4 (Summer 2010), 46–70.

Bordwell, David. "Film Style and Technology, 1930–60." In Bordwell, Staiger, and Thompson, 341–64.

———. "Intensified Continuity: Visual Style in Contemporary American Film." *Film Quarterly* 55: 3 (2002), 16–28.

240   Bordwell, David, and Janet Staiger. "Technology, Style and Mode of Production." In Bordwell, Staiger, and Thompson, 243–61.

Bordwell, David, and Kristin Thompson. *Film Art: An Introduction.* Reading, Mass.: Addison-Wesley, 1979.

Bordwell, David, Janet Staiger, and Kristin Thompson. *The Classical Hollywood Cinema: Film Style and Mode of Production to 1960.* New York: Columbia University Press, 1985.

Bottomore, Stephen. "The Panicking Audience? Early Cinema and the 'Train Effect.'" *Historical Journal of Film, Radio and Television* 19: 2 (1999), 177–216.

Boulding, Kenneth. *The Image: Knowledge in Life and Society.* Ann Arbor: University of Michigan Press, 1956.

Brooks, Max. *The Zombie Survival Guide.* New York: Three Rivers, 2003.

Brown, John. "Land Beyond Brigadoon." *Sight and Sound* 53: 1 (Winter 1983/1984), 40–46.

Burch, Noël. *Theory of Film Practice.* Trans. Helen R. Lane. New York: Praeger, 1973.

Burdeau, Emmanuel. *Vincente Minnelli.* Paris: Éditions Capricci, 2011.

Burke, Kenneth. *A Grammar of Motives.* Berkeley: University of California Press, 1969.

Caillois, Roger. *Man, Play and Games.* Trans. Meyer Barash. Urbana: University of Illinois Press, 2001.

Calvino, Italo. *Invisible Cities.* Trans. William Weaver. New York: Harcourt Brace Jovanovich, 1974.

Canetti, Elias. *Crowds and Power.* New York: Noonday, 1984.

Canutt, Yakima, with Oliver Drake. *Stunt Man: The Autobiography of Yakima Canutt.* New York: Walker and Co., 1979.

Card, James. *Seductive Cinema: The Art of Silent Film.* Minneapolis: University of Minnesota Press, 1994.

Carey, John. "Temporal and Spatial Transitions in American Fiction Films." *Studies in the Anthropology of Visual Communication* 1: 1 (1974), 45–50.

Carr, Robert E., and R. M. Hayes. *Wide Screen Movies.* Jefferson, N.C.: McFarland, 1988.

Cavell, Stanley. "North by Northwest." In *Themes Out of School: Effects and Causes.* Chicago: University of Chicago Press, 1988. 152–72.

———. "What Becomes of Things on Film?" In *Themes Out of School: Effects and Causes.* Chicago: University of Chicago Press, 1988. 173–83.

———. *The World Viewed: Reflections on the Ontology of Film.* Enlarged edition. Cambridge, Mass.: Harvard University Press, 1979.

Chevalier, Michel. *Society, Manners, and Politics in the United States.* Garden City, N.Y.: Doubleday, 1961.

Chion, Michel. *La Toile trouée.* Paris: Éditions de l'étoile, 1988.

Cixous, Hélène. "Fiction and Its Phantoms: A Reading of Freud's *Das Unheimliche* (The 'uncanny')." *New Literary History* 7: 3 (Spring 1976), 525–48, 619–45.

Clark, Danae. *Negotiating Hollywood: The Cultural Politics of Actors' Labor.* Minneapolis: University of Minnesota Press, 1995.

Clarke, Frederick S., and Steve Rubin. "The Making of *Forbidden Planet.*" *Cine-Fantastique* 8: 2–3 (Spring 1979), 4–67.

Colman, Juliet Benita. *Ronald Colman: A Very Private Person.* New York: Morrow, 1975.

Colonnese, Tom Grayson. "Native American Reactions to *The Searchers.*" In *The Searchers: Essays and Reflections on John Ford's Classic Western*, ed. Arthur M. Eckstein and Peter Lehman. Detroit: Wayne State University Press, 2004. 335–42.

Condon, Richard. *The Manchurian Candidate.* 1959. New York: Thunder's Mouth Press, 2003.

Conley, Tom. *Cartographic Cinema.* Minneapolis: University of Minnesota Press, 2006.

Courthion, Pierre. *Georges Seurat.* New York: Harry N. Abrams, 1968.

Crary, Jonathan. *Suspensions of Perception: Attention, Spectacle, and Modern Culture.* Cambridge, Mass.: M.I.T. Press, 1999.

Crowther, Bosley. Review of *Brigadoon. New York Times* (September 17, 1954), online at movies.nytimes.com/movie/review?reg=9Do7EDB1E31E53BBC4F52DFBF66838F649EDE. Accessed June 15, 2012.

Danks, Adrian. "Being in Two Places at the Same Time: The Forgotten Geography of Back Projection." Paper presented at "B for Bad Cinema: Aesthetics, Politics, and Cultural Value," Monash University, Melbourne, Australia, April 2009.

Debord, Guy. *Society of the Spectacle.* New York: Zone, 1994.

Denby, David. "Survivors." *New Yorker* (January 12, 2009), 72–73.

De Valck, Marijke, and Maite Hagener. *Cinephilia: Movies, Love and Memory.* Amsterdam: Amsterdam University Press, 2005.

Doane, Mary Ann. "Indexicality: Trace and Sign: Introduction." *differences* 18: 1 (2007), 1–6.

Donovan, Mark, and Margaret Nelson. "For *Field of Dreams* Fans Who Trek to Don Lansing's Iowa Farm, the Diamond Is Forever." *People* (October 23, 1989), 32: 17. Online at www.people.com/people/archive/article/0,,20121488,00.html.

Durgnat, Raymond. *Durgnat on Film.* London: Faber & Faber, 1976.

During, Simon. *Modern Enchantments: The Cultural Power of Secular Magic.* Cambridge, Mass.: Harvard University Press, 2002.

Dyer, Richard. *Stars.* New ed. London: BFI, 1999.

Edouart, A. Farciot. "History of Background Projection." In *The ASC Treasury of Visual Effects*, ed. George E. Turner. Hollywood, Calif.: American Society of Cinematographers, 1983. 107–15.

Edouart, A. Farciot. "Paramount Triple-Head Transparency Process Projector." *Journal of the Society of Motion Picture Engineers* 33: 2 (August 1939), 171–84.

Elsaesser, Thomas. "Hollywood Berlin." *Sight and Sound* (January 1998), 14–17.

Eyman, Scott. *Empire of Dreams: The Epic Life of Cecil B. DeMille.* New York: Simon & Schuster, 2010.

———. *Lion of Hollywood: The Life and Legend of Louis B. Mayer.* New York: Simon & Schuster, 2005.

———. *Print the Legend: The Life and Times of John Ford.* New York: Simon & Schuster, 1999.

———. *The Speed of Sound: Hollywood and the Talkie Revolution, 1926–1930.* Baltimore: Johns Hopkins University Press, 1997.

Factor, Max. "Make-Up for the New Technicolor Process: An Interview with Max Factor." *American Cinematographer* (August 1936).

Feuer, Jane. "The Self-Reflexive Musical and the Myth of Entertainment." In *Film Genre Reader III*, ed. Barry Keith Grant. Austin: University of Texas Press, 2003. 457–71.

Fielding, Raymond. "Norman O. Dawn: Pioneer Worker in Special-Effects Cinematography." In *A Technological History of Motion Pictures and Television.* Berkeley: University of California Press, 1983. 141–49.

———. *The Technique of Special Effects Cinematography.* New York: Hastings House, 1968.

Fischer, Lucy. "Two-Faced Women: The 'Double' in Women's Melodrama of the 1940s." *Cinema Journal* 23: 1 (Fall 1983), 24–43.

Forster, E. M. *The Longest Journey.* London: Penguin, 2006.

Foucault, Michel. *The Birth of the Clinic.* Trans. A. M. Sheridan Smith. New York: Vintage, 1975.

———. *The Order of Things: An Archaeology of Human Sciences.* New York: Viking, 1973.

Frank, Sam. *Ronald Colman.* Westport, Conn.: Greenwood Press, 1997.

Frazer, Sir James George. *The Golden Bough: A Study in Magic and Religion.* 1911. 3rd ed., New York: Macmillan, 1976.

Friend, Tad. "Funny Is Money: Ben Stiller and the Dilemma of Modern Stardom." *New Yorker* (June 25, 2012), 42–57.

Frodon, Jean-Michel, ed. *Le Cinéma et la Shoah.* Paris: Cahiers du cinéma, 2007.

Fujiwara, Chris. *Jerry Lewis.* Urbana: University of Illinois Press, 2009.

Gallagher, Tag. *John Ford: The Man and His Films.* Berkeley: University of California Press, 1986.

Gay, Peter. *Modernism: The Lure of Heresy.* New York: W. W. Norton, 2008.

Gerstäcker, Friedrich. *Germelshausen.* Boston: D. C. Heath, c. 1902.

Gleber, Anke. *The Art of Taking a Walk: Flanerie, Literature, and Film in Weimar Culture.* Princeton, N.J.: Princeton University Press, 1999.

Goffman, Erving. *Forms of Talk*. Philadelphia: University of Pennsylvania Press, 1981.

———. *Frame Analysis: An Essay on the Organization of Experience*. Cambridge, Mass.: Harvard University Press, 1974.

Goodman, Wendy, and Hutton Wilkinson. *Tony Duquette*. New York: Abrams, 2007.

Gomery, Douglas. *Shared Pleasures: A History of Movie Presentation in the United States*. Madison: University of Wisconsin Press, 1992.

Gorky, Maxim. "The Lumière Cinema." In *The Film Factory: Russian and Soviet Cinema in Documents*, ed. Richard Taylor. Cambridge, Mass.: Harvard University Press, 1988. 25–26.

Gumbrecht, Hans Ulrich. *In 1926: Living at the Edge of Time*. Cambridge, Mass.: Harvard University Press, 1997.

Gunning, Tom. "An Aesthetic of Astonishment: Early Film and the (In)Credulous Spectator." In *Viewing Positions: Ways of Seeing Film*, ed. Linda Williams. New Brunswick, N.J.: Rutgers University Press, 1994. 114–33.

———. "The Cinema of Attractions: Early Film, Its Spectator and the Avant-Garde." In *Early Cinema: Space Frame Narrative*, ed. Thomas Elsaesser. London: BFI, 1990. 56–62.

———. "Moving Away from the Index: Cinema and the Impression of Reality." *differences* 18: 1 (2007), 29–52.

———. "Tracing the Individual Body: Photography, Detectives, and Early Cinema." In *Cinema and the Invention of Modern Life*, ed. Leo Charney and Vanessa R. Schwartz. Berkeley: University of California Press, 1995. 15–45.

Haines, Richard W. *Technicolor Movies: The History of Dye Transfer Printing*. Jefferson, N.C.: McFarland, 1993.

Halberstam, David. *The Fifties*. New York: Fawcett, 1993.

Haralovich, Mary Beth. "Selling *Mildred Pierce*: A Case Study." In *Boom and Bust: American Cinema in the 1940s*, ed. Thomas Schatz. Berkeley: University of California Press, 1999. 196–202.

Hardy, Forsyth. *Scotland in Film*. Edinburgh: Edinburgh University Press, 1990.

Harvey, Stephen. *Directed by Vincente Minnelli*. New York: Harper & Row, 1989.

Heisner, Beverly. *Hollywood Art: Art Direction in the Days of the Great Studios*. Jefferson, N.C.: McFarland, 1990.

Higgins, Scott. *Harnessing the Technicolor Rainbow: Color Design in the 1930s*. Austin: University of Texas Press, 2007.

"Highland Flingding: Bonnie 'Brigadoon' Has Moors Indoors." *Life* 37: 6 (August 9, 1954), 94–97.

Holmes, Eben. "Strange Reality: On Glitches and Uncanny Play." *Eludamos: Journal for Computer Game Culture* 4 (November 2010), online at www.eludamos .org/index.php/eludamos/article/view/vol4no2-9/194.

Hopkins, Albert A. *Magic: Stage Illusions, Special Effects and Trick Photography.* New York: Dover, 1976.

Horne, Gerald. *Class Struggle in Hollywood, 1930–1950: Moguls, Mobsters, Stars, Reds, & Trade Unionists.* Austin: University of Texas Press, 2001.

Husserl, Edmund. *The Paris Lectures.* Trans. Peter Koestenbaum. The Hague: Martinus Nijhoff, 1970.

James, David E., and Rick Berg, eds. *The Hidden Foundation: Cinema and the Question of Class.* Minneapolis: University of Minnesota Press, 1996.

James, William. *The Principles of Psychology.* Vol. 2. New York: Dover, 1950.

Jameson, Fredric. *Signatures of the Visible.* New York: Routledge, 1990.

Kracauer, Siegfried. *Theory of Film: The Redemption of Physical Reality.* 1960. Princeton, N.J.: Princeton University Press, 1997.

Lem, Stanislaw. *The Futurological Congress: From the Memoirs of Ijon Tichy.* Trans. Michael Kandel. New York: Harvest, 1985.

Lightman, Herb A. "Cinematographic Magic for 'A Stolen Life.'" *American Cinematographer* 27: 5 (June 1946), 196–97, 210.

Loncraine, Rebecca. *The Real Wizard of Oz: The Life and Times of L. Frank Baum.* New York: Gotham, 2009.

MacCann, Richard Dyer. "'Brigadoon' Faces CinemaScope Cameras." *Christian Science Monitor* (June 22, 1954), 4C.

Mannoni, Laurent. *The Great Art of Light and Shadow: Archaeology of the Cinema.* Trans. and ed. Richard Crangle. Exeter: University of Exeter Press, 2000.

Marling, Karal-Ann. "Disneyland, 1955: The Place That Was Also a TV Show." In *As Seen on TV: The Visual Culture of Everyday Life in the 1950s.* Cambridge, Mass.: Harvard University Press, 1994. 86–126.

Martin, Andrew. *Going to the Pictures: Scottish Memories of Cinema.* Edinburgh: National Museums of Scotland Publishing, 2000.

Martin-Jones, David. *Scotland: Global Cinema: Genres, Modes and Identities.* Edinburgh: Edinburgh University Press, 2009.

May, Lary. *The Big Tomorrow: Hollywood and the Politics of the American Way.* Chicago: University of Chicago Press, 2000.

McArthur, Colin. *Brigadoon, Braveheart, and the Scots: Distortions of Scotland in Hollywood Cinema.* London: I. B. Taurus, 2003.

McBride, Joseph, ed. *Filmmakers on Filmmaking.* Los Angeles: J. P. Tarcher, 1983.

McCarthy, Todd. *Howard Hawks: The Grey Fox of Hollywood.* New York: Grove Press, 1997.

McLean, Adrienne L. *Dying Swans and Madmen: Ballet, the Body, and Narrative Cinema.* New Brunswick, N.J.: Rutgers University Press, 2008.

Minnelli, Vincente. *I Remember It Well.* Garden City, N.Y.: Doubleday, 1974.

Mishkin, Leo. "'Brigadoon' Misses Magic That Made It Memorable on Stage." *Morning Telegram* (September 17, 1954), n.p.

Moore, Paul S. "So the Public May Know: James M. Sessions' Ads for Balaban & Katz." *Marquee* 38: 1 (2006), 17–24.

Mulvey, Laura. "A Clumsy Sublime." *Film Quarterly* 60: 3 (Spring 2007), 3.

Nabokov, Vladimir. *Despair*. New York: Vintage International, 1989.

———. *King, Queen, Knave*. New York: Vintage International, 1989.

Naremore, James. *Acting in the Cinema*. Berkeley: University of California Press, 1988.

———. *The Films of Vincente Minnelli*. Cambridge: Cambridge University Press, 1993.

Nead, Lynda. *The Haunted Gallery: Painting, Photography, Film c. 1900*. New Haven, Conn.: Yale University Press, 2007.

———. *Victorian Babylon: People, Streets and Images in Nineteenth-Century London*. New Haven, Conn.: Yale University Press, 2000.

"The New Pictures." *Time* (October 4, 1954).

Nye, David E. *Electrifying America: Social Meanings of a New Technology, 1880–1940*. Cambridge, Mass.: MIT Press, 1992.

Oldenburg, Claes. *Proposals for Monuments and Buildings 1965–69*. Chicago: Big Table, 1969.

"On Brigadoon." *Life* 37: 6 (August 9, 1954), 94–97.

Orwell, George. "Boys' Weeklies." In *George Orwell: Essays*. 1940. London: Penguin, 2000. 78–100.

———. "My Country Right or Left." 1940. In *Orwell's England*, ed. Peter Davison. London: Penguin, 2001. 242–48.

———. "Poetry and the Microphone." 1940. In *Orwell's England*, ed. Peter Davison. London: Penguin, 2001. 344–54.

Pearson, Roberta E. *Eloquent Gestures: The Transformation of Performance Style in the Griffith Biograph Films*. Berkeley: University of California Press, 1992.

Pereira, Irene Rice. *The Nature of Space*. Washington, D.C.: Corcoran Gallery of Art, 1968.

Pirandello, Luigi. *Shoot! The Notebooks of Serafino Gubbio, Cinematograph Operator*. 1926. Trans. C. K. Scott Moncrieff. Chicago: University of Chicago Press, 2005.

Polunin, Vladimir. *The Continental Method of Scene Painting*. London: C. W. Beaumont, 1927.

Pomerance, Murray. "Ashes, Ashes: Structuring Emptiness in *All Fall Down*." In *A Little Solitaire: John Frankenheimer and American Film*, ed. Murray Pomerance and R. Barton Palmer. New Brunswick, N.J.: Rutgers University Press, 2011. 184–96.

———. "He Loved What He Did So Much!: An Interview with Evans (Evans) Frankenheimer." *Film International* 9: 3 (2010), 35–50.

———. *The Horse Who Drank the Sky: Film Experience Beyond Narrative and Theory*. New Brunswick, N.J.: Rutgers University Press, 2008.

Pomerance, Murray. "In the Wings." In *Shining in Shadows: Movie Stars of the 2000s*, ed. Murray Pomerance. New Brunswick, N.J.: Rutgers University Press, 2011. 238–42.

———. *Johnny Depp Starts Here*. New Brunswick, N.J.: Rutgers University Press, 2005.

———. "The Laddy Vanishes." In *From Hobbits to Hollywood: Essays on Peter Jackson's Lord of the Rings*, ed. Ernest Mathijs and Murray Pomerance. New York: Editions Rodopi, 2006. 351–72.

———. "Light, Looks, and *The Lodger*." *Quarterly Review of Film and Video* 26 (2009), 425–33.

———. "The Look of Love: Cinema and the Dramaturgy of Kinship." In *A Family Affair: Cinema Calls Home*. London: Wallflower, 2008. 293–303.

———. "The Man-Boys of Steven Spielberg." In *Where the Boys Are: Cinemas of Masculinity and Youth*, ed. Murray Pomerance and Frances Gateward. Detroit: Wayne State University Press, 2005. 133–54.

———. *Michelangelo Red Antonioni Blue: Eight Reflections on Cinema*. Berkeley: University of California Press, 2011.

———. "Notes on Some Limits of Technicolor: The Antonioni Case." *Senses of Cinema* 53 (December 2009). Online at www.sensesofcinema.com/2009/feature-articles/notes-on-some-limits-of-technicolor-the-antonioni-case. Accessed June 21, 2012.

———. "Significant Cinema: The Scene of the Crime." *Senses of Cinema* 61 (December 2011). Online at www.sensesofcinema.com/2011/feature-articles/significant-cinema-the-scene-of-the-crime. Accessed June 21, 2012.

———. "Stark Performance." In *Rebel Without a Cause: Approaches to a Maverick Masterwork*, ed. J. David Slocum. Albany: State University of New York Press, 2005. 35–52.

———. "The Villain We Love: Notes on the Dramaturgy of Screen Evil." In *B Is for Bad Cinema*, ed. Constantine Verevis and Claire Perkins. Albany: State University of New York Press, forthcoming.

Powdermaker, Hortense. *Hollywood the Dream Factory: An Anthropologist Looks at the Movie-Makers*. Boston: Little, Brown, 1950.

Priest, Christopher. *The Prestige*. London: Touchstone, 1995.

Prince, Stephen. *Digital Visual Effects in Cinema: The Seduction of Reality*. New Brunswick, N.J.: Rutgers University Press, 2012.

Ray, Nicholas. *I Was Interrupted: Nicholas Ray on Making Movies*. Berkeley: University of California Press, 1993.

Read, Paul, and Mark-Paul Meyer. *Restoration of Motion Picture Film*. Woburn, Mass.: Butterworth-Heinemann, 2000.

Reeves, Nicholas, and John H. Taylor. *Howard Carter before Tutankhamun*. London: British Museum, 1992.

Reynolds, Jan. *The Williams Family of Painters.* Woodbridge, Suffolk: Antique Collectors Club, 1975.

Rickitt, Richard. *Special Effects: The History and Technique.* New York: Billboard, 2007.

Róheim, Géza. *The Gates of the Dream.* New York: International Universities Press, 1970.

Rosenbaum, Jonathan. *Goodbye Cinema, Hello Cinephilia: Film Culture in Transition.* Chicago: University of Chicago Press, 2010.

Salt, Barry. *Film Style and Technology: History and Analysis.* 2nd ed. London: Starword, 1992.

Sartre, Jean-Paul. "Theatre and Cinema." In *Modern Times: Selected Non-Fiction,* trans. Robin Buss, ed. Geoffrey Wall. London: Penguin, 2000. 199–203.

———. *The Words.* Trans. Bernard Frechtman. New York: Vintage, 1981.

Scarfone, Jay, and William Stillman. *The Wizardry of Oz: The Artistry and Magic of the 1939 M-G-M Classic.* New York: Applause, 2004.

Schatz, Thomas. *The Genius of the System: Hollywood Filmmaking in the Studio Era.* New York: Pantheon, 1988.

———. *Hollywood Genres: Formulas, Filmmaking, and the Studio System.* Philadelphia: Temple University Press, 1981.

Schivelbusch, Wolfgang. *Disenchanted Night: The Industrialization of Light in the Nineteenth Century.* Berkeley: University of California Press, 1995.

———. *The Railway Journey: The Industrialization of Time and Space in the 19th Century.* Berkeley: University of California Press, 1986.

———. *Tastes of Paradise: A Social History of Spices, Stimulants, and Intoxicants.* Trans. David Jacobson. New York: Vintage, 1993.

Schmaltz, Anita. Review of *Brigadoon. Metro Times* (February 5, 2003). Online at www2.metrotimes.com/screens/review.asp?rid=19674. Accessed June 15, 2009.

Schwartz, Evan I. *Finding Oz: How L. Frank Baum Discovered the Great American Story.* Boston: Houghton Mifflin Harcourt, 2009.

Schwartz, Vanessa R. *Spectacular Realities: Early Mass Culture in Fin-de-Siècle Paris.* Berkeley: University of California Press, 1999.

Scott, A. O. "A Visitor from Betwixt Shows Up in Between." *New York Times* (October 29, 2004). Online at movies.nytimes.com.

Sebald, W. G. *On the Natural History of Destruction.* Trans. Anthea Bell. Toronto: Vintage Canada, 2004.

———. *The Rings of Saturn.* Trans. Michael Hulse. New York: New Directions, 1988.

Shiff, Richard. "La marionette et la mire." In *Impressionnisme et naissance du cinématographe,* ed. Sylvie Ramond. Lyon: Fage, 2005. 201–41.

Simmel, Georg. "Sociability as the Autonomous Form of Sociation." In *The*

Sociology of Georg Simmel, trans. and ed. Kurt H. Wolff. New York: Free Press of Glencoe, 1950. 43–57.

Smith, R. Dixon. *Ronald Colman, Gentleman of the Cinema*. Jefferson, N.C.: McFarland, 1991.

Sobchack, Vivian. "The Scene of the Screen: Envisioning Photographic, Cinematic, and Electronic 'Presence.'" In *Carnal Thoughts: Embodiment and Moving Image Culture*. Berkeley: University of California Press, 2004. 135–62.

———. "'Surge and Splendor': A Phenomenology of the Hollywood Historical Epic." In *Film Genre Reader III*, ed. Barry Keith Grant. Austin: University of Texas Press, 2003. 296–323.

Sperb, Jason, and Scott Balcerzak. *Cinephilia in the Age of Digital Reproduction: Film, Pleasure, and Digital Culture*. London: Wallflower Press, 2009.

Sprague, Stephen. "How I See the Yoruba See Themselves." *Studies in the Anthropology of Visual Communication* 5: 1 (Fall 1978), 9–28.

Taylor, Bill. "Rear Projection Takes a Step Forward." *American Cinematographer* 88: 4 (April 2007), 66–75.

Tessé, Jean-Philippe. "La revolution numérique est terminée." *Cahiers du cinéma* 672 (November 2011), 6–8.

Tinkcom, Matthew. "Working Like a Homosexual: Camp Visual Codes and the Labor of Gay Subjects in the MGM Freed Unit." *Cinema Journal* 35: 2 (Winter 1996), 24–42.

Troyan, Michael. *A Rose for Mrs. Miniver: The Life of Greer Garson*. Lexington: University Press of Kentucky, 1999.

Truffaut, François. *Hitchcock*. Trans. Helen Scott. New York: Touchstone, 1985.

———. "Journal of *Fahrenheit 451* [Part 3]." *Cahiers du cinéma* 179 (June 1966), 17–24.

Tuchman, Barbara. *A Distant Mirror: The Calamitous 14th Century*. New York: Knopf, 1978.

Tuchman, Gaye. "The Technology of Objectivity: Doing 'Objective' TV News Film." *Urban Life and Culture* 2: 1 (April 1973), 3–26.

Turnock, Julie. "The Screen on the Set: The Problem of Classical Studio Rear Projection." *Cinema Journal* 51: 2 (Winter 2012), 157–62.

Walters, James. *Alternative Worlds in Hollywood Cinema*. Chicago: University of Chicago Press/Intellect Books, 2008.

Welles, Orson, and Peter Bogdanovich. *This Is Orson Welles*. Ed. Jonathan Rosenbaum. New York: HarperCollins, 1992.

Wilkinson, Alec. "Talk This Way." *New Yorker* (November 9, 2009), 32–38.

Wolfe, Tom. "Loverboy of the Bourgeoisie." In *The Kandy-Kolored Tangerine-Flake Streamline Baby*. New York: Bantam, 1999. 167–73.

———. *The Painted Word*. New York: Farrar, Straus, & Giroux, 1975.

Wollen, Peter. *Paris Hollywood: Writings on Film*, London: Verso, 2002.

Wood, Robin. "*Marnie.*" In *Hitchcock's Films Revisited.* Rev. ed. New York: Colum- 249
bia University Press, 2002. 173–97.

Worringer, Wilhelm. *Abstraction and Empathy: A Contribution to the Psychology of Style.* Trans. Michael Bullock. New York: International Universities Press, 1980.

Yumibe, Joshua. *Moving Color: Early Film, Mass Culture, Modernism.* New Brunswick, N.J.: Rutgers University Press, 2012.

Index

About the Author

Murray Pomerance is professor of sociology at Ryerson University. His many books include *The Horse Who Drank the Sky*, *An Eye for Hitchcock*, and *Johnny Depp Starts Here*, all from Rutgers University Press. As well as editor of the Techniques of the Moving Image series at Rutgers University Press and Horizons of Cinema series at State University of New York Press, he is co-editor (with Lester D. Friedman) of the Screen Decades series and (with Adrienne L. McLean) of the Star Decades series at Rutgers University Press.

Taboo voices: = sound + contact
The Trip: stolid landscapes vs. human mutability